Fundamentals of Conservation Biology: Volume 2

Fundamentals of Conservation Biology: Volume 2

Walter Barlow

Callisto Reference
www.callistoreference.com

Callisto Reference,
118-35 Queens Blvd., Suite 400,
Forest Hills, NY 11375, USA

Visit us on the World Wide Web at:
www.callistoreference.com

ISBN: 978-1-64116-788-8 (Hardback)

Cataloging-in-Publication Data

Fundamentals of conservation biology : Volume 2 / Walter Barlow.
p. cm.
Includes bibliographical references and index.
ISBN 978-1-64116-788-8
1. Conservation biology. 2. Nature conservation. 3. Ecology. I. Barlow, Walter.
QH75 .C66 2023
639.9--dc23

Table of Contents

Preface

The world is advancing at a fast pace like never before. Therefore, the need is to keep up with the latest developments. This book was an idea that came to fruition when the specialists in the area realized the need to coordinate together and document essential themes in the subject. That's when I was requested to be the editor. Editing this book has been an honour as it brings together diverse authors researching on different streams of the field. The book collates essential materials contributed by veterans in the area which can be utilized by students and researchers alike.

Conservation biology refers to the study of the conservation of nature and the preservation of biodiversity on the Earth. Its goal is to safeguard species, their habitats and ecosystems from extinction, and protect biotic interactions from erosion. Conservation biology aims to understand the origins and effects of extinction catastrophe as well as the deterioration of Earth's biodiversity. It involves creating systems of protected areas to conserve indigenous species and natural ecosystems. Conservation biology focuses on the processes affecting the loss, maintenance and restoration of biodiversity. It also studies the negative effect which the loss of biodiversity has on the capacity of humans to sustain their well-being. This book unfolds a detailed explanation of the various fundamentals of conservation biology. Coherent flow of topics, student-friendly language and extensive use of examples make it an invaluable source of knowledge.

Each chapter is a sole-standing publication that reflects each author´s interpretation. Thus, the book displays a multi-facetted picture of our current understanding of application, resources and aspects of the field. I would like to thank the contributors of this book and my family for their endless support.

Walter Barlow

7

Threats to Biodiversity

A pair of southern white rhinoceros (*Ceratotherium simum simum*, NT) in Tshukudu Private Game Reserve, adjacent to South Africa's Kruger National Park. Once nearly extinct due to uncontrolled hunting, this species rebounded to over 20,000 individuals. Now, poaching is taking a toll again, even in premier protected areas such Kruger, where at least 662 rhinos were lost in 2016. Rangers have cut off the horn of one of the rhinos in the photo in a desperate attempt to prevent poaching.

Conservation biologists aim to preserve all the components, interactions, and processes within and between ecosystems, natural communities, species, and populations. The main obstacle to accomplishing this goal is habitat loss, while climate change will also play an increasingly important role. But let us for a moment consider widespread species and migratory populations. These species and populations typically live in different habitats and encounter different climates as they move across the landscape. We might think that tolerance for variety would make these groups robust against habitat loss and climate change. And yet, they are also declining, even in seemingly intact ecosystems and protected areas (Craigie et al., 2010; Lindsey et al., 2014). How can it be that populations apparently buffered from the two main extinction drivers are also subjected to population declines and extirpations?

While habitat loss and climate change are the most prominent threats facing biodiversity at present, they are not alone. Nearly all human activities place additional pressures on populations, even those that already suffer from habitat loss and climate change. These additional pressures are primarily from pollution, overharvesting, **persecution**, invasive species, and disease (Maxwell et al., 2016). Because these threats are associated with and/or exacerbated by human activities, they can be dynamic in their nature, develop rapidly, and persist at such large scales that wildlife populations have little opportunity to adapt or move to safer areas. Moreover, these threats may interact with each other, as well as with climate change and habitat loss, so that their combined impact is greater than their individual effects. In this chapter, we explore how each of these threats impact wildlife and natural communities, and how they could push populations and species to extinction. Methods for lessening the impact of these threats are integrated into Chapters 9–15.

> Comprehensive conservation efforts must recognise that biodiversity faces multiple threats that need to be dealt with at different scales.

7.1 Pollution in Its Many Forms

Rachel Carson's 1962 book, *Silent Spring*, described the dangers of pollution—pesticide pollution in particular—with a clarity that captured the public's attention for many years afterwards. Carson, an American biologist, was particularly successful in drawing attention to **biomagnification** (also called bioaccumulation), a process through which pesticides and other toxins accumulate and become more concentrated in animals at higher levels of the **food chain** (Figure 7.1). Her work drew on research that found that dichlorodiphenyltrichloroethane (DDT), sprayed on crops to kill pest insects and on water bodies to kill malaria mosquito (*Anopheles* spp.) larvae, was also harming non-target organisms that consumed insects and fish exposed to DDT. Of note is that non-target organisms high on food chains, particularly fish-eating birds, such as eagles, pelicans, and egrets, often had high levels of DDT concentrated in their tissues. The affected birds were generally weakened, and the shells of their eggs were thin and prone to cracking during incubation. Consequently, bird populations declined dramatically in areas where DDT was used, as adults died and failed to raise young.

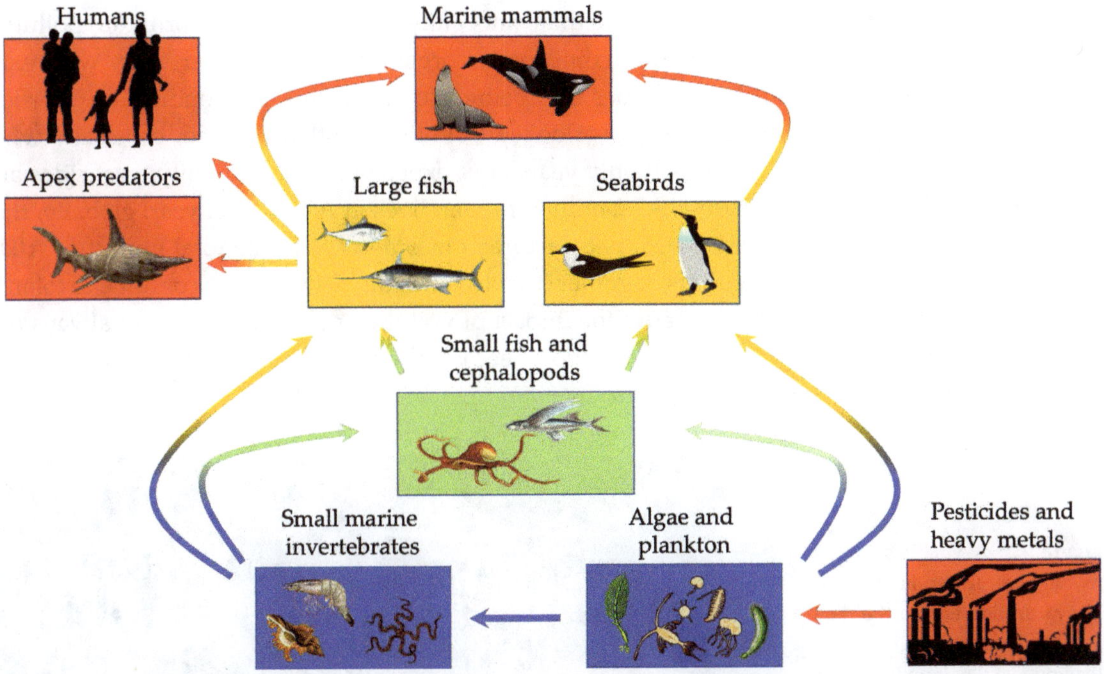

Figure 7.1 A simplified marine food web showing how sharks, marine mammals, seabirds, and even humans are all vulnerable to health problems associated with bioaccumulation where pesticides, heavy metals, and other harmful chemicals become concentrated at higher trophic levels.

In the 1970s, many industrialised countries recognised the dire situation and banned the use of DDT, which eventually allowed for the partial recovery of the affected bird populations. Unfortunately, while some countries have switched to safer alternatives (e.g. Hargrove, 2003), DDT continues to be widely used in Africa to control malaria mosquito, tsetse fly (*Glossina* spp.), and other disease vectors. Researchers recently observed complete absences of breeding fish-eating birds in some African wetlands, and some of the highest-ever recorded DDT levels in seed-eating birds (Bouwman et al., 2013). This is cause for concern, not only for wildlife, but also for the long-term effects on people, particularly the consumers of the food products exposed to these chemicals (e.g. Manaca et al., 2011) and the workers who handle these chemicals in the field.

> Pollution does not always lead to immediate mortality, but instead can have sublethal impacts that compromise organisms' fitness over time, with population declines as the end result.

DDT is however not the only form of pollution we battle today. With the impacts of a growing human population becoming gradually more pervasive, pollution is compromising water, soil, and air quality at rates faster than ever before. Some forms of pollution can be highly visible, and with dramatic consequences (Figure 7.2). But importantly, there are many less detectable forms of pollution. While it may not always lead to immediate mortality, these insidious forms of pollution have sublethal impacts that compromise organisms' fitness over time, with early death and population declines still being the end result. Responding to the silent threats of subtle and easily-overlooked pollution is often delayed, especially when the negative effects are felt only years after exposure. In their totality, pesticides and other pollutants claim 1.4–2.2 million human lives in Africa each year; globally, they claim 9 million lives, which is over three times more than the total impact of AIDS, malaria, and tuberculosis, together (Landrigan et al., 2018). Yet we continue to tolerate these threats, in part because the impact of pollution on our health is not always that apparent, especially when pollution deaths are expressed as a stroke, heart disease, respiratory infections, diarrhoea, or cancer, among other health issues.

Figure 7.2 A young boy next to an open sewer in Nairobi, Kenya. In addition to the dangers to human welfare and livelihoods, polluted waterways kill millions of native animals and plants each year, and harm countless number of ecosystems.

One of the most challenging aspects when trying to prevent pollution is identifying the source. Many forms of pollution can easily be transported away from their source through the air, via rivers, even in groundwater. This transport of pollutants (called **pesticide drift** in the case of pesticides) means that a substantial burden (perhaps as much as 95%, Miller, 2004) of impacts are being felt by non-target species, including economically important non-target organisms. For example, pesticide drift from cotton fields in Benin has caused extirpations of freshwater fish (Agbohessi et al., 2015), while beneficial pollinating insects are also often negatively impacted (Pettis et al., 2013). Studies on fish in Nigeria (Adeogun et al., 2016), large mammals in South Africa (Bornman et al., 2010), and frogs in Kenya (Hayes and Menendez, 1999) have shown that beneficial organisms that survive this secondary pesticide exposure have disrupted reproductive and endocrine systems, and hence reduced fitness. Even humans may be exposed to secondary poisoning from pesticides, as toxic pesticide levels have been found in edible oysters and mussels in Ghana (Dodoo et al., 2013), prawn in Côte d'Ivoire (Roche and Tidou, 2009), and even chickens in South Africa (Barnhoorn et al., 2009).

To make matters worse, many pollutants take many years to **biodegrade** (i.e. break down in nature), and thus continue to pose a threat to wildlife and humans long after entering the environment. One important class of such long-lived pollutants is **persistent organic pollutants (POP)**. Several types of pesticides qualify as POPs, which are prone to bioaccumulation and drift. The most famous POP is DDT; in the USA, biologist continue to see eggshell thinning and bird deaths, nearly 50 years after DDT was banned in that country (Burnett et al., 2013). This is a concern in places like Ethiopia's Lake Koka, where recent studies have found DDT residues in every sample of fish tissue (from several different species) tested (Deribe et al., 2011). More information on POPs, many which are banned from use by signatories of the *Stockholm Convention on Persistent Organic Pollutants,* can be found on the *Stockholm Convention* website (http://pops.int).

There are also many types of persistent inorganic pollutants that find their way into the environment on a daily basis. One important class of persistent inorganic pollutants that also bioaccumulate is heavy metals; these include mercury, cobalt, copper, lead, and arsenic. A study from Zambia traced cobalt contamination in living trees to soil pollution from mining activities that occurred the mid-1970s (Mihaljevič et al., 2011). Some everyday products can also persist in the environment. For example, an aluminium can takes about 200 years to break down, while a plastic bag takes between 100–1,000 years to break down. The continued use of these products should thus raise alarm to anyone concerned about the environment and human health. But it also provides opportunities for any person to contribute to conservation by reducing use of these products and reusing/recycling those products that find their way into the supply chain.

Many pollutants take many years to biodegrade, and thus continue to pose a threat to wildlife and humans long after entering the environment.

7.1.1 Water pollution

Water pollution, the accidental or intentional dumping of pesticides; herbicides; oil products; fertilisers; sewage; industrial waste; detergents; and other foreign chemicals and objects into aquatic environments, is arguably the biggest current pollution concern in Africa (Prüss-Ustün et al., 2016; Landrigan et al., 2018).

The dumping of products containing heavy metals into aquatic environments is particularly concerning because heavy metals are toxic even in small concentrations, and likely to biomagnify. When aquatic organisms process contaminated water, they absorb or ingest the heavy metals along with other essential nutrients. With each additional step along the food chain, organisms ingest and accumulate increasingly higher concentrations of these toxic elements (see Figure 7.1). In this way, even small amounts of heavy metals can become lethal across several levels of the **food web** over time. Biomagnification is especially a concern with long-lived predatory marine fishes that people consumed as food, such as swordfish (*Xiphias gladius*, LC), marlins, sharks, and some tunas and sea basses. For example, mercury (emitted mainly during fossil fuel use), lead, and arsenic have bioaccumulated so much in sharks off South Africa that many species are now considered unsafe for human consumption (McKinney et al., 2016; Bosch et al., 2016; Merly et al., 2019). Recent studies also found unsafe levels of mercury in freshwater fish from regions as wide as Central Africa's Great Lakes (Campbell et al., 2008), Ethiopia's Lake Awassa (Desta et al., 2006), and several reservoirs in West Africa (Quédraogo and Amyot, 2013).

> Because of biomagnification, many long-lived predatory marine fishes are now considered unsafe for human consumption.

Oil pollution involves the release of petroleum products into the environment, which can originate from damaged ships, failed drilling rigs, leaking offshore platforms, or other unexpected events. The released oil causes mammals and birds to lose the insulating abilities of their fur and feathers, leaving those animals vulnerable to hypothermia and drowning. Other aquatic animals, including fish and shellfish, may ingest oil products, causing them to sicken and die. Because of the way oil is extracted and transported, marine ecosystems are particularly at risk. Furthermore, because of the massive amount of oil that are involved in oil extraction and transport, an oil pollution event often represents a serious ecological disaster (Figure 7.3). Africa has been hit hard by oil spills in recent years, particularly around oil-producing countries like Angola and Nigeria, and along shipping lanes passing along the coasts of Namibia, South Africa, and Mozambique. Nigeria is perhaps the biggest victim of oil spills; between 1976 and 2001, there were an estimated 6,817 oil spills around Africa's largest wetland, the Niger Delta (UNDP, 2006)! These oil spills have destroyed thousands of hectares of mangrove swamps, estuarine wetlands, and other coastal ecosystems, causing severe hardship to marginalised local communities who depended on those areas for subsistence fishing and farming (Fentiman and Zabbey, 2015).

Plastic pollution is fast becoming a ubiquitous threat to Africa's environment, its wildlife, and its people. To visualise the magnitude of the problem, consider that there are more than 1.6 trillion pieces of plastic, collectively weighing over 70,000 tonnes, currently floating in the Atlantic and Indian Oceans surrounding Africa (Eriksen et al., 2014). While many of these plastic items were dumped directly in the ocean, many also have a terrestrial origin. For example, if someone throws a plastic wrapper on a sidewalk, there is a good chance that the wrapper will find its way into a nearby stream at some point, carried by wind or rain runoff. From here, the wrapper will float along various

> There are more than 1.6 trillion pieces of plastic, collectively weighing over 70,000 tonnes, currently floating in the Atlantic and Indian Oceans surrounding Africa.

Figure 7.3 (Top) Staff and volunteers from the seabird rescue centre SANCCOB are caring for some of the 19,000 African penguins (*Spheniscus demersus*, EN) that were rescued after a stricken iron ore carrier spilled 1,400 tonnes of oil off South Africa in June 2000 (Wolfaardt et al., 2009). (Bottom) SANCCOB volunteers releasing a group of African penguins that were rescued from the oil spill.

streams and rivers until it reaches the ocean. A recent review found that 88–95% of plastics floating into the world's oceans originated from just 10 rivers, which include West Africa's Niger River and East Africa's Nile River (Schmidt et al., 2017; Lebreton et al., 2017). In the process, thousands of seabirds, dolphins, whales, turtles, seals and fish die each year from suffocation or starvation after ingesting plastics and other pieces of trash that they confused with food (Wilcox et al., 2015). This plastic pollution also impacts humans: researchers recently found microfibers (many of which are plastic) in over 80% of tap water samples from Uganda (Kosuth et al., 2017), as well as food-grade commercial sea salt originating from South Africa (Karami et al., 2017).

Some of the biggest impacts from plastic pollution are caused not by visible scraps of plastic, but by **microplastics**, the collective name for plastic particles smaller than 1 mm (some are microscopic). Microplastics may originate from the breakdown of larger pieces of plastic and polystyrene products, or they may be manufactured intentionally small, such as beads added to cosmetics and other personal care products that are flushed down drains after use. Because microplastics are so small, they easily pass through the standard filters used at sewage treatment plants. Consequently, microplastics generally end up in the aquatic environment, where they are unintentionally consumed by crustaceans (crabs, lobsters, and krill), molluscs (mussels, oysters, and clams), echinoderms (sea stars, sea urchins, sea cucumbers), and baby fish. This consumption can block or damage the victim's digestive and respiratory systems, cause reduced food uptake by creating a false sense of satiation, or even poison animals through leeching of synthetic chemicals. Each of these threats increases death rates and lowers reproductive rates (Sussarellu et al., 2016). Just as with the biomagnification we discussed earlier, the consumption of microplastics also affects other consumers (including humans), because the small organisms that ingest the microplastics are often food for other animals, allowing plastic pollution to move through an entire food chain. For example, a recent study from Lake Victoria found microplastics imbedded in the digestive tracts of perch and tilapia bought at a local market and meant for human consumption (Biginagwa et al., 2016). Because microplastics are so hard to remove once in an ecosystem, the best method for their containment may be to reduce plastic use, to ban products containing microplastics, or to develop microplastics that are biodegradable within a reasonable timeframe. But for this to happen, there is a need to educate the public and lawmakers (Galloway and Lewis, 2016) about the dangers posed by this threat to the environment and local economies.

Nutrient pollution represents another growing threat to Africa's aquatic environments. Many lakes, streams, and other freshwater and marine environments naturally contain low concentrations of essential nutrients, such as nitrates and phosphates. In order to survive, the species living in these nutrient-poor waters must then be adapted to this natural nutrient scarcity. However, raw sewage, agricultural fertilisers, concentrated animal feeding operations, and industrial processes release large amounts of additional nitrates and phosphates into the environment, which are washed into the aquatic environment. Minor additions of essential nutrients stimulate plant growth, providing more food for organisms at higher trophic levels. However, at high concentrations, the system become subjected to nutrient pollution.

> Nutrient pollution, caused in part by excessive fertiliser use, can led to eutrophication, famous for causing algae blooms, aquatic dead zones, and fish kills.

One of the worst outcomes of nutrient pollution is **eutrophication**. During eutrophication, surface algae grow so rapidly (known as an algae bloom) that it starts blocking sunlight from reaching aquatic organisms below the surface. Because each individual alga is short-lived, their rapid growth also adds large amounts of decaying matter to the environment. In response, decomposers that feed on the dead algae can become so abundant that they consume most of the water's dissolved oxygen. Without oxygen and sunlight, aquatic plant and animal life may die off in large numbers. The resultant dead zones are sometimes visibly in the form of fish kills, with large numbers of dead fish floating on the surface of the affected water body. The organisms that die during this process is generally also toxic to humans because of bacteria build-up and other imbalances. Eutrophication is an increasingly common problem in Africa; for example, a recent review found that 41–76% of South Africa's lakes may be eutrophic (Harding, 2015). Eutrophication has already negatively impacted Africa's tourism and fisheries sectors (Nyenje et al., 2010), and even led a temporary shutdown of water supplies on the Kenyan side of Lake Victoria (Sitoki et al., 2012). Preventing further eutrophication should thus be a high priority—not only will it prevent harmful algae blooms but may even play an important role in controlling invasive aquatic plants such as the water hyacinth (*Eichhornia crassipes*) (Coetzee and Hill, 2012; Bownes et al., 2013).

Groundwater pollution—the release of pollutants into aquifers and other sources of groundwater—is also becoming a serious issue across Africa. This type of pollution generally originates from landfills, on-site sanitation systems, leaking sewage systems, mining leachate, **agriculture runoff** (fertiliser, pesticides, animal waste, etc.), and other types of waste dumping. The pollutants may sometimes be released directly into aquifers; however, more often the contaminants and pathogens leak into the soil, from where it seeps into groundwater.

One of the most important emerging threats to groundwater in Africa is **hydrological fracturing** or fracking, in short. During this process, pressurised liquids that contain suspended particles and thickening agents are blasted into rock formations deep underground to break them open. When the pressure and liquids are removed, the suspended particles keep the fractures open, which enables extraction of natural gas and petroleum. While fracking was initially hailed as a method to access previously inaccessible fossil fuels, scientists subsequently found that it poses a wide variety of very serious environmental and health risks. Most importantly, the liquids used in fracking contain toxic chemicals which pose a high risk for groundwater pollution (Osborne et al., 2011), which in turn lead to miscarriages and birth defects (McKenzie et al., 2014), cancer (McKenzie et al., 2012), as well as skin and respiratory diseases (Rabinowitz et al. 2015). In addition, fracking increases greenhouse gas emissions (Howarth, 2014) and induces infrastructure-damaging earthquakes (Ellsworth, 2013). Because of these myriad serious risks, several national governments in Europe, and several local governments in the USA, UK, Canada, and Australia have banned the practice from their lands (https://keeptapwatersafe.org/global-bans-on-fracking). In contrast, and despite opposition from civil society, several countries in Africa (e.g. South Africa: Roelf, 2016; Botswana: Barbee, 2015) recently approved this harmful practice.

> Because fracking poses many serious risks, governments across the world have banned the practice from their lands.

7.1.2 Air pollution

In the past, people and industries thought that the atmosphere was so vast that any gases or particles released into the air would disperse and dilute to the point that they would post no ill effects. But as air quality has diminished over time, scientists have documented that air pollution can cause irreparable harm to ecosystems and human health, often far from the original sources. A striking example comes from West Africa's Lake Chad, which shrank by 95% between 1963 and 1998 (Figure 7.4). Experts generally thought that the shrinkage was caused by unsustainable water use in the region, but recent evidence suggests that air pollution from Europe which reduced rainfall in the Lake's catchment area may also have contributed to this ecological disaster (Hwang et al., 2013). The Lake's water level has risen since 2007, likely due, in part, to clean air regulations implemented by the European Union. Despite this positive turn around, air pollution continues to be a serious problem (Amegah and Agyei-Mensah, 2017) that threatens humans and wildlife throughout Africa.

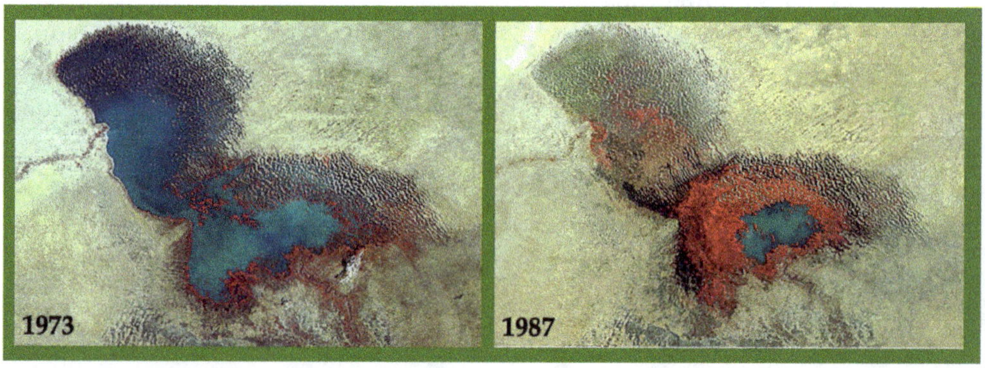

Figure 7.4 Changing rainfall patterns attributed to air pollution may have contributed to West Africa's Lake Chad shrinking by 95% between 1963 and 1998. An ecological disaster ensued, as the 68 million people whose livelihoods were at risk put additional strains on the environment while trying to replace the natural resources the lake previously provided.

An important form of air pollution is **hydrocarbons**, which are released during fossil fuel burning, particularly during transport, power generation, and other industrial activities (Karagulian et al., 2015). Pollution from airborne hydrocarbon compounds can sometimes be sensed without scientific equipment, by the bad smells, high air turbidity, and eye and lung irritation a person may experience in large cities with highly polluted air. When exposed to sunlight, these chemicals can react with other gases and particles in the atmosphere to produce **photochemical smog**, which is made up of ozone and other secondary compounds. In the upper atmosphere, ozone filters harmful ultraviolet radiation, which benefits most living things; but at ground level, high concentrations of ozone pose several dangers. For example, it damages plant tissues which make them brittle; high surface ozone levels have found to cause crop damage in Botswana and South Africa (Zunckel et al., 2004). Hydrocarbon exposure also poses several threats to humans: it altered some people's DNA—often a cancer precursor—in Benin (Fanou et al., 2006), caused lung damage in Côte d'Ivoire (Kouassi et al., 2010), and subjected people to **carcinogenic compounds** in the DRC and Ghana (Tuakuila, 2013; Bortey-Sam et al., 2017). The lack of air monitoring and standards over much of Sub-Saharan (Petkova et al., 2013), and lack of awareness—people often confuse photochemical smog with natural mist and early-morning fog—should thus be of serious concern both to conservation biologists and society at large.

> Air pollution from hydrocarbons often manifests itself as photochemical smog. Hanging like a thick cloud over industrial areas, people sometimes confuse it with natural mist and early-morning fog.

Burning fossil fuels also releases sulphur oxides (SO_x) and nitrogen oxides (NO_x) into the atmosphere, where they combine with water vapor to produce nitric and sulphuric acids. These acids later return to the ground as **acid rain**, with dramatically low pH relative to normal rainwater. Prevailing winds can transport acid rain clouds over long distances, so the effects of acid rain may occur hundreds of kilometres from its sources. Because the acid rain is closely tied to the water cycle, aquatic and soil organisms are particularly vulnerable to the negative effects of acid rain. Plants exposed to acid rain, either directly or after absorbing contaminated water from the ground, are often left severely weakened or even killed: it has even caused plant extirpations in Zambia (UNEP, 2006).

Another important contributor to air pollution is domestic fuel burning (Karagulian et al., 2015). During these activities, very small pollutant particles are released into the air. Because these particles are so small, they are difficult to filter from the air, and can easily be inhaled. Once inhaled, the particles can pass into the victim's bloodstream, from where they negatively impact cardiovascular health, neurodevelopment, and cognitive function (WHO, 2013). Despite the harmful impact of these particles in the environment, their monitoring is virtually non-existent in Africa, making it very hard to guide air quality policy decisions and legislations. In contrast, measures that mitigate pollution from domestic fuel burning may even help slow the rate of habitat loss (Chapter 5), as this type of pollution is associated with inefficient wood stoves, slash-and-burn agriculture, and the artisanal charcoal industry.

7.1.3 Soil pollution

Soil pollution occurs when soil meets foreign chemicals and other pollutants. This type of pollution is often associated with industrial activities that extract resources from the earth, agricultural runoff, pesticide use, oil spills, acid rain, improper treatment of sewage, and improper disposal of waste. People and wildlife can then become sick through direct contact with contaminated soils, or through secondary contamination via polluted groundwater or eating food grown in contaminated soil. For example, a recent review reported how soil pollution has left medicinal plants toxic to humans in countries such as Botswana; Ghana; and Mali, at times with fatal consequences (Street, 2012).

The improper disposal of electronic waste (or e-waste in short) is a particularly serious form of soil pollution. Because electronic products contain toxic heavy metal contaminants that are expensive to recycle, discarded electronic products usually end up in dump yards (Figure 7.5). Here, open burning of electronic and other waste materials releases the toxic compounds into the soil, as well as the air and water (Robinson, 2009), from where it also accumulates in the environment.

Figure 7.5 Nearly all electronic goods contain parts with toxic chemicals that are expensive to recycle. Instead, such components end up in dump yards such as this one in Ghana, from where the toxic compounds pollute the air, water, and soil, posing many human and environmental risks.

7.1.4 Light pollution

Light pollution describes the addition of excessive, ill-timed, or poorly designed artificial light to the natural world. A consequence of an increasingly industrialised world (Falchi et al., 2016), light pollution has increased dramatically over the past decades as more people have gained greater access to electricity (Figure 7.6). Behavioural disruption is perhaps the most well-known consequence of increased light pollution—consider all the moths and other nocturnal insects (and insect predators, such as bats and geckos) attracted to artificial night lights. Light pollution also interferes with the navigation abilities of nocturnal species, which often use the stars, moon, and light reflectance from water surfaces to orientate themselves. For example, work in Gabon has shown how artificial lights disorientate sea turtle hatchlings trying to reach the sea (Bourgeois et al., 2009), while others have highlighted the significance of light-induced seabird mortality (Black, 2005). These and other behavioural disruptions—which include attraction to and repelling away from artificial light—may seem to only affect a small number of individuals around a few lights in your home. But the systemic impact of thousands of lights every night has wide-ranging ecosystem impacts when considering the cumulative impact of reduced reproductive performance (Firebaugh and Haynes, 2016), disrupted predator-prey dynamics (Minnaar et al., 2015) and disturbed night-time pollination services (Knop et al., 2017) on the many thousands of organisms impacted every night.

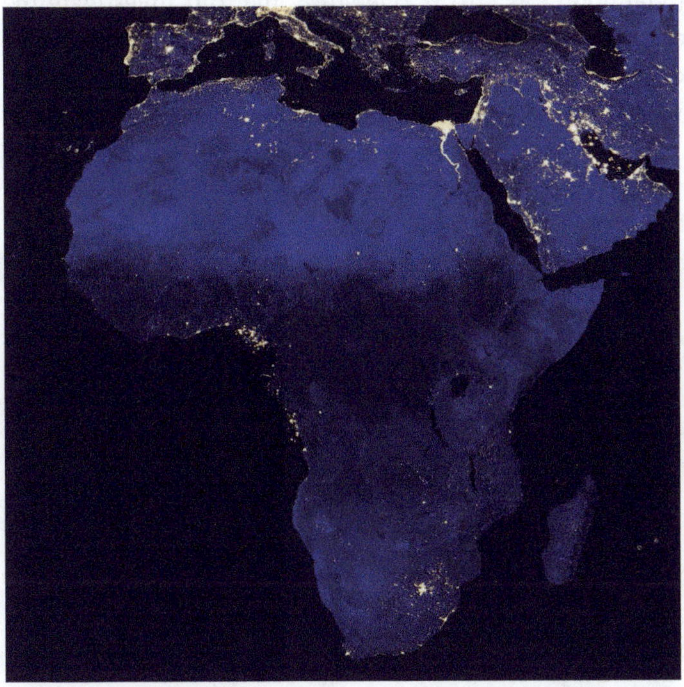

Figure 7.6 Night-time composite of Africa and parts of Europe and Asia, taken by the Suomi NPP satellite in 2012. City lights of every major city in Africa can be seen; lights are particularly concentrated in South Africa and West Africa's Gulf of Guinea.

Light pollution also disrupts the natural day-night cycles with which most species evolved. These disruptions interfere with **circadian rhythms**, which negatively affect living organisms' physiology. For example, one study showed that night-time light pollution disrupted natural sleep patterns in birds, leaving the affected individuals more susceptible to malaria infections (Ouyang et al., 2017). Circadian rhythm disruptions from light pollution (especially from high frequency "blue" light) also impact humans by increasing stress, fatigue, and anxiety, and susceptibility to obesity (Rybnikova et al., 2016) and cancer (Haim and Portnov, 2013). It is important to note that light pollution does not mean that the use of light is inherently bad—light has and will continue to play an important role in our daily lives. However, it does mean that we need to be more thoughtful about the consequences of light pollution and put measures in place to mitigate its impacts on the natural world and our own lives.

7.1.5 Noise pollution

Many people find a sense of freedom when they are in natural surroundings, with peace and quiet facilitating a much-needed connection to nature. These experiences are increasingly being threatened by **noise pollution.** However, noise pollution (also called acoustic pollution)—caused by human activities, such as industrial, military, and transportation systems—affects more than just the appealing tranquillity of nature. It also prevents animals from hearing each other, predators, and prey, all which could interfere with feeding, reproduction, navigation, and predator-avoidance behaviours. While African studies on the impact of noise pollution on wildlife are near-absent (Shannon et al., 2015), one study that did investigate the topic found that traffic noise increased dwarf mongooses' (*Helogale parvula*, LC) alertness but also reduced responsiveness to alarm calls (Kern and Radford, 2016). Such responses could leave the affected individuals less fit and more vulnerable to predators.

One would think that marine organisms living in the vast oceans may be spared from noise pollution, but this is not the case (Koper and Plön, 2012; Kunc et al., 2017). Sound carries much further in salt water than air, so noises from ship propellers; military sonar; seismic activities, and construction have significantly increased the level of ambient noise levels marine organisms experience. This increased level of ambient noise not only disrupts communication in sea animals (e.g. Cerchio et al., 2014), but can even lead to death (some mass whale strandings have been attributed to noise pollution: Morell et al., 2017; Williams et al., 2017). As with light pollution, there is a general need to be more thoughtful about the consequences of sound pollution on the natural world and to put measures in place (see e.g. Koper and Plön, 2012) to mitigate its impacts.

Noise pollution prevents interferes with communication, feeding, reproduction, navigation, and predator-avoidance behaviours; it may even contribute to mass strandings of whales.

7.1.6 Thermal pollution

Thermal pollution describes localised human-induced temperature changes to the natural world. Aquatic ecosystems represent one of the ecosystems most vulnerable to thermal pollution. For example, when water is released from big dams, it comes from the colder middle and lower strata of the reservoir, leading to rapid cooling of aquatic ecosystems further downstream. The opposite is true at power plants that use river water as a coolant; turbines release their heat to the circulating water and then the warmed water is released back into the environment. These abrupt releases of thermally discordant water often lead to **thermal shock** which can be lethal to fish and other aquatic organisms. For example, studies from South Africa have shown that thermal shock can kill fish embryos and larvae and caused deformities in the young of Clanwilliam yellowfish (*Barbus capensis*, VU) (King et al., 1998).

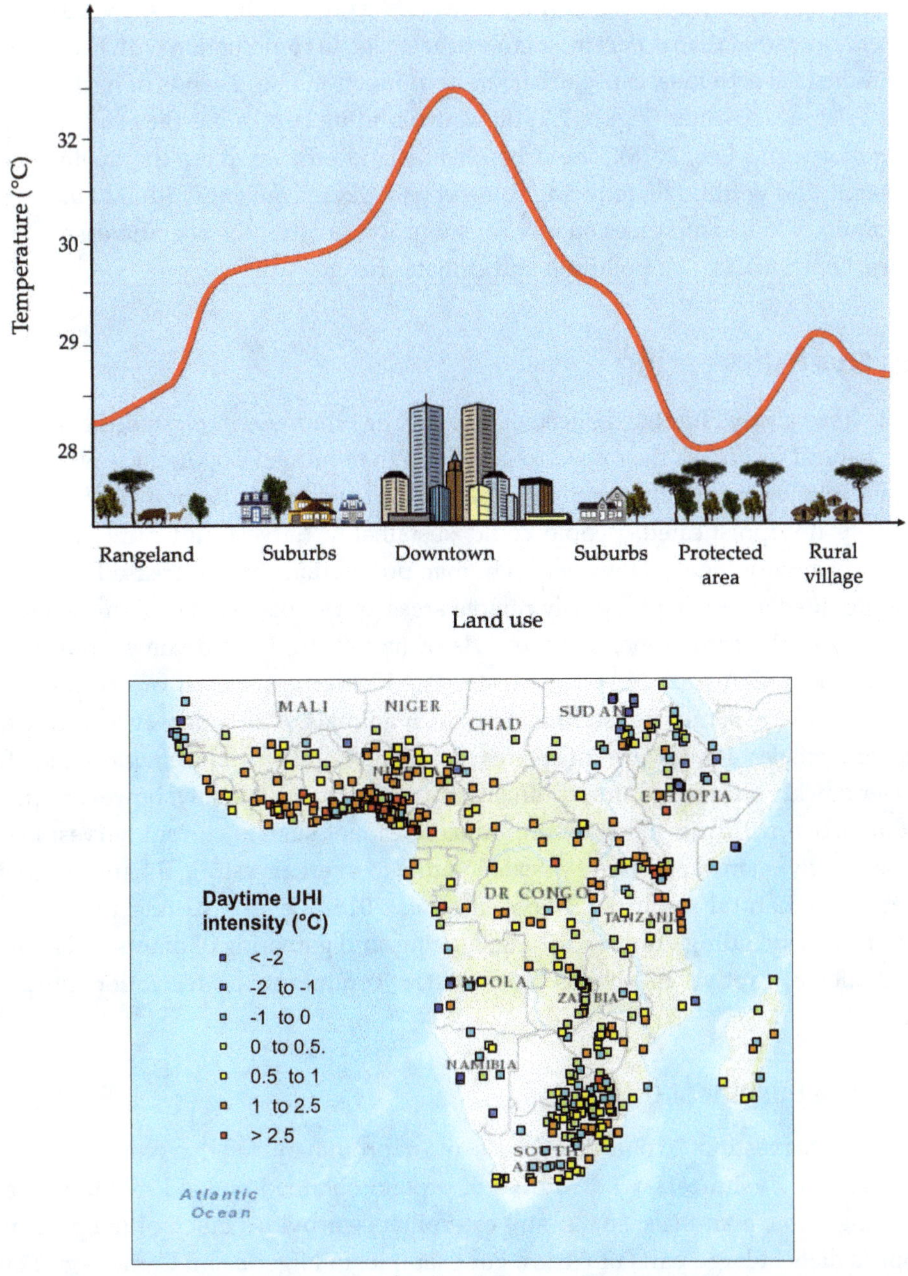

Figure 7.7 (Top) Man-made surfaces such as roofs, roads, and pavements do not reflect, but rather absorb solar energy as heat, causing built-up areas to be warmer than the surrounding rural areas. (Bottom) Data derived from 16-year mean daytime temperatures obtained by TERRA and AQUA satellites show how the urban heat island effect increases daytime temperatures of several African cities (represented as squares). Note how areas with high levels of deforestation (e.g. West Africa and Albertine Rift) also show the highest temperature increases (> 2.5°C). Map by T.C. Chakrabotry, after Chakrabotry and Lee, 2018.

The **urban heat island effect** represents a terrestrial form of thermal pollution. Urban and other developed areas are generally covered with large swaths of man-made surfaces (e.g. asphalt roads, pavement surfaces, and building roofs), which absorb solar energy rather than reflect it. This absorbed heat, in combination with heat outputs from industrial activities, cause urban areas to function like "islands of heat" that are several degrees warmer (Figure 7.7) than surrounding rural areas (Feyisa et al., 2014; Chakraborty and Lee, 2018). The urban heat island effect reduces the quality of life for people and wildlife by reducing comfort and water availability (due to increasing evaporation). It also increases energy consumption to offset the heat increases which, in turn, contributes to air pollution and climate change.

7.2 Overharvesting

People have always hunted, collected, trapped, or otherwise harvested the food and other natural resources they need to survive. When human populations were small, at least relative to the abundance of their resources, and collection methods were relatively unsophisticated, people could sustainably harvest and hunt wildlife in their local environments. However, as human populations have increased, and roads have provided access to previously remote areas, our impact on the environment has escalated. At the same time, our methods of harvesting have become dramatically more efficient. Guns are now used instead of blowpipes, spears, or arrows, while networks of wire snares indiscriminately catch animals of all types, even young and pregnant females. Populations of species that mature and reproduce rapidly can often recover quickly after harvests and can thus be exploited sustainably; however, species that are slow-maturing and slow-reproducing cannot sustain current harvest levels. Consequently, many species are threatened due to **overharvesting**, the unsustainable collection of natural resources (Maxwell et al., 2016). Overharvesting may take on many forms, including hunting, fishing, logging, and gathering of plants and animals for medicine, captive collections, subsistence, commerce, or recreation purposes (Figure 7.8).

7.2.1 The Bushmeat Crisis

Bushmeat harvesting is one of Africa's most prominent overharvesting concerns (see Box 4.1). **Bushmeat**—wild sources of protein obtained on land by hunting and collecting birds, mammals, snails, and caterpillars—provides much of the protein in people's diets in large parts of Africa. For example, in Nigeria and Cameroon, 12,000 tonnes of bushmeat—two tonnes obtained from bay duiker (*Cephalophus dorsalis*, NT) alone—are sold at markets in the Cross-Sanaga rivers region each year (Fa et al., 2006). Similarly, more than 9,000 primates are killed annually for a single market in Côte d'Ivoire (Covey and McGraw, 2014); people from Central Africa harvest an astonishing 5.3 million tonnes of mammalian bushmeat annually (Fa et al., 2002). Usually seen as a conservation challenge in Africa's tropical forests, the **bushmeat crisis** also impacts savannah regions (reviewed in Lindsey et al., 2013). For example, bushmeat hunters, numbering between 1.500 and 2,000, remove over 600,000 kg of herbivore biomass

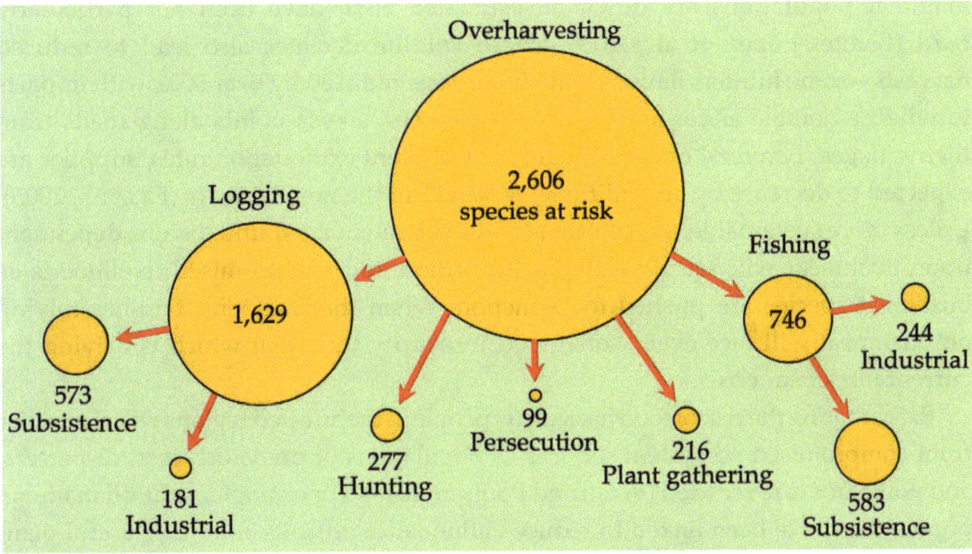

Figure 7.8 Overharvesting in Sub-Saharan Africa at scale: Over 60% of species that are threatened by overharvesting are also threatened (directly and indirectly) by logging. Nearly 30% of all species are threatened by fishing, and 10% by hunting and trapping.

from Botswana's Okavango Delta each year, despite the region's protected status and importance for ecotourism sectors (Rogan et al., 2017).

Outside influences play a prominent role in the harvesting pressure associated with the bushmeat crisis. In Section 5.2, we discussed neocolonialism, where jobs associated with land-grabbing industries are frequently reserved for migrant labourers. Poorly paid and with limited rights, migrant labourers are often forced to turn to local natural resources to fulfil their basic needs (Thibault and Blaney, 2003). The impact of these migrant labourers on the local environment is massive compared to traditional (and many other local) peoples that prioritise sustainability. For example, immigrants working at logging concessions in the northern parts of the Republic of the Congo hunt 72% of all bushmeat harvested in the region (Poulsen et al., 2009). The increased commercialisation of bushmeat also poses challenges (Lindsey et al., 2013); for example, in the broader Congo Basin, commercial hunters are exploiting bushmeat at scales 27 times that of the area's traditional peoples (Fa et al., 2016). In addition to hunting for local markets, illegal exports also play an important role. For example, more than 50 tonnes of wild fish and bushmeat enters France from Africa each week (Chaber et al., 2010); similar amounts were also estimated for airports in Switzerland (Wood et al., 2014).

> The massive wildlife declines caused by the bushmeat crisis are also threatening ecosystem services, food security and people's livelihoods.

Very few animal populations can withstand such high extraction rates. Consequently, regions dependent on bushmeat have already seen substantially wildlife declines (Lindsey et al., 2013). West Africa, where forest mammal populations are down an estimated 80%, have been hot particularly hard (Benítez-López et al., 2019). These wildlife declines also lead to reduced harvests—some hunters have seen their harvests reduced by over 80%, with impacts to wildlife notable as far as 40 km from hunters' access points along roads from their villages (Benítez-López et al., 2017). At current exploitation rates, supplies are expected to decrease by an additional 80% within the next 50 years (Fa et al., 2003). Unless more sustainable, alternative sources of protein are found, people dependent upon bushmeat will see increased malnutrition and compromised livelihoods as bushmeat species are pushed to extinction. When that happens, families relying on bushmeat will face even worse food insecurity than that which is driving the current bushmeat crisis.

Exacerbating the risk of food insecurity, people in the affected regions will also suffer from compromised ecosystem services as populations of predators, seed dispersers, and pollinators are reduced (Rosin and Poulsen, 2016). For example, reduced mammal populations have been linked to reduced abundance of fruits and other useful plant products available for human consumption (Vanthomme et al., 2010). Some areas are already suffering from "empty forest syndrome"—a condition where a forest appears to be green and healthy, but is practically devoid of animals, and in which ecological processes have been irreversibly altered such that the forest's species composition will change over subsequent decades (Nasi et al., 2011; Benítez-López et al., 2019). The bushmeat crisis is thus a major concern to people concerned about biodiversity and/ or human well-being.

7.2.2 Overfishing

Pressure on biodiversity in aquatic environments is also increasing as people continue to harvest fish, sea turtles, dolphins, shellfish, and manatees for meat at increasing rates. Modernised fishing methods play a major role. For example, a motorised fishing fleet that faces few restrictions has caused a 75% decline in fish populations at Ethiopia's Lake Tana in recent years (de Graaf et al., 2004). Also, in the marine environment, motorised fleets and enormous factory ships can now spend months at sea where they catch fish to sell at local and global markets (Ramos and Grémillet, 2013; Pauly et al., 2014). Some estimates suggest that wild-caught seafood could be virtually absent by 2050 if current exploitation levels persist (Worm et al., 2006).

For many aquatic organisms, the indirect impacts of modern commercial fishing methods outweigh direct exploitation (Figure 7.9). One example is **ghost fishing,** which causes thousands of animals to die each year after becoming entangled in dumped, abandoned, and lost fishing gear. Similarly, approximately 25% of fish harvests are considered **bycatch**—animals that are accidentally caught, injured, or killed during fishing operations. Recent declines in skates, rays, turtles, sharks, dolphins, and seabirds have all been linked to incidental deaths as bycatch (Cox et al., 2007; Carruthers et al., 2009). Seabird biologists from South Africa have been at the forefront of solving bycatch problems in recent years (Box 7.1).

Box 7.1 Solving Seabird Bycatch Problems: From Theory to Practice

Ross Wanless

DST-NRF Centre of Excellence at the FitzPatrick Institute of African Ornithology, University of Cape Town, South Africa.

✉ *rosswanless@gmail.com*

The global problem of seabird bycatch in fisheries—the accidental death of seabirds during fishing—is one of the biggest threats to pelagic seabirds (Croxall et al., 2012). Ironically, it is both one of the easiest and one of the most challenging problems to solve. How so? Simple technical fixes to stop birds from getting snagged on fishing gear and drowning can work amazingly well, but fishermen must be convinced to use them.

Techniques for preventing bycatch break down into two basic approaches. The first approach is to prevent access to the danger point (the baited hook or the cables that birds strike). Fishing only at night eliminates up to 80% of the problem, but still jeopardises nocturnal foragers and diurnal species during a full moon. Another option is bird-scaring lines (Figure 7.A) consisting of a mainline flown from the stern of a boat with hanging streamers that scare birds away from danger areas behind the vessel. The second approach, primarily used in longline fishing, is to remove the risky gear (baited hooks) as quickly as possible; essentially this involves adding weights to lines to sink them faster. It has reduced seabird bycatch on some fisheries by 90–95%.

Despite clear harm to seabirds caused by fisheries and the simple, effective fixes at hand, implementing these mitigation measures has been patchy at best in most fisheries where seabird bycatch occurs. There are some exceptions, and it is useful to examine what elements led certain fisheries to fix the problem. A good case study is in South Africa, where BirdLife South Africa's Albatross Task Force (ATF) demonstrated in 2006 that trawl fishing for hake (*Merluccius* spp.) was killing around 18,000 seabirds each year (Watkins et al., 2008). The fishery involved had Marine Stewardship Council (MSC) certification, which gives a fishery access to premium European markets on the condition that it meets environmentally friendly and sustainable metrics, including no significant bycatch impacts. This provided a powerful incentive for fleet-wide implementation of a bycatch mitigation measure; failure to do so would have resulted in a loss of certification, with catastrophic financial implications.

Despite this strong incentive, it required another five years of work from the ATF to assess bird scaring lines and refine the design, overcome resistance to their use, and close loopholes in regulations. In 2014, the ATF published an assessment of the effectiveness of their bird scaring lines—a single measure to

Figure 7.A Bird-scaring lines (in orange) keep a variety of albatross, petrels, and gannets at a safe distance from the baited hooks deployed off a trawler off South Africa.

prevent the accidental and avoidable deaths of around 10,000 albatrosses and large numbers of other species. When used correctly, the system eliminated 90–95% of seabird bycatch (Maree et al., 2014). Why did it take so long for the fleet to adopt this measure, despite it costing almost nothing, requiring no skill or time to use, and posing no meaningful operational problems? And why have identical fishing industries in many other countries failed to follow suite?

The answer is complex. ATF teams are present in South Africa (and now also in Namibia), providing sustained pressure and constant presence. South Africa had standing legislation, yet compliance from the South African fleet was initially minimal (and remains less than perfect today). MSC certification certainly created an enabling environment (Wanless and Maree, 2014) and incentive to drive change, yet it took more than that to change the entire fleet. Constant lobbying from BirdLife and regular dialogue from deck to boardroom were also critical ingredients. A legislative framework that provides some hope of censure against non-compliant vessels meant that there was internal pressure within the industry to "*tow* the line"—pun intended. Ultimately, widespread change became possible when there was a credible, independent observer programme to verify deck practice and give teeth to agencies when addressing non-compliance.

Figure 7.9 (Top) Discarded fishing gear, such as this ghost net, poses an entanglement hazard to marine wildlife.

(Bottom) A wandering albatross (*Diomedea exulans*, VU) that was a victim of bycatch, the accidental catching of non-target species during fishing operations.

7.2.3 The impact of traditional medicine

Africa has a long history of sustainable use of traditional medicines. Unfortunately, as the number of people living in Africa has increased, so has the demand for traditional medicine. Today, harvesting for traditional medicine is putting unsustainable pressure on species exploited for this purpose (Williams et al., 2014). One prominent example is vultures: the demand of vulture body parts, believed to bestow clairvoyant abilities, is driving massive vulture population declines across Africa (see Box 4.4). The growth in traditional medicine markets in East Asian countries such as China, Thailand, Cambodia, and Vietnam exacerbates these problems. For example, as tigers (*Panthera tigris*, EN) and rhinoceros have become scarce in Asia, Asian traditional healers are increasingly targeting African predators and rhinoceros to satisfy their market demands. Another group of species threatened by the Asian traditional medicine trade is sea horses (*Hippocampus* spp.). Due to population declines from overharvesting, sea horse exports from Kenya and Tanzania to East Asia have halved over recent years; yet, more than 600 kg of dried sea horses (over 254,000 individuals) continue to be exported annually (McPherson and Vincent, 2004). Exploitation for Asian traditional medicine markets has already pushed the western black rhinoceros (*Diceros bicornis longipes*, EX) to extinction. In a similarly perilous position is the northern white rhinoceros (*Ceratotherium simum cottoni*, CR); with only two non-reproductive females left in the world, this species is now considered **committed to extinction** (see Section 8.3; Box 11.4). A group of species sought after by both African and Asian traditional medicine markets is pangolins, thought to be the most heavily poached animals on Earth. For example, between 2012 and 2016, more than 20 tonnes of African pangolin scales (involving up to 30,000 animals) were seized during law enforcement operations across the region (Andersen, 2016). The problem is also getting worse: authorities intercepted 13 tonnes of scales in Singapore in 2019, all from a single shipment believed to travel from Nigeria to Vietnam (Geddie, 2019). With such a large active operational scale, it comes as no surprise that all four African pangolin species are now threatened with extinction (IUCN, 2019).

7.2.4 The impact of live animal trade

Millions of non-domesticated animals are sold as pets around the world each year (Table 7.1). Given that many of these pets were originally collected in the wild, it is no surprise that the most popular species tend to be at a high risk of extinction (Bush et al., 2014). These huge numbers are magnified by the extra millions of animals needed to compensate for deaths during collection and shipping. Collection of wild animals for pets and other purposes has a massive impact of biodiversity in Africa, the world's largest pet trade exporter (Bush et al. 2014).

Among the most popular groups of wildlife traded are Africa's parrots (Figure 7.10). For example, 32,000 wild-sourced African grey parrots (*Psittacus erithacus*, EN) were imported into the European Union in 2005 (UNEP-WCMC, 2007). Combined with habitat loss, the wild bird trade has already caused extirpations of this species in some areas of West Africa (Annorbah et al., 2015). Similarly, 82 of the 291 species of African freshwater fish known to occur in the pet trade are considered threatened with extinction (UNEP-WCMC, 2008). While it is true that collecting wild animals for the pet trade sustains many people's livelihoods, research on harvesting of ornamental fish in Cameroon has shown that this practice is not sustainable in the long term (Brummet et al., 2010). It is therefore critical to find ways to make these practices more sustainable, for the sake of the pet collectors and biodiversity.

Table 7.1 Examples of groups targeted in global wildlife trade, and their levels of exploitation.

Group	Number traded each year	Notes
Orchids	250 million	Mainly cultivated, but about 10% sourced from the wild. Illegal trade—and mislabelling to avoid regulation—a major problem.
Succulent plants	35 million	Mainly cultivated, but about 15% sourced from the wild. Illegal trade remains a major problem.
Corals	13 million	Collected using destructive methods; used for aquarium decor and jewellery.
Reptiles	7.2 million	Mainly sourced from the wild for zoos and pet trade, but increasingly from farms. Does not include large skin trade.
Birds	2.3 million	Mostly perching birds destined for zoos and pet trade. Also includes legal and illegal trade of parrots.
Ornamental fish	2 million	Most originate from wild reefs, caught by illegal methods that damage the surrounding coral reef and other wildlife.
Primates	148,000	Used for biomedical research, while many also destined for pets, circuses, zoos, and private collections.

Sources: http://cites-dashboards.unep-wcmc.org, data presented as live specimens exported from 2011–2015. Data generally do not include illegal traded specimens, which are usually not reported to CITES.

Figure 7.10 Wild-caught African grey parrots crammed into a travel crate before export to Asia. Researchers estimate that over 60% of smuggled parrots die from stress, dehydration, and smothering during transit (Mcgowan, 2008). Because of trade-driven population declines, CITES banned all international trade in this species in October 2016.

7.2.5 Overharvesting of plant products

Overharvesting is not restricted to animals and animal products. While legal and illegal timber and firewood extraction is a major source of deforestation throughout Africa, it is also an important extinction driver. In fact, logging and other forms of wood harvesting have already contributed to the extinction of at least six plant species in Sub-Saharan Africa, with an additional 116 species considered *Critically Endangered* in part due to these threats (IUCN, 2019). Other plant species face extinction due to exploitation for medicines, spices, fragrances, and ornaments. For example, White's ginger (*Mondia whitei*)—reputed to have aphrodisiac and antidepressant properties—has been harvested to extirpation in parts of central Kenya and South Africa (Aremu et al., 2011). Similarly, harvesting rates of African blackwood (*Dalbergia melanoxylon*, NT)—popular for making musical instruments and fine furniture—are currently unsustainable because the tree is slow-growing, has low germination rates, and extractions are seldom offset with planting of new seeds or seedlings (Amri et al., 2009).

7.2.6 Challenges in managing overharvesting

One of the biggest challenges in combatting overharvesting is the non-enforcement and/or outright absence of legal controls to protect exploited species. But even where strong regulatory frameworks exist, the sheer scale of the problem poses practical challenges for effective enforcement (discussed in Chapter 12), as billions of dollars flow among participants in illegal wildlife trade, which include local people trying to make a living, professional poachers, corrupt government officials, unethical dealers, and wealthy buyers who are not concerned about how the wildlife products they use were obtained. The illegal wildlife trade has hit Africa's megafauna particularly hard. For example, even though there has been an international ban on the ivory trade since 1989, thousands of African elephants continue to be illegally killed on an annual basis (Box 7.2). Similarly, despite a ban on rhinoceros horn trade since 1977, an increasing number of rhinoceros succumb to poaching every year (Figure 7.11). Worse yet, the illegal wildlife trade shares many characteristics and practices with the illegal trade in drugs and weapons; in some cases, the same syndicates run these various criminal enterprises (Christy and Stirton, 2015). Apprehending these criminal networks is generally very dangerous, requiring vast resources.

Now, consider a hypothetical conservationist concerned about the bushmeat crisis' impact on biodiversity. This person may very well think that effective enforcement of a hunting ban would be the best solution to prevent further overharvesting. Unfortunately, solving complex challenges with simplistic steps runs a high risk of being counterproductive. For example, local bushmeat markets provide important contributions to food and financial security in many rural parts of Africa (van der Merwe et al., 2015). Replacing bushmeat with livestock and crops production—two primary drivers of habitat loss (Chapter 5)—also carries risks. For example, an estimated 250,000 km^2 of forest will need to be converted to pastureland to replace the bushmeat trade just

Box 7.2 Conserving Elephants in the Anthropocene

David H.M. Cumming[1,2]

[1]*FitzPatrick Institute of African Ornithology, University of Cape Town, Cape Town, South Africa.*

[2]*Tropical Resource Ecology Programme, University of Zimbabwe, Harare, Zimbabwe.*

✉ *cummingdhm@gmail.com*

As our increasingly human-dominated planet enters a new geological era, will there still be room for Earth's largest land mammals? Or will there be, as happened to mammoths, sabre-toothed cats, and giant sloths during the Pleistocene (see Box 8.1), another hominid-induced extinction of large mammals? Our new human-dominated era has become known as the Anthropocene (Waters et al., 2015), and the animals are, of course, Africa's elephants.

Elephants encapsulate the dilemmas of conserving large charismatic mammals. They are dominant ecosystem engineers that, depending on their densities, can facilitate or adversely impact species diversity and ecosystem processes (Section 4.2.1). They are also economically important to ecotourism industries and revered by many; ivory ornaments and carvings have been valued highly by many cultures past and present. But elephants are also regarded as dangerous pests by expanding small-scale farming communities, responsible for destroying crops and killing people. While retaliatory killings and habitat loss (primarily through agricultural expansion) certainly contribute to the endangerment of elephants, poaching to supply Asian markets (see Figure 12.1) is the primary cause behind massive population reductions we are currently witnessing (Wittemyer et al., 2014).

Africa's elephants have, in the past, been greatly exploited, first for their meat and later also for their ivory. In 1887, about 1,000 tonnes of ivory were being exported from Africa (Spinage, 1973) and, by 1900, elephant populations in many African countries had all but collapsed. In Southern Africa, for example, it was feared that they might soon go extinct. However, with effective protection, elephant populations increased twentyfold, to more than 200,000, south of the Zambezi River by the 1970s. Elsewhere, elephant numbers also recovered, and, in the mid-1970s, the continental elephant population was estimated to be more than 1 million (Table 7.B). But a rapid escalation of the illegal killing of elephants for ivory and meat soon followed, accompanied by a steep rise in the price of ivory. In response, African elephants were placed on CITES Appendix II in 1976 to control the international trade in ivory. Elephants in some Southern African countries were well protected, so numbers continued to grow. However, elsewhere poaching and illegal trade in ivory continued and, in 1989, the African elephant was placed on CITES Appendix I, which banned all international trade in elephants and elephant products. The result was a decline in the price of ivory, and recovery of many populations.

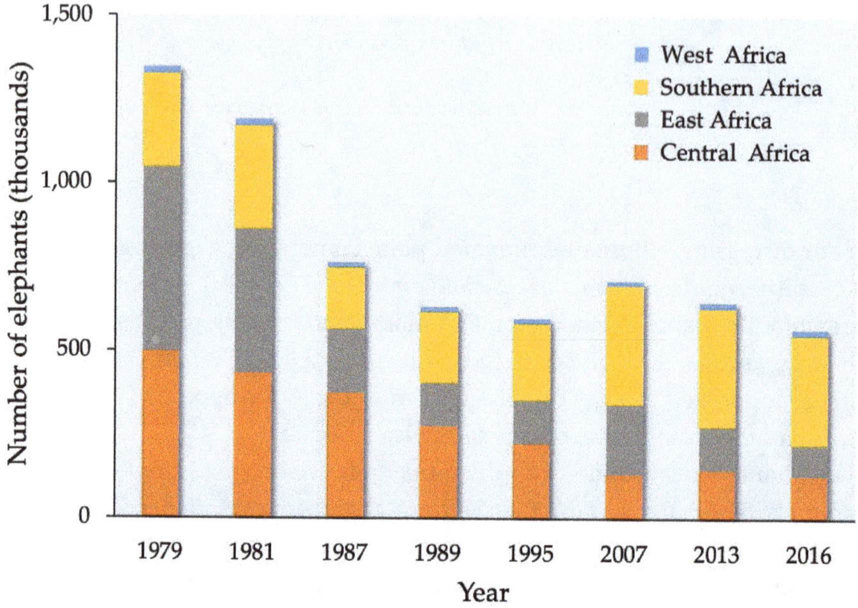

Figure 7.B Estimated number of elephants in West, Central, East and Southern Africa between 1979 and 2016.

Conservationists, and the world at large, traditionally regarded the African elephant as a single species. Recent morphometric and genetic evidence has revealed that forest and savannah elephants represent two distinct species, with forest elephants (*Loxodonta cyclotis*) occupying the West and Central African forests, and the larger savannah elephants (*Loxodonta africana*) being widespread in non-forested regions of Sub-Saharan Africa (Roca et al., 2015). The distinction has important implications for their conservation, as each of these elephant species now viewed on its own is even more sensitive to population declines (CBD, 2015).

Since about 2006, poaching of elephants again began to escalate, in part a response to an increase in the price of ivory, poorly funded wildlife agencies, and corruption (Hauenstein et al., 2019). The scale of these killings is extraordinary. For example, an estimated 30,000 elephants were killed in 2013 alone. Forest elephants declined by about 60% (Maisel et al., 2013). While population trends for savannah elephants vary across the region, they too face increased poaching pressure (Chase et al., 2016). Due to these large-scale killings, combined with the impact of habitat loss from agricultural expansion, West Africa's elephants are today confined to small isolated protected areas with a total population of about 17,000 (Maisel et al., 2013). Elephant population trends in East Africa vary: numbers are increasing in Uganda and Kenya, but Tanzania has lost some 60,000 elephants in the last few years. In Southern Africa, Botswana has the largest elephant population, estimated in 2014 to number at least 130,000. Neighbouring Zimbabwe has a population of 83,000 elephants, much the same number as it had in 2001. However, two of Zimbabwe's four regional populations declined significantly between 2006 and 2014 with a loss of at least 20,000 elephants (Figure 7.C).

Figure 7.C Savannah elephants at a waterhole in Hwange National Park. Hwange, Zimbabwe's flagship protected area, has been a hotspot of poacher activity in recent years. By lacing waterholes and salt licks with cyanide during the dry season, poachers killed over 100 elephants here in 2013 (Cruise, 2017); several elephant poisoning events have occurred since then.

Global and national efforts to curb elephant poaching are currently focused on improving law enforcement on the ground, intercepting ivory shipments to Asia, closing ivory markets in Africa and Asia, and leading campaigns to reduce demand for ivory in major consuming countries in Asia, particularly in China. Importantly, while these initiatives are relieving poaching pressure on African elephant populations, they fail to address core issues relating to the interactions between people and elephants in the rural areas of Africa. A high proportion of elephant ranges lie outside protected areas where they overlap with people. Relieving continued pressures on elephants, outside as well as inside protected areas, would only happen if people who are harmed by elephants derive enough benefits from elephants and other wildlife to outweigh the direct and indirect costs of sharing land with them. Community-based natural resource management (CBNRM) projects, such as those in Namibia (Section 14.3) show that this can be achieved. Establishing secure and sustainable funding streams through payments for ecosystem services (Section 15.3), or payments for co-existing with large dangerous mammals such as elephants (Section 14.4), could extend these promising initiatives even further.

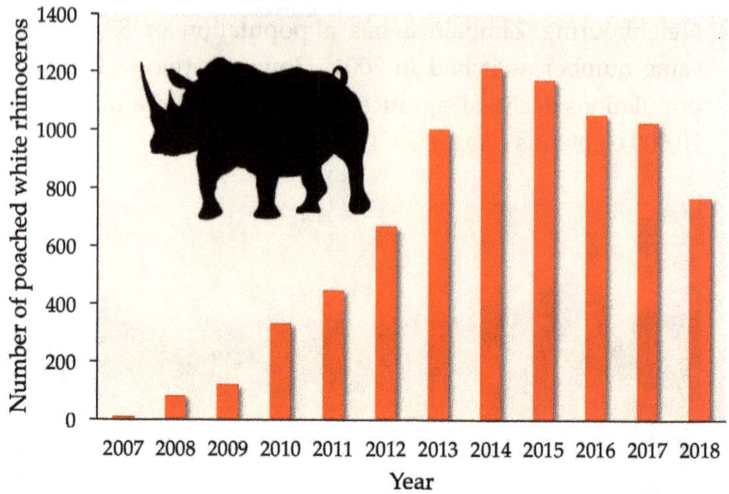

Figure 7.11 More than 7,200 rhinoceros were illegally killed in South Africa between 2007 and 2017. Fortunately, illegal killings have declined in recent years, thanks to massive anti-poaching campaigns and increased law enforcement efforts.

for the Congo Basin (Nasi et al., 2011). Clearly, there is a need for the bushmeat trade, albeit in a sustainable manner to ensure long-term viability of the local biodiversity, as well as the prosperity of the people who inhabit these areas. We delve deeper into solutions for these kinds of complex challenges from Chapter 9 onwards.

7.3 Persecution

Persecution involves the indiscriminate abuse or killing of a group of animals, generally used as a strategy to prevent property damage (e.g. crop-raiding elephants) and livestock depredation (e.g. lions endangering cattle). Some animals are also persecuted because of the real or perceived dangers they pose to humans; this includes the indiscriminate killing of sharks, snakes, and spiders to avoid bites, and culling of bats to prevent spread of **zoonotic diseases** (Schneeberger and Voigt, 2016). Lastly, local folklore also contributes to persecution: animals, such as moles, chameleons, and owls are sometimes indiscriminately killed because of cultural beliefs that they bring bad luck.

While killing a (potential or perceived) problem animal may bring a certain instant gratification, it is a short-term solution that often causes more harm than good. Culling bats, for example, may in fact increase the prevalence of the same zoonotic diseases people are trying to control (Schneeberger and Voigt, 2016). Persecution also leads to the loss of ecosystem services, as it often targets ecosystem engineers and keystone species (Section 4.2.1). Retaliatory poisoning is particularly harmful for all the other useful organisms that may be killed in the process. One study in Namibia estimated that about 100 non-target animals are killed for every target animal, putting harmless species such

While killing a (potential or perceived) problem animal may bring a certain instant gratification, it is a short-term solution that often causes more harm than good.

as aardwolf (*Proteles cristatus*, LC), bat-eared fox (*Otocyon megalotis*, LC), and Cape fox (*Vulpes chama*, LC) also at risk (Brown, 2006). Among the most vulnerable to such poisoning are vultures, which may be accidentally poisoned by bait set out for problem predators, or directly targeted for traditional medicine and to hide poaching activities. In June 2019, 537 vultures (comprising five different *Endangered* and *Critically Endangered* species) were killed in Botswana after scavenging from three poisoned elephant carcass (de Greef, 2019). This mass poisoning event was particularly devastating because it was during the vulture breeding season, so many vulture chicks likely also died from starvation if not from eating tainted meat brought back to the nest by their parents.

7.4 Invasive Species

An **exotic species** is a species that occurs beyond its native range, most often because humans have moved it, whether intentionally or not. Most exotic species do not establish viable populations in the new areas to which they have been moved because the new environments may not meet their needs, because native species may outcompete them or otherwise displace them, or because there may not be a sufficient number of individuals to become established. However, a small number of exotic species go on to become **invasive species**—exotic species that rapidly spread and increase in abundance at the expense of native species and ecosystems. While there is no definitive list of qualities that predict which exotic species can become invasive, many invasive species have the following in common: (1) they begin to reproduce at an early age; (2) they can reproduce rapidly; (3) they lack sufficient predators in their introduced range; (4) they disperse easily; (5) and they are generalist species, able to survive in a variety of ecosystems.

> Invasive species displace native species through competition, predation, and habitat alterations. They often thrive in environments disturbed by human activities.

7.4.1 Spread of invasive species

As stated above, invasive species spread and invade new areas because human activities move them there. Some of the most prominent means by which human activities facilitate the spread of invasive species include:

- *Agriculture*: Large industries exist to grow agricultural plants for crop production, ornamental plants for gardens, grasses for pastures, and livestock for food. Many of these organisms later escape from cultivation and captivity and go on to invade and harm local ecosystems. Other species spread when industry workers accidentally harvest the seeds of weedy plants along with commercial seeds, and then sow those seeds in new localities, while microbes, parasitic organisms, and insects may be transported with plant leaves and roots, in potting soil, or even attached to transported animals. One of Africa's worst plant invaders, the triffid weed (*Chromolaena odorata*), continues to spread because of its sustained use to boost soil fertility on agricultural lands (Uyi et al., 2014).

- *Accidental transport*: Many invasive species spread to new areas because people transported them unintentionally. Domestic rats (*Rattus* spp.) and mice (*Mus* spp.) are classic examples: they have spread around the world as stowaways aboard ships (Box 7.3). A great number of invasive plants that currently occur in South Africa's Cape Floristic Province arrived by accident by clinging onto the luggage and hiking gear of tourists (Anderson et al., 2015). The ballast tanks of ships are also common hiding places for invasive aquatic species: DNA analyses have shown how a German ship carried tiny snails in this way along the entire length of Africa's Atlantic coast, providing invasion opportunities across this entire shipping route (Ardura et al., 2015).
- *Biological control*: Environmental and agricultural organisations sometimes use biological control (Section 4.2.7) to manage the spread of, and harm caused by, invasive species. While this approach can be very effective, in rare cases the biocontrol agent can become invasive and harm native species, rather than its intended target. For example, domestic cats that were introduced to Marion Island off Africa's south coast feasted on native seabirds—in some cases, even causing seabird extirpations—instead of the rats and mice they were meant to control (Bloomer and Bester, 1992). For this reason, very careful research is necessary to test the appropriateness of a biocontrol agent before being released.
- *Deliberate introductions*: Soon after their arrival, colonists released hundreds of European birds and mammals into countries like South Africa and Kenya to make the African countryside feel more familiar. Other species, especially fish (e.g. trout, bass, and carp), were released to provide food and recreational opportunities. Many of these species have subsequently become so successful that they harm native species. For example, mesquite (*Prosopis juliflora*), introduced to Ethiopia from Mexico to reduce soil salinity, proved such a successful invader that it completely displaced local plants; the subsequent encroachment even threatens the viability of Ethiopia's few remaining Grevy's zebras (*Equus grevyi*, EN) (Kebede and Coppock, 2015). The introduction of the Nile perch (*Lates niloticus*, LC) to the Rift Valley to boost local fisheries likely led to the extinction of hundreds of fish species endemic in Lake Victoria (Pringle, 2005).
- *Captive escapees*: Many invasive species were originally kept as pets or ornamental plants but have escaped from captivity to establish feral populations that harm local wildlife. Some of the most problematic aquatic invasive species are common pets that people dumped in streams, lakes, or storm drains because they could not care for them anymore. Finding these

escapees before they establish should thus be a priority. For example, a recent survey found that 258 alien ornamental plant species growing in South Africa's Kruger National Park are at risk of becoming invasive—most of these plants were subsequently removed from the park (Foxcroft et al., 2008).

Box 7.3 Aliens on Islands: Damage and Control

Peter Ryan

FitzPatrick Institute of African Ornithology, DST-NRF Centre of Excellence, University of Cape Town, South Africa.

peter.ryan@uct.ac.za

Invasive species are one of the main threats to biodiversity. Island ecosystems are particularly vulnerable; of the 156 bird species that have gone extinct in the last 500 years, more than 90% lived on oceanic islands (IUCN, 2019). This vulnerability is mainly due to species on oceanic islands evolving in the absence of competing species or predators, and thus lacking adequate defences against introduced species (including humans).

Invasive species pose many threats to island biodiversity. Newly arrived mammalian predators have exacted the greatest toll. Seemingly unable to appreciate the danger posed by these strange new arrivals, the ecologically-naïve adult birds simply remain on their nests to be eaten rather than fleeing. Introduced herbivores can have devastating impacts, because many island plants lack defences like tough leaves or thorns. Most devastating are domestic goats and rabbits, introduced by early island explorers to provide a source of food in the case of shipwreck, that have grazed many once-lush islands down to the ground. Introduced plants can also outcompete native plants. For example, the Mexican thorn (also called mesquite, *Prosopis juliflora*) has formed dense thickets on the once sparsely vegetated lowlands of Ascensión Island, making those areas unsuitable for both nesting seabirds and sea turtles.

Some of Africa's least-transformed islands are the sub-Antarctic Prince Edward Islands, 2,000 km southeast of Cape Agulhas, and Gough Island, 2,800 km west of Cape Town. Their small size, isolation, and lack of sheltered harbours prevented human settlement. Nevertheless, their large seal and seabird populations were frequently exploited for oil and skins in the 19th and early 20th centuries. In the 19th century, sealing parties accidentally introduced house mice (*Mus musculus*) to Marion Island, the larger of the two Prince Edward Islands, and Gough Island. The mice flourished by eating native invertebrates and plants, probably causing the local extinction of one flightless moth on Marion Island. A few domestic cats were brought in to control the mice at Marion Island's weather station, established in 1948. Instead, the cats targeted the island's birds, which were easier prey. By the 1970s, some 2,000 cats were killing an estimated 450,000 seabirds each year, greatly reducing the island's burrow-nesting petrels and even driving some species to local extinction (Bloomer and Bester, 1992). The events on Marion contrasted with nearby predator-free Prince Edward Island that continued to support vast breeding populations of burrowing petrels.

A pioneering initiative eradicated Marion Island's cats in 1991, using a combination of introduced cat influenza, hunting, trapping, and poisoning (Bloomer and Bester, 1992). Researchers hoped Marion's seabird populations would recover within a decade but had not considered the impact of mice once the cats were removed. The precedent was set on Gough Island; in 2001, introduced mice were discovered to predate on large numbers of seabird chicks, including Tristan albatross (*Diomedea dabbenena*, CR) chicks more than 100 times larger than themselves (Davies et al., 2015; Dilley et al., 2015a). It was hypothesised that mice are more likely to attack seabirds when they are the sole introduced predators on an island. Sure enough, the first attacks on Marion's albatross chicks were recorded in 2003 (Figure 7.D); by 2015, the attacks had increased dramatically (Dilley et al., 2015b).

Figure 7.D Two grey-headed albatross fledglings (*Thalassarche chrysostoma*, EN), still on the nest, suffering from injuries after predatory mouse attacks on Marion Island, southern Indian Ocean. The bird in the foreground already has its scalp exposed. Attacks usually occur at night; mice will come back to the attack site over successive nights until the victims succumb to their injuries.

Fortunately, it is possible to eradicate invasive species from islands. In 2014, Australia removed mice, rats, and rabbits from sub-Antarctic Macquarie Island (Parks and Wildlife Service, 2014), which is almost twice the size of Gough Island. Plans are now also in place to eradicate Gough's mice in 2019. The island's isolation facilitates this effort—damage to other species can be minimized, and possible spread of toxins or diseases will be confined. To access areas inaccessible on foot, helicopters will be used to spread poison bait from specially designed hoppers slung under the aircraft. Some poisoning of non-target native individuals is inevitable, but this is a small price to pay compared to extinctions of those species. If adequate measures are put in place to prevent subsequent reintroductions, there is hope of restoring at least part of the island's natural balance.

7.4.2 Impact of invasive species

Invasive species have many negative consequences for native biodiversity: they displace native species through competition, alter the structure and composition of natural communities, and sometimes also hybridise with native species. These impacts may also translate to financial losses, as invasive species compromise ecosystem services (Figure 7.12), damage infrastructure, and spread infectious diseases.

Figure 7.12 The tickberry (*Lantana camara*) may be pretty, but it is a serious invasive species across Africa. Where it invades, it reduces the productivity of natural ecosystems and agricultural lands by forming dense thickets that outcompete native plants. This plant is also toxic to animals, including livestock and pets.

Invasive species often become pervasive because they outcompete and displace native species. One such example is the Mediterranean mussel (*Mytilus galloprovincialis*), which was accidentally introduced to South Africa in the mid-1970s via European ships. A superior competitor, the exotic mussel soon started displacing native mussels and limpets, especially in the inter-tidal zone of South Africa's west coast (Branch and Steffani, 2004). Considered South Africa's most successful marine invasive, recent evidence suggests that the Mediterranean mussel is continuing to spread north into Namibia and along South Africa's east coast towards Mozambique.

Another superior competitor is the water hyacinth. A native to South America's Amazon forest, this species was intentionally introduced as a showy ornamental plant to dams, ponds, and lakes across Africa in the early 20th century. The plant established well, but then started reproducing and spreading at such rapid rates that water bodies across the region were soon covered by a dense mat of leaves. With little surface exposure and water movement, eutrophication and suffocation followed, leading to the deaths of countless fish and other aquatic organisms (Villamagna and Murphy, 2010). A biological control program targeting hyacinth showed promise during the 1990s; however, eutrophication from fertiliser overuse (which stimulate growth of hyacinth and other invasive aquatic plants) may be contributing to this species' recent resurgence (Coetzee and Hill, 2012; Bownes et al., 2013).

Natural communities are at particular risk in cases where invasive species change ecosystem structure and functioning so much that native species can no longer survive. Such is the case across many parts of Africa, where invasive Australian gum (*Eucalyptus* spp.) and pine (*Pinus* spp.) trees (both widely planted for timber) transpire so much water through their leaves (as much as 50,000 litres of water per tree/year; Dzikiti et al., 2016) that they can reduce the availability of surface- and groundwater in an area by as much as 70% (le Maitre et al., 2016). In addition to creating drought conditions, the closed canopies created by these invasive trees reduce the amount of solar radiation reaching the ground, greatly limiting thermoregulatory opportunities for taxa such as reptiles (Schreuder and Clusella-Trullas, 2016). Habitat degradation caused by invasions of the cinnamon tree (*Cinnamomum verum*), originally from Sri Lanka, has already caused at least ten invertebrate extinctions in the Seychelles (IUCN, 2019).

A single gum or pine tree can transpire as much as 50,000 litres of water per year, while plantations of these trees can reduce water resources in an area by as much as 70%.

While many of the invasive species mentioned earlier originated from outside Africa, it is important to note that African species can also become invasive in other parts of Africa when they are moved outside of their native ranges. When invading nearby areas, non-native species can come in close contact with closely-related species, creating a high risk of genetic mixing—also called **genetic pollution** or genetic swamping—which describes the hybridisation of invasive species with native species. For example, hybridisation with the widespread banded tilapia (*Tilapia sparmanii*, LC) threatens the survival of Namibia's Otjikoto tilapia (*Tilapia guinasana*, CR), globally restricted to the < 1 km^2 Lake Guineas (Bills 2007). The Cape platanna (*Xenopus gilli*, EN), an endemic to South Africa's Cape Floristic Region, is similarly threatened by hybridisation with the widespread African clawed frog (*Xenopus laevis*, LC) (Fogell et al., 2013).

7.4.3 Genetically modified organisms

A topic of conflict among conservation biologists is the increased popularity of **genetically modified organisms (GMO)**. A GMO is an organism whose genetic material has been altered to provide useful or improved products and services. To do this, scientists typically use genome editing technologies to transfer genes from a "source" organism into the DNA of the target organism. For example, scientists can transfer a bacterial gene that produces an insect toxin into a crop, such as maize, to obtain a GMO that can resist insect herbivory. Farmers using this GMO maize would then be able to increase production *and* reduce pesticide use (Gewin, 2003). While GMOs are usually associated with the development of pest-resistant and drought-resistant crops, uses are highly varied. For example, in Senegal, GMO technologies are used to produce tilapia that are better adapted to local ecosystems (Eknath et al., 2007). GMO technologies are being used to develop new and cheaper medicines (Concha et al., 2017), and to combat important diseases: trials in Burkina Faso shows that fungi genetically engineered to produce spider toxins caused a 99% collapse in malaria-carrying *Anopheles* mosquito populations within 45 days (Lovett et al., 2019). GMOs can even be used for conservation purposes, like developing new methods to combat invasive species (Esvelt et al., 2014), creating more effective bioenergy sources (Beer et al., 2009), and making vulnerable species more **resistant** to climate change (Piaggio et al., 2017). Some scientists even hope to combat plastic pollution by creating a genetically modified bacterium able to consume plastic waste (Austin et al., 2018).

GMOs offer benefits such as increased production and reduced pesticide use, but there are concerns about unknown and unintended consequences like hybridisation and invasiveness.

The use of GMOs is not a new phenomenon. Selective breeding, hybridisation, and other forms of artificial selection—techniques that have been used for much of human history—all result in different forms of genetically modified crops and animal species. However, technological advances in genetic engineering have enabled scientists to transfer genes from and between different taxa that have not previously been used in selective breeding programmes (i.e. viruses, bacteria, insects, fungi, and shellfish). GMO technologies that transfer genetic material between wholly disparate taxa has led to concern about the unknown and unintended consequences of such "crossovers". Some people are also concerned that GMOs that escape from captivity or cultivation (e.g. Gilbert, 2010) could hybridise with closely-related wild species, endangering native wildlife while resulting in new, aggressive weeds and virulent diseases. Additionally, the use of GMO crops could potentially harm non-crop species (e.g. insects, birds, and soil organisms) that live in, on, or near the GMO crops. Concerns have also been raised about the potential effects to people eating GMO foods, leading some governments to regulate GMO research and commercial applications differently than traditional agriculture. However, after decades of research, it appears that GMO food is safe to eat (Blancke, 2015).

Clearly, GMOs offer a wide range of opportunities which could directly and indirectly benefit biodiversity conservation. However, the benefits of GMOs must be examined and weighed against the potential risks on a case by case basis. It is probably wise to proceed cautiously, to study GMOs thoroughly, and to monitor their impacts on ecosystems and human health in the areas where they are used. These investigations could involve workshops where experts come together to perform **environmental impact assessments (EIA)** (Section 12.2.2). The potential but unknown impacts of GMOs can also be mitigated by limiting the ability of these organisms to spread or reproduce (Muir and Howard, 2004).

7.6 Parasites and Diseases

Parasites and diseases have always been an important natural factor in regulating the ecology of wildlife, especially in wild populations that have become unsustainably large. Today, however, human activities are facilitating increased spread and transmission of parasites (Box 7.4) and other pathogens, sometimes even creating conditions for epidemics to develop (Figure 7.13). Consequently, parasites and diseases have become a major threat to wildlife, including those already suffering under low population sizes and densities.

Box 7.4 Promoting African and Global Honeybee Health

Vincent Dietemann

Agroscope, Swiss Bee Research Center, Schwarzenburgstrasse, Switzerland.

✉ *vincent.dietemann@alp.admin.ch*

Modern society imposes increased pressure on animals and plants to secure the food needed for a growing human population. Honeybees especially contribute to crop productivity in a crucial way thanks to their pollination services. Unfortunately, the number of bee colony losses has surged in recent years in several regions of the world (Goulson et al., 2015), worrying scientists, politicians, and the public. Some regions in Africa, however, have maintained healthy domesticated and wild honeybee colonies (Pirk et al., 2016), which continue to pollinate flowers and enhance the production of many fruit and vegetable crops.

The power of comparisons

Comparative studies have always been important to biological research. Studying a model organism or system under different conditions allows scientists to identify how these organisms or systems react and adapt to their environment. This can even be done at the continental scale and could help us understand the effect of human pressure exerted on honeybees. In general, beekeeping in North America and Europe has been widely industrialised, involving large-scale operations and modern technology, whereas in Africa beekeeping has remained small-scale and mostly low-tech. This gives us an opportunity to determine the effects of beekeeping management and trade on honeybee health.

Different contexts

The varroa mite (*Varroa destructor*) originally parasitised the eastern honeybee (*Apis cerana*). In the wake of global honeybee trade, this parasite has invaded most regions of the world that are home to the western honeybee (*Apis mellifera*) and resulted in major colony losses (Figure 7.E). Although eastern and western honeybees are closely-related species, the western honeybee did not coevolve with this parasite and, thus, has few natural defences against it, with colonies dying within a few years after infestation. Consequently, only those colonies treated against the parasite by beekeepers can survive, and most wild honeybee populations have been decimated. However, there have been exceptions: colonies of the western honeybee in the southern parts of Africa are resistant to the parasite, and large wild populations remain. Several international teams have now turned their attention to resistant African honeybee populations to understand the basis of their survival (Strauss et al., 2016). Researchers hope to use this knowledge to promote the breeding of surviving colonies in currently susceptible populations both within and outside of Africa.

Figure 7.E During its development, this young honey bee worker has been damaged by the varroa mite it carries on the front end of its abdomen. Its deformed wings are a consequence of this parasitism.

Africa also differs strongly in land use and crop management techniques that are likely to influence honeybees' nutrition and health. In many areas, small-scale farming prevails, with a lower use of pesticides than in other areas of the world. Understanding how pesticide and other chemical use, as well as how nectar and pollen variety and quality, impact these pollinators will be key to their survival. Therefore, the rest of the world may learn how to maintain healthy honeybees from Africa. Africa, in return, might benefit from global efforts to maintain sustainable pollination services and promote food security.

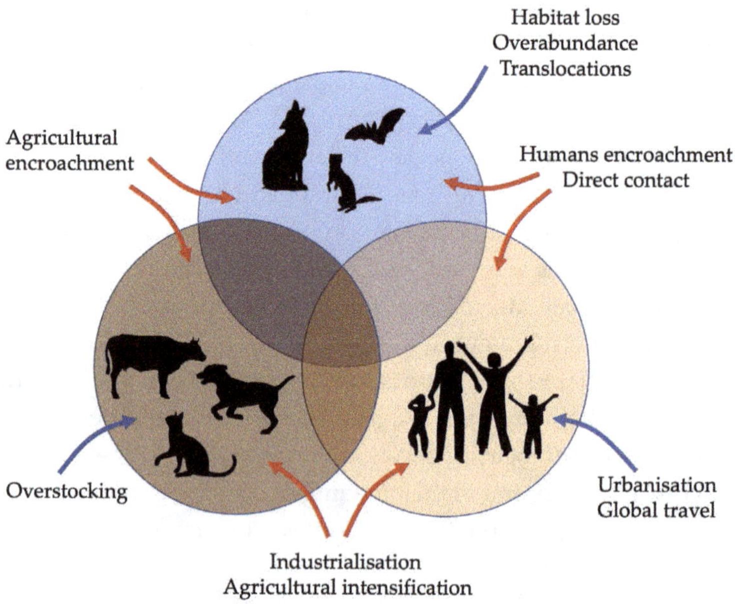

Figure 7.13 Habitat loss and encroachment of human activities into natural areas increase the rates of transmission of infectious diseases such as influenza, rabies, canine distemper virus, and Ebola between wildlife, domestic animals, and human. This figure illustrates the infection and transmission routes of rabies. Blue arrows represent factors that leads to higher infection rates, while red allows represent factors that contribute to the spread of the disease among the three vulnerable groups. After Daszak et al., 2000.

One way in which humans elevate the impact of parasites and diseases on wildlife is by exposing native species to harmful organisms that they have never previously encountered, and thus have no evolved coping mechanisms. For example, population declines and extirpations of about 200 frog species across the world, including in Africa (Tarrant et al., 2013; Hirschfeld et al., 2016), is due, in part, to a disease caused by the chytrid fungus (*Batrachochytrium dendrobatidis*). This disease, known as chytridiomycosis (Figure 7.14), affects a frog's ability to absorb water and electrolytes through the skin (Alroy, 2015). It likely originated in the Korean Peninsula (O'Hanlon et al., 2018), and spread across the world through trade with African clawed frogs (*Xenopus laevis*, LC) (Weldon et al., 2004). As of yet, there is no cure for this disease, and it continues to be seen as one of the biggest threats currently facing the world's amphibians.

Figure 7.14 Biologists swabbing an olive striped frog (*Phlyctimantis leonardi,* LC) in Gabon to screen for the chytrid fungus. Frogs from Cameroon has tested positive (Baláž et al., 2012) which suggests the species might be at risk; however, thus far no ill effects have been observed.

Disease transmissions can also occur when humans and their pets or livestock interact with wildlife (Cumming and Cumming, 2015). For example, during the early 1990s about 25% of lions in Tanzania's Serengeti National Park were killed by canine distemper virus which they contracted from domestic dogs living near the park (Kissui and Packer, 2004). Because of the many biological similarities between apes and humans, gorillas (*Gorilla* spp.), chimpanzees (*Pan troglodytes,* EN) and bonobos (*P. paniscus,* EN) are particularly vulnerable to **anthroponotic diseases,** such as measles, influenza, and pneumonia which can be transferred from humans to animals. But even chytridiomycosis (discussed above) can become an anthroponotic disease, transferred from frog to frog by a careless biologist that handles a healthy frog after a sick one without taking precautions against transmission. Some diseases (e.g. Ebola; flu; and tuberculosis) can be anthroponotic and **zoonotic** (transferred from animals to humans). While the impact of Ebola on humans in Africa is well-known, it is worth noting that gorillas suffer > 90% mortality when exposed to Ebola, compared to 50% mortality in humans. In fact, it was an Ebola outbreak in 2004 that caused the western lowland gorilla (*Gorilla gorilla gorilla,* CR) to be classified as highly threatened by the IUCN (Genton et al., 2012).

Humans also indirectly facilitate the transmission and spread of parasites and pathogens. While there are some exceptions (notably social insects), transmission and infection rates are typically low for wildlife living in large, complex ecosystems because they have space to move away from disease-carrying droppings, saliva, old skin, and other sources of infection. However, these natural buffers against pathogens and parasites are removed when humans confine those organisms to small areas (such as small fenced reserves) or keep them in crowded conditions. In addition to forcing those organisms to remain in close

> Human activities often facilitate the emergence and spread of infectious diseases, which threaten wildlife, domestic species, and humans alike.

contact with potential sources of infection, crowded conditions lead to deterioration of habitat quality and food availability. Both these factors increase the organisms' stress levels and reduce their body conditions which, in turn, lowers their resistance to parasites and diseases (reviewed in Gottdenker et al., 2014).

Human-induced extirpations indirectly facilitate the transmission and spread of parasites and pathogens, even to humans. Such is the case with schistosomiasis (also known as bilharzia), a zoonotic disease carried by a few freshwater snail species. In the 1980s, health care professionals observed an increased incidence of human schistosomiasis around Lake Malawi after overfishing depleted snail-eating fish populations, followed by decreased incidence of schistosomiasis as fish populations recovered in the 1990s (Stauffer et al., 2006). A similar situation occurred in East Africa, where the elimination of apex predators resulted in increased olive baboon (*Papio anubis*, LC) populations, which not only worsened crop raiding, but also increased parasite infection rates among local peoples (Brashares et al., 2010).

Parasites and diseases also threaten captive wildlife populations, including those kept at zoos and other **ex situ conservation** facilities (Section 11.5). Because of the proximity in which different species are kept, captive conditions may allow for easier spread of diseases. An added complication with captive populations is that some individuals may function as disease reservoirs. These individuals generally appear healthy because they are fairly resistant to the disease they carry, yet they are able to infect other susceptible individuals. Disease reservoirs frequently limit opportunities for translocation of captive populations (Section 11.2), even when dealing with threatened species. For example, well-meaning people often bring raggedy-looking yet healthy penguins in moult to rehabilitation centres, hoping the penguins will be released once "better". Yet, those animals might never be released back in the wild to avoid the risk of transmitting diseases to wild penguin populations (Brossy et al., 1999).

The impacts of diseases are bound to become more important in the future of conservation biology, especially as growing human populations and increased competition for space increase the need for single-species management and ex situ conservation (Chapter 11). Disease management should therefore always be taken very seriously, and appropriate steps taken to avoid disease transmissions.

7.7 Summary

1. Many threats to biodiversity do not lead to immediate and/or direct mortality, but instead have sublethal impacts that compromise organisms' fitness over time. Responses to these silent, insidious, and easily-overlooked threats are often delayed, especially when the negative effects are felt only years after exposure.
2. Environmental pollution leaves ecosystems uninhabitable for native wildlife, and cause sickness and death in wildlife and people. Common causes of

pollution include pesticides, heavy metals, plastic, fossil fuels, fertilisers, light, heat, and noise, leading to pollution of water, groundwater, air, and soil.

3. Overharvesting is becoming an increasingly damaging threat to biodiversity because people have better access to previously unexploited areas and are adopting increasingly efficient methods for harvesting wildlife products. Persecution, which has its roots in human-wildlife conflict, is becoming an important threat because a growing human population is increasingly encroaching on the shrinking remaining natural habitats.
4. Invasive species outcompete local species and change the structure and composition of their native ecosystems. Human activity is responsible for these invasions, by accidentally or deliberately moving wildlife to new regions of the world. Some invasive species require a great amount of effort and resources to manage.
5. Disease transmission and spread increase when wildlife is confined to small areas and/or crowded conditions. Diseases may also be transmitted between wildlife, domesticated species, and even humans. Managing for diseases is also important in zoos and other ex situ facilities, because diseases spreading from one individual to another can prevent those individuals from being released into the wild.

7.8 Topics for Discussion

1. Which forms of environmental pollution are most prominent in the region where you live? Which natural ecosystems are impacted most severely by this pollution? How are humans affected? What do you think can be done to reduce or even eliminate this pollution?
2. Consider all the fishing, hunting, trapping, collecting, logging, and other wildlife harvesting activities in your region. Which activities are well managed, and which are not? Why is it so difficult to regulate these activities, when so many people know that overharvesting would eventually harm local economies, their families, and their livelihoods? What measures do you think can be put in place to control overharvesting in your region, or at least reduce its impact?
3. Briefly describe what biological control is, and what its benefits are. What are the risks involved in biological control? How can these risks be predicted and avoided?
4. Can you name a few diseases that can be transmitted from people to wildlife, and from wildlife to people? Which species are involved in each of these diseases? How does the transmission of each of these diseases impact the conservation management of species involved?

7.9 Suggested Readings

Benítez-López, A., L. Santini, A.M. Schipper, et al. 2019. Intact but empty forests? Patterns of hunting-induced mammal defaunation in the tropics. *PLoS ONE* 17: e3000247. https://doi.org/10.1371/journal.pbio.3000247 African mammals are undergoing catastrophic declines due to unregulated hunting.

Bouwman, H., I.M. Viljoen, L.P. Quinn, et al. 2008. Halogenated pollutants in terrestrial and aquatic bird eggs: Converging patterns of pollutant profiles and impacts and risks from high level. *Environmental Research* 126: 240–52. https://doi.org/10.1016/j.envres.2013.06.003 DDT threaten African biodiversity and people even today

Campbell, L., P. Verburg, D.G. Dixon, et al. 2008. Mercury biomagnification in the food web of Lake Tanganyika (Tanzania, East Africa). *Science of The Total Environment* 402: 184–91. https://doi.org/10.1016/j.scitotenv.2008.04.017 Biomagnification of heavy metals are making some fish unsafe to eat.

Galloway, T.S., and C.N. Lewis. 2016. Marine microplastics spell big problems for future generations. *Proceedings of the National Academy of Sciences* 113: 2331–33. https://doi.org/10.1073/pnas.1600715113 The threat of plastic pollution to ocean life.

Gottdenker, N.L., D.G. Streicker, C.L. Faust, et al. 2014. Anthropogenic land use change and infectious diseases: A review of the evidence. *EcoHealth* 11: 619632. https://doi.org/10.1007/s10393-014-0941-z Linking environmental degradation to disease risk in humans and wildlife.

le Maitre, D.C., G.G. Forsyth, S. Dzikiti, et al. 2016. Estimates of the impacts of invasive alien plants on water flows in South Africa. Water SA 42: 659–72. http://dx.doi.org/10.4314/wsa.v42i4.17 The impact of invasive plants on water cycles

Maxwell, S.L., R.A. Fuller, T.M. Brooks, et al. 2016. The ravages of guns, nets and bulldozers. *Nature* 536: 143–45. https://doi.org/10.1038/536143a Biodiversity faces many anthropogenic threats.

Pringle, R.M. 2005. The origins of the Nile perch in Lake Victoria. *BioScience* 55: 780–87. https://doi.org/10.1641/0006-3568(2005)055[0780:TOOTNP]2.0.CO;2 The devastating impact of invasive fish in Lake Victoria.

Stauffer, J.R., H. Madsen, K. McKaye, et al. 2006. Schistosomiasis in Lake Malawi: Relationship of fish and intermediate host density to prevalence of human infection. *EcoHealth* 3: 22-27. https://doi.org/10.1007/s10393-005-0007-3 Trophic cascades can even affect human health.

Bibliography

Adeogun, A.O., O.R. Ibor, S.D. Adeduntan, et al. 2016. Intersex and alterations in reproductive development of a cichlid, *Tilapia guineensis*, from a municipal domestic water supply lake (Eleyele) in southwestern Nigeria. *Science of the Total Environment* 541: 372–82. https://doi.org/10.1016/j.scitotenv.2015.09.061

Agbohessi, P.T., I.I. Toko, A. Ouédraogo, et al. 2015. Assessment of the health status of wild fish inhabiting a cotton basin heavily impacted by pesticides in Benin (West Africa). *Science of the Total Environment* 506: 567–84. https://doi.org/10.1016/j.scitotenv.2014.11.047

Alroy, J. 2015. Current extinction rates of reptiles and amphibians. *Proceedings of the National Academy of Sciences* 112: 13003–08. https://doi.org/10.1073/pnas.1508681112

Amegah, A.K., and S. Agyei-Mensah. 2017. Urban air pollution in Sub-Saharan Africa: Time for action. *Environmental Pollution* 220: 738–43. https://doi.org/10.1016/j.envpol.2016.09.042

Amri, E., Z.L. Kanyeka, H.V.M. Lyaruu, et al. 2009. Evaluation of genetic diversity in *Dalbergia elanoxylon* populations using random amplified polymorphic DNA markers. *Research Journal of Cell and Molecular Biology* 3: 71–79. https://doi.org/10.15406/mojbm.2017.01.00015

Andersen, I. 2016. *Seizure of huge African pangolin scale shipment points to worrying increase in trafficking* (Gland: IUCN). https://www.iucn.org/news/secretariat/201606/seizure-huge-african-pangolin-scale-shipment-points-worrying-increase-trafficking

Anderson L.G., S. Rocliffe, N.R. Haddaway, et al. 2015. The role of tourism and recreation in the spread of non-native species: A systematic review and meta-analysis. *PLoS ONE* 10: e0140833. https://doi.org/10.1371/journal.pone.0140833

Annorbah, N.N.D., N.J. Collar, and S.J. Marsden. 2016. Trade and habitat change virtually eliminate the Grey Parrot *Psittacus erithacus* from Ghana. *Ibis* 158: 82–91. https://doi.org/10.1111/ibi.12332

Ardura, A., A. Zaiko, J.L. Martinez, et al. 2015. Environmental DNA evidence of transfer of North Sea molluscs across tropical waters through ballast water. *Journal of Molluscan Studies* 81: 495–501. https://doi.org/10.1093/mollus/eyv022

Aremu, A.O., L. Cheesman, J.F. Finnie, et al. 2011. *Mondia whitei* (Apocynaceae): A review of its biological activities, conservation strategies and economic potential. *South African Journal of Botany* 77: 960–71. https://doi.org/10.1016/j.sajb.2011.06.010

Austin, H.P., M.D. Allen, B.S. Donohoe, et al. 2018. Characterization and engineering of a plastic-degrading aromatic polyesterase. *Proceedings of the National Academy of Sciences* 2018: 201718804. https://doi.org/10.1073/pnas.1718804115

Baláž, V., O. Kopecký, and V. Gvoždík. 2012. Presence of the amphibian chytrid pathogen confirmed in Cameroon. *Herpetological Journal* 22: 191–94.

Barbee, J. 2015. Botswana sells fracking rights in national park. *Guardian*. https://gu.com/p/4eck4

Barnhoorn, I.E.J., M.S. Bornman, C. Jansen van Rensburg, et al. 2009. DDT residues in water, sediment, domestic and indigenous biota from a currently DDT-sprayed area. *Chemosphere* 77: 1236–41. https://doi.org/10.1016/j.chemosphere.2009.08.045

Beer, L.L., E.S. Boyd, J.W. Peters, et al. 2009. Engineering algae for biohydrogen and biofuel production. *Current Opinion in Biotechnology* 20: 264–71. https://doi.org/10.1016/j.copbio.2009.06.002

Benítez-López, A., L. Santini, A.M. Schipper, et al. 2019. Intact but empty forests? Patterns of hunting-induced mammal defaunation in the tropics. *PLoS ONE* 17: e3000247. https://doi.org/10.1371/journal.pbio.3000247

Benítez-López, A., R. Alkemade, A.M. Schipper, et al. 2017. The impact of hunting on tropical mammal and bird populations. *Science* 356: 180–83. https://doi.org/10.1126/science.aaj1891

Biginagwa, F.J., B.S. Mayoma, Y. Shashoua, et al. 2016. First evidence of microplastics in the African Great Lakes: Recovery from Lake Victoria Nile perch and Nile tilapia. *Journal of Great Lakes Research* 42: 146–49. https://doi.org/10.1016/j.jglr.2015.10.012

Bills, R. 2007. *Tilapia guinasana. The IUCN Red List of Threatened Species* 2007: e.T63354A12662434. http://doi.org/10.2305/IUCN.UK.2007.RLTS.T63354A12662434.en

Black, A. 2005. Light induced seabird mortality on vessels operating in the Southern Ocean: Incidents and mitigation measures. *Antarctic Science* 17: 67–68. https://doi.org/10.1017/S0954102005002439

Blancke, S. 2015. Why people oppose GMOs even though science says they are safe. *Scientific American.* https://www.scientificamerican.com/article/why-people-oppose-gmos-even-though-science-says-they-are-safe

Bloomer, J.P., and M.N. Bester. 1992. Control of feral cats on sub-Antarctic Marion Island, Indian Ocean. *Biological Conservation* 60: 211–19. https://doi.org/10.1016/0006-3207(92)91253-O

Bornman, M.S., I.E.J. Barnhoorn, C. de Jager, et al. 2010. Testicular microlithiasis and neoplastic lesions in wild eland (*Tragelaphus oryx*): possible effects of exposure to environmental pollutants? *Environmental Research* 110: 327–33. https://doi.org/10.1016/j.envres.2010.02.003

Bortey-Sam, N., Y. Ikenaka, O. Akoto, et al. 2017. Oxidative stress and respiratory symptoms due to human exposure to polycyclic aromatic hydrocarbons (PAHs) in Kumasi, Ghana. *Environmental Pollution* 228: 311–20. https://doi.org/10.1016/j.envpol.2017.05.036

Bosch, A.C., B. O'Neill, G.O. Sigge, et al. 2016. Heavy metal accumulation and toxicity in smoothhound (*Mustelus mustelus*) shark from Langebaan Lagoon, South Africa. *Food Chemistry* 190: 871–78. https://doi.org/10.1016/j.foodchem.2015.06.034

Bourgeois, S., E. Gilot-Fromont, A. Viallefont, et al. 2009. Influence of artificial lights, logs and erosion on leatherback sea turtle hatchling orientation at Pongara National Park, Gabon. *Biological Conservation* 142: 85–93. https://doi.org/10.1016/j.biocon.2008.09.028

Bouwman, H., I.M. Viljoen, L.P. Quinn, et al. 2008. Halogenated pollutants in terrestrial and aquatic bird eggs: Converging patterns of pollutant profiles and impacts and risks from high level. *Environmental Research* 126: 240–52. https://doi.org/10.1016/j.envres.2013.06.003

Bownes, A., M.P. Hill, and M.J. Byrne. 2013. The role of nutrients in the responses of water hyacinth, *Eichhornia crassipes* (Pontederiaceae) to herbivory by a grasshopper *Cornops aquaticum* Brüner (Orthoptera: Acrididae). *Biological Control* 67: 555–62. https://doi.org/10.1016/j.biocontrol.2013.07.022

Branch, G.M., and C.N. Steffani. 2004. Can we predict the effects of alien species? A case-history of the invasion of South Africa by *Mytilus galloprovincialis* (Lamarck). *Journal of Experimental Marine Biology and Ecology* 300: 189–215. https://doi.org/10.1016/j.jembe.2003.12.007

Brashares J.S., C.W. Epps, and C.J. Stoner. 2010. Ecological and conservation implications of mesopredator release. In: *Trophic Cascades*, ed. by J. Terborgh and J. Estes (Washington: Island Press).

Brossy, J.J., A.L. Plös, J.M. Blackbeard, et al. 1999. Diseases acquired by captive penguins: What happens when they are released into the wild? *Marine Ornithology* 27: 185–86.

Brown, C.J. 2006. *Historic distribution of large mammals in the Greater Fish River Canyon Complex, southern Namibia, and recommendations for re-introductions* (Windhoek: Namibia Nature Foundation). http://www.the-eis.com/data/literature/Greater%20Fish%20River%20Canyon%20Complex%20Historic%20distribution%20of%20mammals.pdf

Brummet, R.E., C. Cargill, L.M. Lekunze, et al. 2010. Stream degradation, fish abundance and the potential viability of ornamental fisheries in south-western Cameroon. *African Journal of Aquatic Science* 35: 155–64. https://doi.org/10.2989/16085914.2010.497650

Burnett, L.J., K.J. Sorenson, J. Brandt, et al. 2013. Eggshell thinning and depressed hatching success of California Condors reintroduced to central California. *Condor* 115: 477–91. https://doi.org/10.1525/cond.2013.110150

Bush, E.R., S.E. Baker, and D.W. Macdonald. 2014. Global trade in exotic pets 2006–2012. *Conservation Biology* 28: 663–76. https://doi.org/10.1111/cobi.12240

Campbell, L., P. Verburg, D.G. Dixon, et al. 2008. Mercury biomagnification in the food web of Lake Tanganyika (Tanzania, East Africa). *Science of The Total Environment* 402: 184–91. https://doi.org/10.1016/j.scitotenv.2008.04.017

Cannon, J.C. 2018. Half a ton of pangolin scales seized on the way to Asia from Benin. *Mongabay*. https://news.mongabay.com/2018/04/half-a-ton-of-pangolin-scales-seized-on-the-way-to-asia-from-benin

Carruthers, E.H., D.C. Schneider, and J.D. Neilson. 2009. Estimating the odds of survival and identifying mitigation opportunities for common bycatch in pelagic longline fisheries. *Biological Conservation* 142: 2620–30. https://doi.org/10.1016/j.biocon.2009.06.010

Carson, R. 1962. *Silent Spring* (Boston: Houghton Mifflin).

CBD (Center for Biological Diversity). 2015. *Petition to reclassify and uplist African elephants from Threatened to Endangered under the Endangered Species Act as two separate species: Forest elephants* (Loxodonta cyclotis) *and savannah elephants* (Loxodonta africana) (Tucson: Center for Biological Diversity). https://www.biologicaldiversity.org/species/mammals/pdfs/African_Elephant_Uplisting_Petition.pdf

Cerchio, S., S. Strindberg, T. Collins, et al. 2014. Seismic surveys negatively affect humpback whale singing activity off northern Angola. *PloS ONE* 9: e86464. https://doi.org/10.1371/journal.pone.0086464

Chaber, A.-L., A. Allebone-Webb, Y. Lignereux, et al. 2010. The scale of illegal meat importation from Africa to Europe via Paris. *Conservation Letters* 3: 317–21. https://doi.org/10.1111/j.1755-263X.2010.00121.x

Chakraborty, T., and X. Lee. 2018. A simplified urban-extent algorithm to characterise surface urban heat islands on a global scale and examine vegetation control on their spatiotemporal variability. *International Journal of Applied Earth Observation and Geoinformation* 74: 269–80. https://doi.org/10.1016/j.jag.2018.09.015

Chase, M.J., S. Schlossberg, C.R. Griffin, et al. 2016. Continent-wide survey reveals massive decline in African savannah elephants. *PeerJ* 4:e2354. https://doi.org/10.7717/peerj.2354

Christy, B., and B. Stirton. 2015. How killing elephants finances terror in Africa. *National Geographic*. http://on.natgeo.com/1I5N2aO

Coetzee, J.A., and M.P. Hill. 2012. The role of eutrophication in the biological control of water hyacinth, *Eichhornia crassipes*, in South Africa. *BioControl* 57: 247–61. https://doi.org/10.1007/s10526-011-9426-y

Concha, C., R. Cañas, J. Macuer, et al. 2017. Disease prevention: An opportunity to expand edible plant-based vaccines? *Vaccines* 5: 14. https://doi.org/10.3390/vaccines5020014

Covey, R., and W.S. McGraw. 2014. Monkeys in a West African bushmeat market: Implications for Cercopithecid conservation in eastern Liberia. *Tropical Conservation Science* 7: 115–25. https://doi.org/10.1177/194008291400700103

Cox, T.M., R.L. Lewison, R. Zydelis, et al. 2007. Comparing effectiveness of experimental and implemented bycatch reduction measures: The ideal and the real. *Conservation Biology* 21: 1155–64. https://doi.org/10.1111/j.1523-1739.2007.00772.x

Craigie, I.D., J.E.M. Baillie, A. Balmford, et al. 2010. Large mammal population declines in Africa's protected areas. *Biological Conservation* 143: 2221–28. https://doi.org/10.1016/j.biocon.2010.06.007

Croxall, J.P., S.H. Butchart, B. Lascelles, et al. 2012. Seabird conservation status, threats and priority actions: A global assessment. *Bird Conservation International* 22: 1–34. https://doi.org/10.1017/S0959270912000020

Cruise, A. 2017. Ten more elephants poisoned by poachers in Zim. *Guardian*. https://gu.com/p/6k6tx

Cumming, D.H.M., and G.S. Cumming. 2015. One Health: An ecological and conservation perspective. In: *One Health: The Theory and Practice of Integrated Health Approaches*, ed. by J. Zinsstag, et al. (Wallingford: CAB International).

Daszak, P., A.A. Cunningham, and A.D. Hyatt. 2000. Emerging infectious diseases of wildlife—threats to biodiversity and human health. *Science* 287: 443–49. https://doi.org/10.1126/science.287.5452.443

Davies, D., B.J. Dilley, A.L. Bond, et al. 2015. Trends and tactics of mouse predation on Tristan Albatross *Diomedea dabbenena* chicks at Gough Island, South Atlantic Ocean. *Avian Conservation and Ecology* 10: 5. http://doi.org/10.5751/ACE-00738-100105

de Graaf, M., M.A.M. Machiels, T. Wudneh, et al. 2004. Declining stocks of Lake Tana's endemic *Barbus* species flock (Pisces, Cyprinidae): Natural variation or human impact? *Biological Conservation* 116: 277–87. http://doi.org/10.1016/S0006-3207(03)00198-8

de Greef, K. 2019. 500 vultures killed in Botswana by poachers' poison, government says. *New York Times*. https://nyti.ms/2FpkfTf

Deribe, E., B.O. Rosseland, R. Borgstrøm, et al. 2011. Bioaccumulation of persistent organic pollutants (POPs) in fish species from Lake Koka, Ethiopia: The influence of lipid content and trophic position. *Science of The Total Environment* 410–11: 135–45. http://doi.org/10.1016/j.scitotenv.2011.09.008

Desta, Z., R. Borgstrøm, B.O. Rosseland, et al. 2006. Major difference in mercury concentrations of the African big barb, *Barbus intermedius* (R.) due to shifts in trophic position. *Ecology of Freshwater Fish* 15: 532–43. https://doi.org/10.1111/j.1600-0633.2006.00193.x

Dilley, B.J., D. Davies, A.L. Bond, et al. 2015a. Effects of mouse predation on burrowing petrel chicks at Gough Island. *Antarctic Science* 27: 543–53. https://doi.org/10.1017/S0954102015000279

Dilley, B.J., S. Schoombie, J. Schoombie, et al. 2015b. 'Scalping' of albatross fledglings by introduced mice spreads rapidly at Marion Island. *Antarctic Science* 28: 73–80. https://doi.org/10.1017/S0954102015000486

Dodoo, D.K., D.K. Essumang, and J.W.A. Jonathan. 2013. Accumulation profile and seasonal variations of polychlorinated biphenyls (PCBs) in bivalves *Crassostrea tulipa* (oysters) and *Anadara senilis* (mussels) at three different aquatic habitats in two seasons in Ghana. *Ecotoxicology and Environmental Safety* 88: 26–34. http://doi.org/10.1016/j.ecoenv.2012.10.013

Dzikiti, S., M.B. Gush, D.C. le Maitre, et al. 2016. Quantifying potential water savings from clearing invasive alien *Eucalyptus camaldulensis* using in situ and high resolution remote sensing data in the Berg River Catchment, Western Cape, South Africa. *Forest Ecology and Management* 361: 69–80. https://doi.org/10.1016/j.foreco.2015.11.009

Eknath, A.E., H.B. Bentsen, P.W. Ponzoni, et al. 2007. Genetic improvement of farmed tilapias: Composition and genetic parameters of a synthetic base population of *Oreochromis niloticus* for selective breeding. *Aquaculture* 273: 1–14. https://doi.org/10.1016/j.aquaculture.2007.09.015

Ellsworth, W.L. 2013. Injection-induced earthquakes. *Science* 341: 1225942. https://doi.org/10.1126/science.1225942

Eriksen M., L.C.M. Lebreton, H.S. Carson, et al. 2014. Plastic pollution in the world's oceans: More than 5 trillion plastic pieces weighing over 250,000 tons afloat at sea. *PLoS ONE* 9: e111913. https://doi.org/10.1371/journal.pone.0111913

Esvelt, K.M., A.L. Smidler, F. Catteruccia, et al. 2014. Emerging technology: Concerning RNA-guided gene drives for the alteration of wild populations. *eLife* 3: e03401. https://doi.org/10.7554/eLife.03401.001

Fa, J.E., C.A. Peres, and J. Meeuwig. 2002. Bushmeat exploitation in tropical forests: An intercontinental comparison. *Conservation Biology* 16: 232–37. https://doi.org/10.1046/j.1523-1739.2002.00275.x

Fa, J.E., D. Currie, and J. Meeuwig. 2003. Bushmeat and food security in the Congo Basin: Linkages between wildlife and people's future. *Environmental Conservation* 30: 71–78. https://doi.org/10.1017/S0376892903000067

Fa, J.E., J. Olivero, M.A. Farfán, et al. 2016. Differences between Pygmy and non-Pygmy hunting in Congo Basin forests. *PLoS ONE* 11: e0161703. https://doi.org/10.1371/journal.pone.0161703

Fa, J.E., S. Seymour, J.E.F. Dupain, et al. 2006. Getting to grips with the magnitude of exploitation: Bushmeat in the Cross-Sanaga rivers region, Nigeria and Cameroon. *Biological Conservation* 129: 497–510. https://doi.org/10.1016/j.biocon.2005.11.031

Falchi, F., P. Cinzano, D. Duriscoe, et al. 2016. The new world atlas of artificial night sky brightness. *Science Advances* 2: e1600377. https://doi.org/10.1126/sciadv.1600377

Fanou, L.A., T.A. Mobio, E.E. Creppy, et al. 2006. Survey of air pollution in Cotonou, Benin—air monitoring and biomarkers. *Science of The Total Environment* 358: 85–96. https://doi.org/10.1016/j.scitotenv.2005.03.025

Fentiman, A., and N. Zabbey. 2015. Environmental degradation and cultural erosion in Ogoniland: A case study of the oil spills in Bodo. *Extractive Industries and Society* 2: 615–24. https://doi.org/10.1016/j.exis.2015.05.008

Feyisa, G.L., K. Dons, and H. Meilby. 2014. Efficiency of parks in mitigating urban heat island effect: An example from Addis Ababa. *Landscape and Urban Planning* 123: 87–95. https://doi.org/10.1016/j.landurbplan.2013.12.008

Firebaugh, A., and K.J. Haynes. 2016. Experimental tests of light-pollution impacts on nocturnal insect courtship and dispersal. *Oecologia* 182: 1203–11. https://doi.org/10.1007/s00442-016-3723-1

Fogell, D.J., K.A. Tolley, and G.J. Measey. 2013. Mind the gaps: Investigating the cause of the current range disjunction in the Cape Platanna, *Xenopus gilli* (Anura: Pipidae). *PeerJ* 1: e166. https://doi.org/10.7717/peerj.166

Foxcroft, L.C., D.M. Richardson, and J.R.U. Wilson. 2008. Ornamental plants as invasive aliens: Problems and solutions in Kruger National Park, South Africa. *Environmental Management* 41: 32–51. https://doi.org/10.1007/s00267-007-9027-9

Galloway, T.S., and C.N. Lewis. 2016. Marine microplastics spell big problems for future generations. *Proceedings of the National Academy of Sciences* 113: 2331–33. https://doi.org/10.1073/pnas.1600715113

Geddie, J. 2019. Singapore seizes record haul of pangolin scales enroute to Vietnam. *Reuters*. https://reut.rs/2WMDtsh

Genton, C., R. Cristescu, S. Gatti, et al. 2012. Recovery potential of a western lowland gorilla population following a major Ebola outbreak: Results from a ten-year study. *PLoS ONE* 7: e37106. https://doi.org/10.1371/journal.pone.0037106

Gewin, V. 2003. Genetically modified corn—Environmental benefits and risks. *PLoS Biology* 1: e8. https://doi.org/10.1371/journal.pbio.0000008

Gilbert, N. 2010. GM crop escapes into the American wild. *Nature News* https://doi.org/10.1038/news.2010.393

Gottdenker, N.L., D.G. Streicker, C.L. Faust, et al. 2014. Anthropogenic land use change and infectious diseases: A review of the evidence. *EcoHealth* 11: 619632. https://doi.org/10.1007/s10393-014-0941-z

Goulson, D., E. Nicholls, C. Botías, et al. 2015. Bee declines driven by combined stress from parasites, pesticides, and lack of flowers. *Science* 347: 1255957. https://doi.org/10.1126/science.1255957

Haim, A., and B.A. Portnov. 2013. *Light Pollution as a New Risk Factor for Human Breast and Prostate Cancers* (Dordrecht: Springer). https://doi.org/10.1007/978-94-007-6220-6

Harding, W.R. 2015. Living with eutrophication in South Africa: A review of realities and challenges. *Transactions of the Royal Society of South Africa* 70: 155–71. https://doi.org/10.1080/0035919X.2015.1014878

Hargrove, J.W. 2003. *Tsetse eradication: Sufficiency, necessity and desirability* (Edinburgh: DFID Animal Health Programme, Centre for Tropical Veterinary Medicine, University of Edinburgh). https://assets.publishing.service.gov.uk/media/57a08d1be5274a31e0001656/RLAHtsetse_Erad.pdf

Hauenstein, S., M. Kshatriya, J. Blanc, et al. 2019. African elephant poaching rates correlate with local poverty, national corruption and global ivory price. *Nature Communications* 10: 2242. https://doi.org/10.1038/s41467-019-09993-2

Hayes, T.B., and K.P. Menendez. 1999. The effect of sex steroids on primary and secondary sex differentiation in the sexually dichromatic reedfrog (*Hyperolius argus*: Hyperolidae) from the Arabuko Sokoke Forest of Kenya. *General and Comparative Endocrinology* 115: 188–99. https://doi.org/10.1006/gcen.1999.7321

Hirschfeld M., D.C. Blackburn, T.M. Doherty-Bone, et al. 2016. Dramatic declines of montane frogs in a central African biodiversity hotspot. *PLoS ONE* 11: e0155129. https://doi.org/10.1371/journal.pone.0155129

Howarth, R.W. 2014. A bridge to nowhere: Methane emissions and the greenhouse gas footprint of natural gas. *Energy Science and Engineering* 2: 47–60. https://doi.org/10.1002/ese3.35

Hwang, Y.-T., D.M.W. Frierson, and S.M. Kang. 2013. Anthropogenic sulfate aerosol and the southward shift of tropical precipitation in the late 20th century. *Geophysical Research Letters* 40: 2845–50. https://doi.org/10.1002/grl.50502

IUCN. 2019. *The IUCN Red List of Threatened Species.* http://www.iucnredlist.org

Karagulian, F., C.A. Belis, C.C.C. Dora, et al. 2015. Contributions to cities' ambient particulate matter (PM): A systematic review of local source contributions at global level. *Atmospheric Environment* 120: 475–83. https://doi.org/10.1016/j.atmosenv.2015.08.087

Karami, A., A. Golieskardi, C.K. Choo, et al. 2017. The presence of microplastics in commercial salts from different countries. *Scientific Reports* 7: 46173. https://doi.org/10.1038/srep46173

Kebede, A.T., and D.L. Coppock. 2015. Livestock-mediated dispersal of *Prosopis juliflora* imperils grasslands and the endangered Grevy's zebra in northeastern Ethiopia. *Rangeland Ecology and Management* 68: 402–07. https://doi.org/10.1016/j.rama.2015.07.002

Kern, J.M., and A.N. Radford. 2016. Anthropogenic noise disrupts use of vocal information about predation risk. *Environmental Pollution* 218: 988–95. http://doi.org/10.1016/j.envpol.2016.08.049

King J., J.A. Cambray, and N.D. Impson. 1998. Linked effects of dam-released floods and water temperature on spawning of the Clanwilliam yellowfish *Barbus capensis*. *Hydrobiologia* 384: 245–65. https://doi.org/10.1023/A:1003481524320

Kissui, B.M., and C. Packer. 2004. Top-down population regulation of a top predator: Lions in the Ngorogonro Crater. *Proceedings of the Royal Society B* 271: 1867–74. https://doi.org/10.1098/rspb.2004.2797

Knop, E., L. Zoller, R. Ryser, et al. 2017. Artificial light at night as a new threat to pollination. *Nature* 548: 206–09. https://doi.org/10.1038/nature23288

Koper, R.P., and S. Plön. 2012. The potential impacts of anthropogenic noise on marine animals and recommendations for research in South Africa. *EWT Research and Technical Paper* 1 (Johannesburg: EWT).

Kosuth, M., S.A. Mason, and C. Tyree. 2017. *Synthetic Polymer Contamination in Global Drinking Water* (Washington: Orb Media). https://orbmedia.org/stories/Invisibles_plastics

Kouassi, K.S., S. Billet, G. Garçon, et al. 2010. Oxidative damage induced in A549 cells by physically and chemically characterized air particulate matter (PM2. 5) collected in Abidjan, Côte d'Ivoire. *Journal of Applied Toxicology* 30: 310–20. https://doi.org/10.1002/jat.1496

Kunc, H.P., K.E. McLaughlin, and R. Schmidt. 2016. Aquatic noise pollution: Implications for individuals, populations, and ecosystems. *Proceedings of the Royal Society B* 283: 20160839. https://doi.org/10.1098/rspb.2016.0839

Landrigan, P.J., R. Fuller, N.J.R. Acosta, et al. 2018. The Lancet Commission on pollution and health. *Lancet* 391: P462–P512. https://doi.org/10.1016/S0140-6736(17)32345-0

le Maitre, D.C., G.G. Forsyth, S. Dzikiti, et al. 2016. Estimates of the impacts of invasive alien plants on water flows in South Africa. *Water SA* 42: 659–72. http://dx.doi.org/10.4314/wsa.v42i4.17

Lebreton, L.C.M., J. van der Zwet, J.-W. Damsteeg, et al. 2017. River plastic emissions to the world's oceans. *Nature Communications* 8: 15611. https://doi.org/10.1038/ncomms15611

Lindsey P.A., V.R. Nyirenda, J.L. Barnes, et al. 2014. Underperformance of African protected area networks and the case for new conservation models: Insights from Zambia. *PLoS ONE* 9: e94109. https://doi.org/10.1371/journal.pone.0094109

Lindsey, P.A., G. Balme, M. Becker, et al. 2013. The bushmeat trade in African savannas: Impacts, drivers, and possible solutions. *Biological Conservation* 160: 80–96. https://doi.org/10.1016/j.biocon.2012.12.020

Lovett, B., E. Bilgo, S.A. Millogo, et al., 2019. Transgenic *Metarhizium* rapidly kills mosquitoes in a malaria-endemic region of Burkina Faso. *Science* 364: 894897. https://doi.org/10.1126/science.aaw8737

Maisels, F., S. Strindberg, S. Blake, et al. 2013. Devastating decline of forest elephants in Central Africa. *PLoS ONE* 8: e59469. https://doi.org/10.1371/journal.pone.0059469

Manaca, M.N., J.O. Grimalt, J. Sunyer, et al. 2011. Concentration of DDT compounds in breast milk from African women (Manhiça, Mozambique) at the early stages of domestic indoor spraying with this insecticide. *Chemosphere* 85: 307–14. https://doi.org/10.1016/j.chemosphere.2011.06.015

Maree, B.A., R.M. Wanless, T.P. Fairweather, et al. 2014. Significant reductions in mortality of threatened seabirds in a South African trawl fishery. *Animal Conservation* 17: 520–29. https://doi.org/10.1111/acv.12126

Maxwell, S.L., R.A. Fuller, T.M. Brooks, et al. 2016. The ravages of guns, nets and bulldozers. *Nature* 536: 143–45. https://doi.org/10.1038/536143a

Mcgowan, P. 2008. *WG6 CS1: African grey parrot* Psittacus erithacus *case study* (Cancun: NDF Workshop). https://www.cites.org/sites/default/files/ndf_material/WG6-CS1-S.pdf

McKenzie, L.M., R. Guo, R.Z. Witter, et al. 2014. Birth outcomes and maternal residential proximity to natural gas development in rural Colorado. *Environmental Health Perspectives* 122: 412–17. https://doi.org/10.1289/ehp.1306722

McKenzie, L.M., R.Z. Witter, L.S. Newman, et al. 2012. Human health risk assessment of air emissions from development of unconventional natural gas resources. *Science of the Total Environment* 424: 79–87. https://doi.org/10.1016/j.scitotenv.2012.02.018

McKinney, M.A., K. Dean, N.E. Hussey, et al. 2016. Global versus local causes and health implications of high mercury concentrations in sharks from the east coast of South Africa. *Science of the Total Environment* 541: 176–83. https://doi.org/10.1016/j.scitotenv.2015.09.074

McPherson, J.M., and A.C.J. Vincent. 2004. Assessing East African trade in seahorse species as a basis for conservation under international controls. *Aquatic Conservation* 14: 521–38. https://doi.org/10.1002/aqc.629

Merly, L., L. Lange, M. Meÿer, et al. 2019. Blood plasma levels of heavy metals and trace elements in white sharks (*Carcharodon carcharias*) and potential health consequences. *Marine Pollution Bulletin* 142: 85–92. https://doi.org/10.1016/j.marpolbul.2019.03.018

Mihaljevič, M., V. Ettler, O. Šebek, et al. 2011. Lead isotopic and metallic pollution record in tree rings from the Copperbelt mining-smelting area, Zambia. *Water, Air, and Soil Pollution* 216: 657–68. http://doi.org/10.1007/s11270-010-0560-4

Miller, G.T., and S. Spoolman 2011. *Sustaining the Earth* (Pacific Grove: Thompson Learning).

Minnaar, C., J.G. Boyles, I.A. Minnaar, et al. 2015. Stacking the odds: Light pollution may shift the balance in an ancient predator-prey arms race. *Journal of Applied Ecology* 52: 522–31. https://doi.org/10.1111/1365-2664.12381

Morell, M., A. Brownlow, B. McGovern, et al., 2017. Implementation of a method to visualize noise-induced hearing loss in mass stranded cetaceans. *Scientific Reports* 7: 41848. https://doi.org/10.1038/srep41848

Muir, W.M., and R.D. Howard. 2004. Characterization of environmental risk of genetically engineered (GE) organisms and their potential to control exotic invasive species. *Aquatic Sciences* 66: 414–20. https://doi.org/10.1007/s00027-004-0721-x

Nasi, R., A. Taber, and N. van Vliet. 2011. Empty forests, empty stomachs? Bushmeat and livelihoods in the Congo and Amazon Basins. *International Forestry Review* 13: 355–68. http://doi.org/10.1505/146554811798293872

Nyenje, P.M., J.W. Foppen, S. Uhlenbrook, et al. 2010. Eutrophication and nutrient release in urban areas of sub-Saharan Africa—a review. *Science of The Total Environment* 408: 447–55. https://doi.org/10.1016/j.scitotenv.2009.10.020

O'Hanlon, S.J., A. Rieux, R.A. Farrer, et al. 2018. Recent Asian origin of chytrid fungi causing global amphibian declines. *Science* 360: 621–27. https://doi.org/10.1126/science.aar1965

Osborn, S.G., A. Vengosh, N.R. Warner, et al. 2011. Methane contamination of drinking water accompanying gas-well drilling and hydraulic fracturing. *Proceedings of the National Academy of Sciences* 108: 8172–76. https://doi.org/10.1073/pnas.1100682108

Ouyang, J.Q., M. de Jong, R.H.A. van Grunsven, et al. 2017. Restless roosts: Light pollution affects behavior, sleep, and physiology in a free-living songbird. *Global Change Biology* 23: 4987–94. https://doi.org/10.1111/gcb.13756

Parks and Wildlife Service 2014. *Evaluation report August 2014: Macquarie Island pest eradication project* (Hobart: DPIPWE). https://www.parks.tas.gov.au/file.aspx?id=31160

Pauly, D., D. Belhabib, R., Blomeyer, et al., 2014. China's distant-water fisheries in the 21st century. *Fish and Fisheries* 15: 474–88. https://doi.org/10.1111/faf.12032

Petkova, E.P., D.W. Jack, N.H. Volavka-Close, et al. 2013. Particulate matter pollution in African cities. *Air Quality, Atmosphere and Health* 6: 603–14. https://doi.org/10.1007/s11869-013-0199-6

Pettis, J.S., E.M. Lichtenberg, M. Andree, et al. 2013. Crop pollination exposes honey bees to pesticides which alters their susceptibility to the gut pathogen *Nosema ceranae*. *PloS ONE* 8.7: e70182. https://doi.org/10.1371/journal.pone.0070182

Piaggio, A.J., G. Segelbacher, P.J. Seddon, et al. 2017. Is it time for synthetic biodiversity conservation? *Trends in Ecology and Evolution* 32: 97–107. https://doi.org/10.1016/j.tree.2016.10.016

Pirk, C.W.W., U. Strauss, A.A. Yusuf, et al. 2015. Honeybee health in Africa—a review. *Apidologie* 1–25. https://doi.org/10.1007/s13592-015-0406-6

Poulsen, J.R., C.J. Clark, G. Mavah, et al. 2009. Bushmeat supply and consumption in a tropical logging concession in northern Congo. *Conservation Biology* 23: 1597–608. https://doi.org/10.1111/j.1523-1739.2009.01251.x

Pringle, R.M. 2005. The origins of the Nile perch in Lake Victoria. *BioScience* 55: 780–87. https://doi.org/10.1641/0006-3568(2005)055[0780:TOOTNP]2.0.CO;2

Prüss-Ustün, A., J. Wolf, C. Corvalán, et al. 2016. *Preventing disease through healthy environments: A global assessment of the burden of disease from environmental risks* (Geneva: WHO). http://apps.who.int/iris/bitstream/10665/204585/1/9789241565196_eng.pdf

Quédraogo, O., and M. Amyot. 2013. Mercury, arsenic and selenium concentrations in water and fish from sub-Saharan semi-arid freshwater reservoirs (Burkina Faso). *Science of The Total Environment* 444: 243–54. https://doi.org/10.1016/j.scitotenv.2012.11.095

Rabinowitz, P.M., I.B. Slizovskiy, V. Lamers, et al. 2015. Proximity to natural gas wells and reported health status: Results of a household survey in Washington County, Pennsylvania. *Environmental Health Perspectives* 123: 21–26. https://doi.org/10.1289/ehp.1307732

Ramos, R., and D. Grémillet. 2013. Overfishing in West Africa by EU vessels. *Nature* 496: 300. https://doi.org/10.1038/496300a

Robinson, B.H. 2009. E-waste: An assessment of global production and environmental impacts. *Science of The Total Environment* 408: 183–91. https://doi.org/10.1016/j.scitotenv.2009.09.044

Roca, A.L., Y. Ishida, A.L. Brandt, et al. 2015. Elephant natural history; a genomic perspective. *Annual Review of Animal BioScience* 3: 139–67. https://doi.org/10.1146/annurev-animal-022114-110838

Roche, H., and A. Tidou. 2009. First ecotoxicological assessment assay in a hydroelectric reservoir: The Lake Taabo (Côte d'Ivoire). *Bulletin of Environmental Contamination and Toxicology* 82: 322–26. https://doi.org/10.1007/s00128-008-9572-9

Roelf, W. 2016. South Africa to start shale gas exploration in next year. *Reuters*. http://reut.rs/1U1RNZQ

Rogan, M.S., P.A. Lindsey, C.J. Tambling, et al. 2017. Illegal bushmeat hunters compete with predators and threaten wild herbivore populations in a global tourism hotspot. *Biological Conservation* 210: 233–42. https://doi.org/10.1016/j.biocon.2017.04.020

Rosin, C., and J.R. Poulsen. 2016. Hunting-induced defaunation drives increased seed predation and decreased seedling establishment of commercially important tree species in an Afrotropical forest. *Forest Ecology and Management* 382: 206–13. https://doi.org/10.1016/j.foreco.2016.10.016

Ross, P.S., and L.S. Birnbaum. 2003. Integrated human and ecological risk assessment: A case study of persistent organic pollutants (POPs) in humans and wildlife. *Human and Ecological Risk Assessment* 9: 303–24. https://doi.org/10.1080/727073292

Rybnikova, N.A., A. Haim, and B.A. Portnov. 2016. Does artificial light-at-night exposure contribute to the worldwide obesity pandemic? *International Journal of Obesity* 40: 815–23. https://doi.org/10.1038/ijo.2015.255

Schmidt, C., T. Krauth, and S. Wagner. 2017. Export of plastic debris by rivers into the sea. *Environmental Science and Technology* 51: 12246–53. https://doi.org/10.1021/acs.est.7b02368

Schneeberger, K., and C.C. Voigt. 2016. Zoonotic viruses and conservation of bats. In: *Bats in the Anthropocene: Conservation of Bats in a Changing World*, ed. by C.C. Voigt and T. Kingston (Cham: Springer). https://doi.org/10.1007/978-3-319-25220-9

Schreuder, E., and S. Clusella-Trullas. 2016. Exotic trees modify the thermal landscape and food resources for lizard communities. *Oecologia* 182: 1213–25. https://doi.org/10.1007/s00442-016-3726-y

Shannon, G., M.F. McKenna, L.M. Angeloni, et al. 2015. A synthesis of two decades of research documenting the effects of noise on wildlife. *Biological Reviews* 91: 982–1005. https://doi.org/10.1111/brv.12207

Sitoki, L., R. Kurmayer, and E. Rott. 2012. Spatial variation of phytoplankton composition, biovolume, and resulting microcystin concentrations in the Nyanza Gulf (Lake Victoria, Kenya). *Hydrobiologia* 691: 109–22. https://doi.org/10.1007/s10750-012-1062-8

Spinage, C.A. 1973. A review of ivory exploitation trends in Africa. *East African Wildlife Journal* 11: 281–89. https://doi.org/10.1111/j.1365-2028.1973.tb00093.x

Stauffer, J.R., H. Madsen, K. McKaye, et al. 2006. Schistosomiasis in Lake Malawi: Relationship of fish and intermediate host density to prevalence of human infection. *EcoHealth* 3: 22–27. https://doi.org/10.1007/s10393-005-0007-3

Strauss, U, V. Dietemann, H. Human, et al. 2016. Resistance rather than tolerance explains survival of savannah honeybees (*Apis mellifera scutellata*) to infestation by the parasitic mite, *Varroa destructor*. *Parasitology* 143: 374–87. https://doi.org/10.1017/S0031182015001754

Street, R.A. 2012. Heavy metals in medicinal plant products—an African perspective. *South African Journal of Botany* 82: 67–74. https://doi.org/10.1016/j.sajb.2012.07.013

Sussarellu, R., M. Suquet, Y. Thomas, et al. 2016. Oyster reproduction is affected by exposure to polystyrene microplastics. *Proceedings of the National Academy of Sciences* 113: 2430–35. https://doi.org/10.1073/pnas.1519019113

Tarrant, J, D. Cilliers, L.H. du Preez, et al. 2013. Spatial assessment of amphibian chytrid fungus (*Batrachochytrium dendrobatidis*) in South Africa confirms endemic and widespread Infection. *PLoS ONE* 8: e69591. https://doi.org/10.1371/journal.pone.0069591

Thibault, M., and S. Blaney. 2003. The oil industry as an underlying factor in the bushmeat crisis in Central Africa. *Conservation Biology* 17: 1807–13. https://doi.org/10.1111/j.1523-1739.2003.00159.x

Tuakuila, J. 2013. S-phenylmercapturic acid (S-PMA) levels in urine as an indicator of exposure to benzene in the Kinshasa population. *International Journal of Hygiene and Environmental Health* 216: 494–98. https://doi.org/10.1016/j.ijheh.2013.03.012

UNDP. 2006. *Niger Delta human development report* (Abuja: UNDP). http://hdr.undp.org/sites/default/files/nigeria_hdr_report.pdf

UNEP-WCMC. 2007. *Wildlife Trade 2005: An analysis of the European community and candidate countries' annual reports to CITES* (Cambridge: UNEP-WCMC). http://ec.europa.eu/environment/cites/pdf/2007_yearbook.pdf

UNEP-WCMC. 2008. *Monitoring of international trade in ornamental fish* (Cambridge: UNEP-WCMC). http://ec.europa.eu/environment/cites/pdf/reports/ornamental_fish.pdf

UNEP. 2006. Report on atmosphere and air pollution. In: *African Regional Implementation Review for the 14th Session of the Commission on Sustainable Development* (New York: UNEP). https://sustainabledevelopment.un.org/content/documents/ecaRIM_bp2.pdf

Uyi, O.O., F. Ekhator, C.E. Ikuenobe, et al. 2014. *Chromolaena odorata* invasion in Nigeria: A case for coordinated biological control. *Management of Biological Invasions* 5: 377–93. http://doi.org/10.3391/mbi.2014.5.4.09

van der Merwe, P., Saayman, M., and Rossouw, R. 2015. The economic impact of hunting in the Limpopo Province. *Journal of Economic and Financial Sciences* 8: 223–42. https://hdl.handle.net/10520/EJC170564

Vanthomme, H., B. Bellé, and P.M. Forget. 2010. Bushmeat hunting alters recruitment of large-seeded plant species in Central Africa. *Biotropica* 42: 672–79. https://doi.org/10.1111/j.1744-7429.2010.00630.x

Villamagna, A.M., and B.R. Murphy. 2010. Ecological and socio-economic impacts of invasive water hyacinth (*Eichhornia crassipes*): A review. *Freshwater Biology* 55: 282–98. https://doi.org/10.1111/j.1365-2427.2009.02294.x

Wanless, R.M., and B.A. Maree. 2014. Problems and solutions for seabird bycatch in trawl fisheries. *Animal Conservation* 17: 534. https://doi.org/10.1111/acv.12183

Waters, C.N., J. Zalasiewicz, C. Summerhayes, et al. 2016. The Anthropocene is functionally and stratigraphically distinct from the Holocene. *Science* 351: aad2622. https://doi.org/10.1126/science.aad2622

Watkins, B.P., S.L. Petersen, and P.G. Ryan. 2008. Interaction between seabirds and deep-water hake trawl gear: An assessment of impacts in South African waters. *Animal Conservation* 11: 247–54. http://doi.org/10.1111/j.1469-1795.2008.00192.x

Weldon, C, L.H. Du Preez, A.D. Hyatt, et al. 2004. Origin of the amphibian chytrid fungus. *Emerging Infectious Diseases* 10: 2100–05. https://doi.org/10.3201/eid1012.030804

WHO (World Health Organisation). 2013. *Review of evidence on health aspects of air pollution—REVIHAAP project* (Bonn: WHO). http://www.euro.who.int/__data/assets/pdf_file/0004/193108/REVIHAAP-Final-technical-report.pdf

Wilcox, C., E. van Sebille, and B.D. Hardesty. 2015. Threat of plastic pollution to seabirds is global, pervasive, and increasing. *Proceedings of the National Academy of Sciences* 112: 11899–904. https://doi.org/10.1073/pnas.1502108112

Williams V.L., A.B. Cunningham, A.C. Kemp, et al. 2014. Risks to birds traded for African traditional medicine: A quantitative assessment. *PLoS ONE* 9: e105397. https://doi.org/10.1371/journal.pone.0105397

Williams, T.M., T.L. Kendall, B.P. Richter, et al. 2017. Swimming and diving energetics in dolphins: A stroke-by-stroke analysis for predicting the cost of flight responses in wild odontocetes. *Journal of Experimental Biology* 220: 1135–45. https://doi.org/10.1242/jeb.154245

Wittemyer, G., J.M. Northrup, J. Blanc, et al. 2014. Illegal killing for ivory drives global decline in African elephants. *Proceedings of the National Academy of Sciences* 111: 13117–21. https://doi.org/10.1073/pnas.1403984111

Wolfaardt, A.C., A.J. Williams, L.G. Underhill, et al. 2009. Review of the rescue, rehabilitation and restoration of oiled seabirds in South Africa, especially African penguins *Spheniscus demersus* and Cape gannets *Morus capensis*, 1983–2005. *African Journal of Marine Science* 31: 31–54. https://doi.org/10.2989/AJMS.2009.31.1.3.774

Wood, K.L., B. Tenger, N.V. Morf, et al. 2014. *Report to CITES: CITES-listed species at risk from the illegal trafficking of bushmeat; Results of a 2012 study in Switzerland's international airports* (Bonn CITES). https://doi.org/10.5167/uzh-111850

Worm, B., E.B. Barbier, N. Beaumont, et al. 2006. Impacts of biodiversity loss on ocean ecosystem services. *Science* 314: 787–90. https://doi.org/10.1126/science.1132294

Zunckel, M., K. Venjonoka, J.J. Pienaar, et al. 2004. Surface ozone over southern Africa: Synthesis of monitoring results during the Cross-border Air Pollution Impact Assessment Project. *Atmospheric Environment* 38: 6139–47. http://doi.org/10.1016/j.atmosenv.2004.07.029

8

Small Populations and Extinction

Extinctions are seldom attributable to only one threat; rather, multiple stressors may act synergistically to drive the demise of a species. Pictured here is a Hewitt's ghost frog (*Heleophryne hewetti*, EN), which is globally restricted to an area of 140 km^2 in the Cape Floristic Region. It is threatened by alien vegetation, overly frequent fires, erosion, siltation, and construction of roads and reservoirs, all of which deteriorate its clear, fast-flowing stream habitat.

Species have evolved and disappeared since the very first species (thought to be microorganisms living in hydrothermal vents) made an appearance on Earth. Some species outcompeted others for access to limiting resources; some were driven to extinction by dangerous pathogens; some just found it hard to survive in constantly evolving ecosystems. While many extinction events have been rather limited in scope and, hence, caused only one or a few extinctions at a time, there have been instances where perturbations were so impactful that they drove very large numbers of species to extinction over a short period of time. There have been five such past **mass extinction events**—periods marked by the sudden and dramatic loss of a large percentage of species (Figure 8.1). But these mass extinctions have also been followed by periods that favoured increased rates of speciation, during which new species evolved to fill the niches left empty by the extinctions.

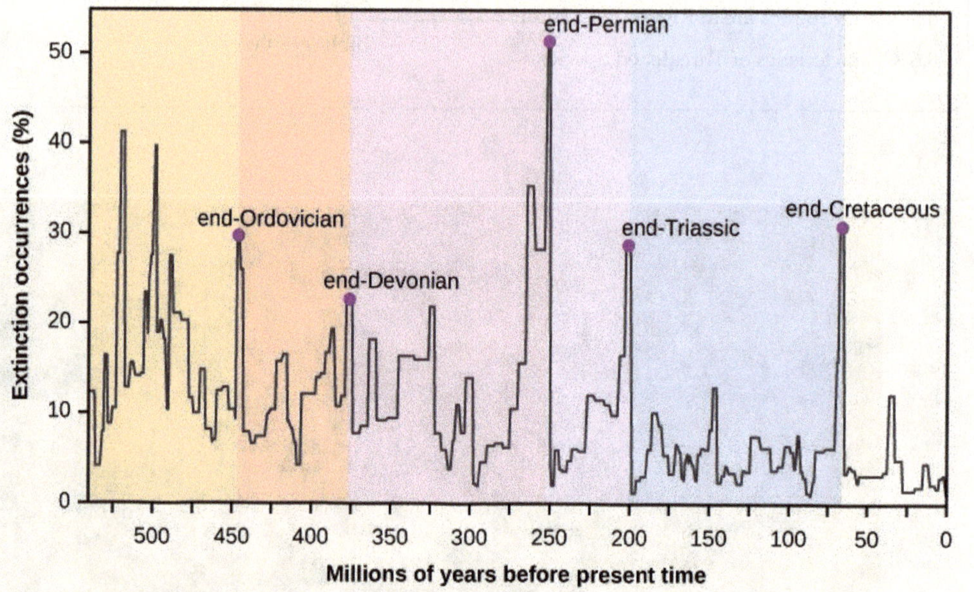

Figure 8.1 There have been five past mass extinction events—periods when natural events changed Earth's environment so dramatically that between 60–95% of species were wiped away forever—over Earth's geological history. So far, the most dramatic extinction event occurred at the end of the Permian period, about 250 million years ago, and thought to be the result of widespread volcanic activity and climate change. The most recent mass extinction, at the end of the Cretaceous period about 65 million years ago and thought to be the result of a massive asteroid impact, saw the disappearance of non-avian dinosaurs.

Nature's ability to balance extinctions with speciation was greatly disturbed around 300,000 years ago, when *Homo sapiens* made their appearance on Earth. Since then, humans have gradually increased their dominance on the natural world, leading to large-scale restructuring and destruction of biological communities. Human modifications of Earth's climatic, biological, and geochemical environments accelerated greatly during the rise of agriculture (12,000–15,000 years ago) and again during the **Industrial Revolution** (1760–1840), when fossil fuel usage and urbanisation became the norm. Now, many scientists recognise today's new and distinct human-dominated **geological epoch**, the **Anthropocene** (Waters et al., 2015). One notable feature of the Anthropocene is that species extinctions are increasing at such rapid rates that many conservation biologists now recognise that we are also witnessing the beginnings of Earth's **sixth extinction episode** (Barnosky et al., 2011; Ceballos et al., 2017). However, unlike previously, this extinction episode is caused by human activities rather than natural events.

8.1 What is Extinction?

The term "extinct" has several nuances in conservation biology, and its meaning can vary somewhat depending on the context:

> Over ninety-nine percent of recent extinctions have been caused by human activities.

- A species is **globally extinct** when no individuals of that species remains alive anywhere in the world. The bluebuck (*Hippotragus leucophaeus*, EX) has been globally *Extinct* since the last individual was shot around 1800 (Kerley et al., 2009).
- Four (possibly seven) species of cycad (*Encephalartos* spp.)—ancient seed plants that were dominant in the age of the dinosaurs—are currently considered **extinct in the wild**; in other words, they exist only in cultivation; in captivity; or another human-managed situation (IUCN, 2019).
- A species is **locally extinct**, also called **extirpated**, when it is extinct in a part of its historic range but can still be found elsewhere in the world. Cheetahs (*Acinonyx jubatus*, VU) once roamed throughout much of Africa, but are now extirpated in over 90% of their historical range (Durant et al., 2017).
- A species is **ecologically extinct** (also called **functionally extinct**) if it persists at such low numbers that its role in an ecosystem is negligible. Africa's vultures are ecologically extinct over much of their range and thus unable to remove diseased carcasses from the environment, posing both an ecological and socio-economic hazard (see Box 4.4).

8.2 Rates of Extinction

If extinction and speciation are natural processes, an obvious question follows: "Why should we care about the loss of biodiversity?" The answer concerns not individual species extinctions as much as the *increasing rate* of these extinctions (Figure 8.2). While a species can be wiped off Earth over a relatively short period of time, speciation typically occurs slowly as the genetic makeup of a population shifts over thousands of years. Unfortunately, we are currently losing species 1,000 times faster than natural **background extinction rates** (for mammals estimated to be 1.8 extinctions per 10,000 species per 100 years, Barnosky et al., 2011), and future rates may be 10,000 times higher that background rates (de Vos et al., 2015). Because over 99% of current species extinctions have been linked to human activity rather than natural processes (Pimm et al., 2014), observations on past extinctions and subsequent speciation may not apply to the present. Moreover, unlike before, humans now share the planet with the species we are wiping out. These losses mean that we are also losing the benefits we gain from nature (Chapter 4) at unprecedented rates.

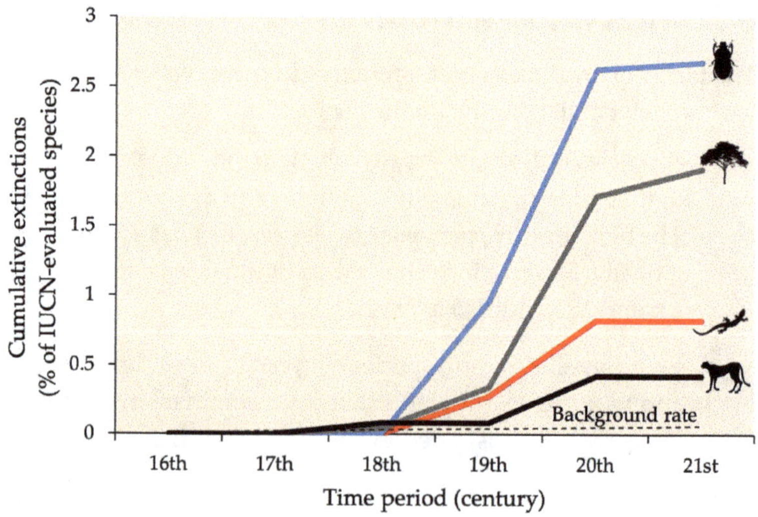

Figure 8.2 Percentage of Sub-Saharan Africa invertebrates, plants, reptiles, and mammals that have gone *Extinct*, *Extinct in the Wild*, and likely *Extinct* since the year 1500. Dashed line represents the natural rate of extinctions expected without human influences. After Ceballos et al., 2015.

8.3 When is a Species Extinct?

While the term "extinction" is relatively easy to define (Section 8.1), determining whether a species is indeed extinct is a more difficult task. One of the most important questions conservation biologists grapple with is deciding how long to wait after the *last* observation before declaring a species extinct. Answering this question is particularly complicated when considering cryptic and shy species that are difficult to survey, sparsely distributed animals that are hard to find, or plants that are difficult to identify when not in flower.

To complicate matters, over the last few decades, biologists and their colleagues have rediscovered several species that were once thought to be extinct. These rediscovered species are often called **Lazarus species**, in reference to their apparent return to life. Recent examples include Burundi's Bururi long-fingered frog (*Cardioglossa cyaneospila*. NT) rediscovered after a 60-year absence (Blackburn et al., 2016), a Tanzanian coral tree, (*Erythrina schliebenii*, CR) originally known from only one specimen collected from a deforested region in the 1930s (Clarke et al., 2011), and the coelacanth (*Latimeria chalumnae*, CR), a fish that was once thought to be extinct for millions of years (Balon et al., 1988). To avoid declaring more extant species as extinct, there is currently a practice of only declaring a species extinct after several decades of intensive searching and "there is no reasonable doubt that the last individual has died" (IUCN, 2012). Consequently, species, such as the black-spotted false shieldback katydid (*Aroegas nigroornatus*, CR) and the Ethiopian sedge, *Cyperus chionocephalus*, *Critically Endangered*, last seen in 1916 (Bazelet and Naskrecki, 2014) and 1836 (Contu, 2013) respectively, have not yet been declared extinct, even though the last individual may have died a long time ago. Similarly, as many as 15 African orchid species—a group that includes some of the most beautiful and specialised plants on Earth, some of which have not seen since 1890—are currently considered *Critically Endangered* but may actually be extinct (IUCN, 2019).

The rediscovery of species once thought to be extinct should not necessarily be considered a sign of conservation progress. In many cases, Lazarus species were simply overlooked because they were extremely rare and restricted to isolated locations. Such is the case for two forest birds from the island nation of São Tomé and Príncipe, namely the São Tomé grosbeak (*Crithagra concolor*, CR) and Newton's fiscal (*Lanius newtoni*, CR). The grosbeak, the world's largest canary (50% larger than the second largest canary), was for a long time known only from three specimens collected in 1888–1890; it was thus considered extinct, until its rediscovery over 100 years later, in 1991 (BirdLife International, 2018a). The fiscal shares a remarkably similar history: it was previously known only from records in 1888 and 1928, until its rediscovery in 1990 (BirdLife International, 2018b). Despite these rediscoveries, both species persist as very small (< 250 individuals) populations that are at risk from extinction due to ongoing habitat loss and the impact of invasive predators.

Because extinctions may not always happen immediately after a disturbance, conservation biologists must also consider the lag time between destructive human activities and eventual extinctions. This is illustrated in a study from Kenya's Kakamega Forest, which found that only half of the species that will eventually go extinct due to habitat loss do so in the first 50 years following habitat fragmentation (Figure 8.3). Long-lived plants can have particularly long extinction lag times, sometimes of several centuries. For example, populations of the Saint Helena olive (*Nesiota elliptica*, EX) fell below viable levels in the mid-1800s, but the last individual died only in 2003, when the species was officially declared extinct (Cronk, 2016). Species that are doomed to eventual extinction are considered **committed to extinction** (also called functionally extinct), while the total number of species committed to extinction is referred to as an area's **extinction debt**. In one study, researchers used the island biogeography theory to estimate that the average extinction debt for African forest primates was over 30%—that is, more than 30% of forest primates are predicted to go extinct because of habitat destruction and other human activities that have already happened (Cowlishaw, 1999).

On a more positive note, extinction debts may also provide hope for conservation biologists, as the lingering presence of seriously imperilled species affords

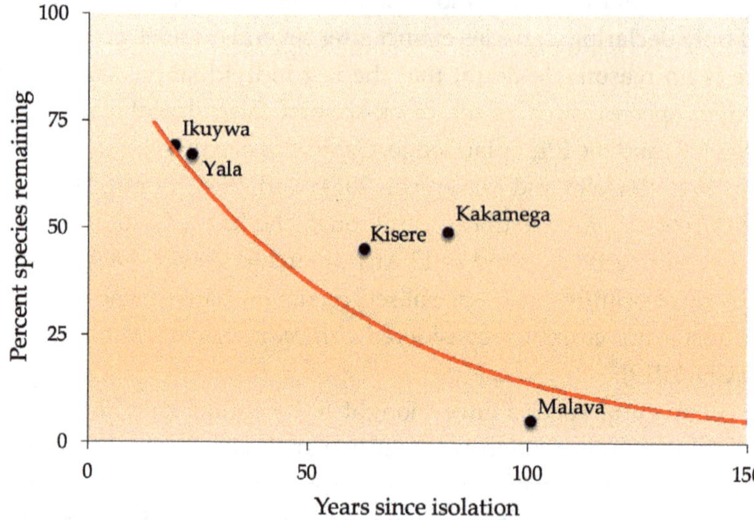

Figure 8.3 Percentage of bird species expected to persist over time in isolated forest patches in western Kenya. Because of extinction debt, not all species are expected to be extirpated immediately after fragmentation; instead there is a time lag between habitat loss and species losses. The image also illustrates how forest size and degree of isolation influences the speed of losses: Kakamega (the largest forest) loses species much slower than Malava, the smallest and most isolated forest. After Brooks et al., 1999.

opportunities to prevent impending extinctions. Conservation biologists are currently illustrating how this can be done by preventing the extinction of three species of pale-coated, desert-adapted ungulates that were formerly common and widespread across the Sahel-Sahara region, namely the scimitar-horned oryx (*Oryx dammah*, EW), dama gazelle (*Nanger dama*, CR), and addax (*Addax nasomaculatus*, CR) (Durant et al., 2014; Brito et al., 2018; IUCN, 2019). The oryx once numbered around one million individuals, with herds of 10,000 seen as recently as 1936. But a population collapse soon followed: by 1985 only 500 oryx survived, and by 2000 it was declared *Extinct in the Wild*. The addax, relatively common as recently as in the 1970s, also experienced precipitous declines; today fewer than 30 individuals remain in the wild. Similarly, the once-common dama gazelle's current global population numbers fewer than 250 individuals, fragmented among five subpopulations in Chad, Mali, and Niger. Conservationists noted initial declines already in the 1960s and 1970s, when wild individuals of all three species were caught to initiate captive breeding programmes. Luckily, all three species responded well to these programmes, and captive populations have grown so strong that reintroduction programmes (Section 11.2) have been initiated for the addax (in 1985, in Tunisia), dama gazelle (in 2015, in Morocco), and oryx (in 2016, in Chad). With several reintroductions seemingly successful, there is hope that viable populations of these iconic species may one day again roam free in their previous strongholds. This will only happen if we can reverse or mitigate the threats that causes their population collapses in the first place, namely uncontrolled and illegal hunting, as well as disturbances associated with agriculture, oil exploration, and inconsiderate drilling of wells for groundwater extraction.

8.4 History of Extinctions in Sub-Saharan Africa

Many people hold on to the romanticised belief that historical human societies lived in harmony with nature. Accumulated evidence however indicates that this is not true; early humans have caused extensive ecosystem changes and species extinctions since *Homo sapiens* appeared on Earth about 300,000 years ago. In fact, even before the arrival of humans, our ancestors had made a mark, by driving species to extinction as early as during the Pleistocene period, which started about 2.5 million years ago (Box 8.1). The impact of early humans was particularly devastating to the wildlife of North America, South America, and Australia, which saw the demise of nearly all their large (> 100 kg) mammals, most famously megaherbivores such as the mammoths (*Mammuthus* spp.). The Pleistocene extinctions were somewhat less devastating to wildlife in Africa, Europe, and Asia, possibly because large mammals on these continents evolved with human predators, allowing them to develop appropriate defence/escape mechanisms. Nevertheless, Africa's wildlife did not completely escape the Pleistocene extinctions, as increasingly-sophisticated human activities during that time ensured the demise of as many as 28 large mammal groups, which included Africa's sabre-toothed cats (Barbourofelidae), nearly all the elephant relatives (Proboscidae), as well as giant hartebeests (*Megalotragus* spp.), giant buffaloes (*Pelorovis* spp.), giant hyenas (*Pachycrocuta* spp.), and giant giraffes (*Sivatherium* spp.).

Early humans have caused extensive ecosystem changes and species extinctions even before *Homo sapiens* appeared on Earth about 300,000 years ago.

Box 8.1 Pleistocene Extinctions: Climate Change, Hominin Predation, or Both?

David H.M. Cumming[1,2]

[1]*FitzPatrick Institute of African Ornithology, University of Cape Town, South Africa.*

[2]*Tropical Resource Ecology Programme, University of Zimbabwe, Harare, Zimbabwe.*

✉ *cummingdhm@gmail.com*

Many scientists consider the present rapid loss of biodiversity to be the start of the 6th mass extinction following five previous extinction episodes (see Figure 8.1), each of which led to large-scale restructuring of Earth's biodiversity. The 5th global mass extinction took place 65 million years ago (Ma) when a massive meteorite collided with the Earth, and resulted in the extinction of all non-avian dinosaurs, and much else besides. This 5th mass extinction event also marked the transition from the Cretaceous to the Tertiary epoch (65 to 2.5 Ma). The Tertiary epoch was followed by the Quaternary, which includes the Pleistocene period (2.5 million to ~ 12 thousand years ago) and more recently the Holocene period—marked by the development of agriculture, and the subsequent domination of the Earth's resources by *Homo sapiens*. The Pleistocene is known for a mini mass-extinction of sorts, which saw the demise of species such as mammoths and sabre-tooth cats. However, unlike previous comprehensive mass extinctions, the Pleistocene was characterised by the extinction of mostly large mammals and very large island birds.

Attempts by scientists to explain these Pleistocene extinctions have been characterised by two centuries of controversy over whether they were caused by climate change or by predatory hominins—the evolutionary line of primates that gave rise to modern humans. The four main hypotheses advanced to account for the loss of Pleistocene fauna are: (i) climate change with minimal if any hominin influence (e.g. Faith et al., 2018); (ii) climate change together with some hominin influence (e.g. Barnosky et al., 2004); (iii) selective hominin predation aided by climate change (e.g. Bartlett et al., 2015), and (iv) hominin predation helped by other large predators without the influence of climate change (e.g. Janzen, 1983, Ripple and Van Valkenburgh, 2010).

The very close relationship between the dispersal of hominins out of Africa, the timing of their arrival elsewhere in the world, and the subsequent extinction of large mammals and birds, provided the primary (if challenged) evidence for human agency in non-African Late- Pleistocene extinctions (e.g. Surovell et al., 2005; Johnson, 2009; Ripple and Van Valkenburgh, 2010). As Haynes (2018) has remarked, "...the proponents of climate change as the only cause of the Late Pleistocene extinctions have not clearly explained how or why so many of the extinct megafaunal genera had survived numerous earlier climate changes."

Similarly, Faith et al. (2018) have stated that the failure of Pleistocene megaherbivores to adapt to the emergence of C4 grasses was the primary driver of their extinction. However, this claim ignores evidence that many extinct herbivore genera and species previously survived changes in diet over time (Ripple and Van Valkenburgh, 2010), that the diets of particular species were known to vary with location (Ferranec, 2004), and that many large species, which are typically highly mobile generalists, would have had little trouble adapting their ranges and diets to changing climates.

Research and debate on Pleistocene extinctions have tended to focus on the demise of non-African large mammals in the Late Pleistocene, which coincided with the period when hominins (*Homo erectus* and later also *H. sapiens*) dispersed across the globe starting at about 2 Ma. In Africa, however, earliest hominins appeared some 7 Ma. It didn't take long for these early African hominins to develop the skills necessary to manipulate the environment to their advantage. Setting the pace were the Australopithecines, who used stone tools to butcher mammalian carcasses between 4–3 Ma. The Australopithecines and the rest of a diverse group of large predators were joined by *H. erectus* at the beginning of the Pleistocene, about 2 Ma. This new, qualitatively unique, hunter was able to hunt collaboratively in bands, and was anatomically adapted to throw projectiles forcefully and accurately at large prey (Lombardo and Deaner, 2018). A large brain also placed high nutritional and energetic demands on *H. erectus*, that could best be met by obtaining meat and bone marrow from proboscidians, the elephant relatives (Surovell et al., 2005; Boschian et al., 2019). Early African hominins were thus well adapted to hunt large prey and contribute to the demise of wildlife, particularly megaherbivores (those over 1,000 kg), through the Early and Middle Pleistocene (Figure 8.A). Other large carnivores at the time may very well have helped hominins drive many Pleistocene herbivores to extinction (Janzen, 1983, Ripple and Van Valkenburgh, 2010; Van Valkenburgh et al., 2016). But this combination may ironically also have led to demise of many of the large Pleistocene predators, through co-extinctions, after their main prey base disappeared (Werdelin and Lewis, 2013).

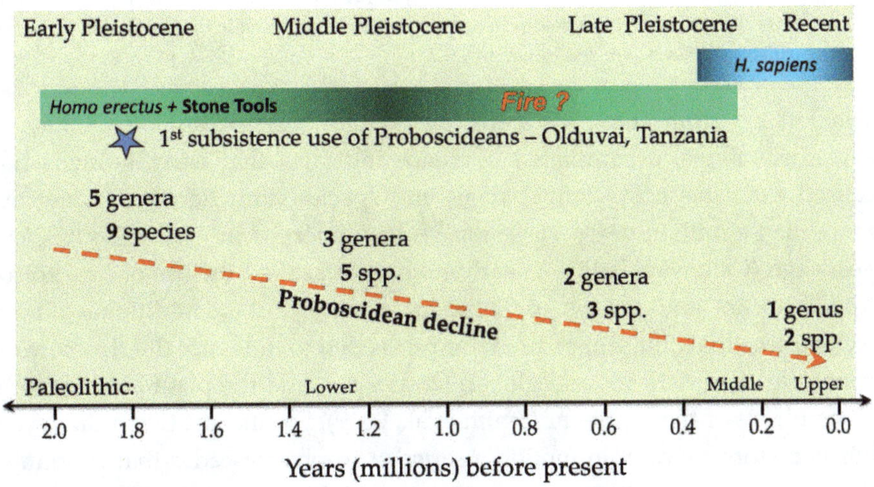

Figure 8.A Decline in African proboscidian (i.e. elephant relatives) diversity through the Early, Middle and Late Pleistocene in relation to the emergence of *Homo erectus* and *H. sapiens*. Similar patterns also occurred in the extinction of large carnivores and giant pigs/hogs.

It thus seems likely that the emergence of a novel and increasingly effective predator during the Early Pleistocene, rather than climate change, was the ultimate factor that tipped the balance against the iconic species that disappeared soon after hominins appeared on Earth. It is worth noting that there is a clear relationship between body size and extinction risk (Figure 8.B), the result of large animals' relatively long generation lengths, long gestation periods, long periods of caring for young, and an abundance of meat presented to eager hunters. Consequently, even a small increase in mortality may very well result in a large animal's annual mortality exceeding its generational mortality, the end result being extinction. This relationship also partly explains why present-day elephant populations are unable to withstand poaching in many parts of Africa (Box 7.2).

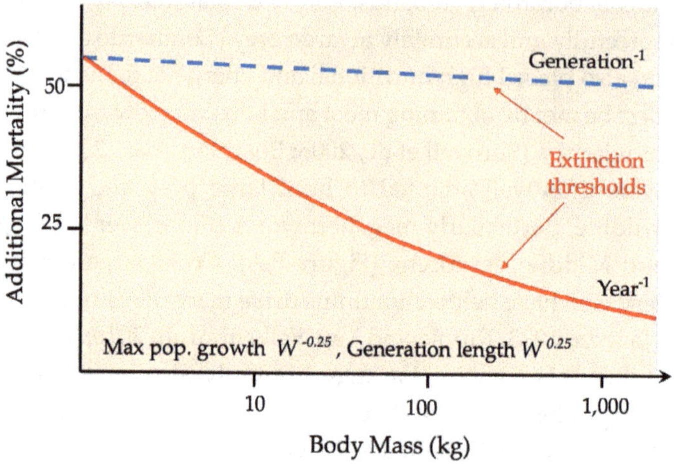

Figure 8.B The impact of additional mortality per year, as it relates to mammalian body mass. The graph shows how even slight increases in annual mortality can rapidly drive megaherbivore species to extinction. After Brook and Bowman, 2005.

The lessons from the Pleistocene extinctions are relevant also today. As explained above, accumulated evidence indicates that early humans have caused extensive ecosystem changes and species extinctions extending over more than a million years. *Homo sapiens* had emerged in Africa about 300,000 years ago (Callaway, 2017). As early humans mastered the use of fire, poison-tipped spears and arrows, pitfall traps, and a host of additional hunting techniques, this unique apex predator proceeded to influence the structure and composition of African (and global) landscapes, and the plant and vertebrate assemblages of the continent (Smith et al., 2019). For the last two million years our ancestors have set in motion a series of trophic cascades that continue to this day and are resulting in increasing loss of diversity of the flora and fauna of the African continent and the rest of the world.

While early extinctions were generally isolated and selective, extinction rates increased rapidly after the rise of agriculture, and especially after European settlers started colonising Africa from the 17th century onward. By no coincidence, the area where most of the extinctions and extirpations during colonialism occurred was on the southwestern tip of Africa, the location of the earliest intensive European settlements on the continent. For example, by 1700, hunting caused the extirpation of every single land animal over 50 kg within 200 km of Cape Town (Rebelo, 1992). As hunters moved further afield in search of targets, Africa saw its first post-colonial large mammal extinctions, namely the bluebuck (Figure 8.4), quagga (*Equus quagga quagga*, EX), and Cape warthog (*Phacochoerus aethiopicus aethiopicus*, EX).

Figure 8.4 One of only four remaining skins of the bluebuck at the Vienna Museum of Natural History, Austria. Once a prized hunting target, it was the first known African antelope hunted to extinction. In the background is a quagga (*Equus quagga quagga*, EX), another African animal hunted to extinction.

Following the demise of many of the Cape Floristic Province's large animals, humans have driven African species to extinction at an increasing pace. Today, at least 84 Sub-Saharan African species have been confirmed *Extinct* (Figure 8.5), nine species are *Extinct in the Wild*, and as many as 202 species are considered possibly *Extinct* (IUCN, 2019). Among the extinct species are two wildflowers (*Acalypha dikuluwensis*, EX; *Basananthe cupricola*, EX) wiped out by mining activities in the DRC; and from Seychelles, an endemic parakeet (*Psittacula wardi*, EX) that was hunted to extinction. Among the species that persist only in captivity is the Kihansi spray toad (*Nectophrynoides asperginis*, EW), whose population crashed from more than 20,000 individuals in June 2003 to only five individuals in January 2004 after the establishment of a hydropower plant in eastern Tanzania (Channing et al., 2006). While some species that are *Extinct in the Wild* may be released back into the wild at some point in future, the four (or possibly seven) cycad species that persist only in captivity will probably not be reintroduced due to ongoing concerns about poaching by plant collectors (Okubamichael et al., 2016).

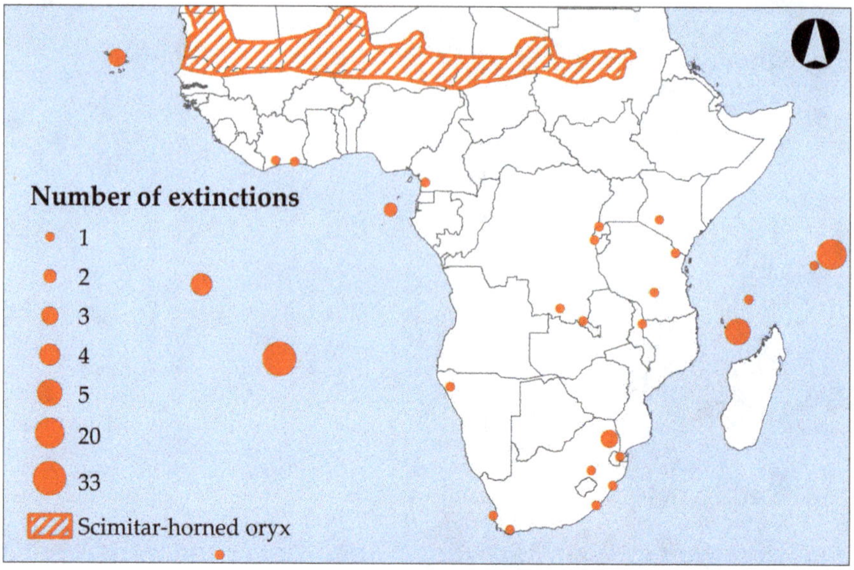

Figure 8.5 The locations of Sub-Saharan Africa's wildlife extinctions (including *Extinct* and *Extinct in the Wild* species) since 1500. Note how the largest number of extinctions involve species with restricted distributions, particularly those that occurred on islands. The scimitar-horned oryx is an example of mainland species that went extinct despite its large original range.

While most of Africa's extinctions—at least until now—were isolated events involving one or two species at a time, the region also provides one of the best-studied examples of a recent man-made mass-extinction event. In the mid-1950s, the Uganda Game and Fisheries Department introduced the predatory Nile perch (*Lates niloticus*) to Lake Victoria to bolster the local fishery industry (Pringle, 2005). An ecological and economic disaster followed, pushing the entire ecosystem to the brink of collapse. First, the local people continued to prefer smaller endemic cichlids—which they could preserve by drying in the sun—to the perch with its oily flesh. This allowed the predatory perch's population to grow unchecked which, in turn, reduced over 500 endemic cichlid species' populations by 80% in just a few years (Witte et al., 1992). As the cichlid populations crashed, some local people started consuming perch for protein; however, they preferred smoking the perch over wood fires. To obtain firewood and charcoal, trees were logged around the lake, which in turn increased eutrophication, as well as erosion and **siltation**. Despite this array of emerging ecological threats, the local fishery continued to harvest the rapidly declining cichlid population. Consequently, as many as 200 cichlid species may have been driven to extinction in the decade following the perch introduction (Goldschmidt et al., 1993).

Judging by the number of extirpations over the last few decades, Africa will undoubtedly see more species pushed to extinction in the coming decades. Of particular concern is West and Southern Africa, which have lost over 75% of its large mammal populations over the past few decades; losses across Sub-Saharan Africa as a whole generally amount to over 50% (Ceballos et al., 2017). Some species will hopefully be spared this fate with the help of people and organisations fighting for their continued survival (Box 8.2). Many species will not be so lucky. The world's last western black rhinoceros (*Diceros bicornis longipes*, EX) died in Cameroon in 2011; the northern white rhinoceros (*Ceratotherium simum cottoni*, CR) may follow this fate within the next few years (see Box 11.4). Lions (*Panthera leo*, EN) have been extirpated from as many as 16 African nations (Bauer et al., 2015), while cheetahs (Figure 8.6) occur in less than 9% of their historic range (Durant et al., 2017).

Box 8.2 Swimming Dangerously Close to Extinction: Population Crash in Lesotho's Endemic Maloti Minnow

Jeremy Shelton

Freshwater Research Centre (FRCSA), Kommetji, South Africa.

✉ *jembejem@gmail.com*

Lesotho's iconic Maloti minnow (*Pseudobarbus quathlambae*, EN) (Figure 8.C) is a small, stream-dwelling cyprinid, and is the only freshwater fish species endemic to the country. Historically, the species was widespread, but its distribution has become increasingly restricted and fragmented in recent times due to interactions with non-native fishes and habitat degradation (Skelton et al., 2001), leading to it being classified as *Endangered* by the IUCN (Chakona and Kubheka, 2018). Genetic research has revealed that what was previously considered a single widespread species comprises two genetically distinct lineages: a "Mohale lineage" found in the Mohale catchment, and an "Eastern lineage" which includes populations in five catchments east of the Mohale catchment (Skelton et al., 2001). The genetic divergence between the two Maloti minnow lines is a result of a long period of geographic isolation and warrants that they be conserved as separate evolutionary significant units (ESU). Furthermore, the Mohale lineage, which comprises 77% of the species' known distribution, is of critical importance for continued survival of the species (Skelton et al., 2001).

Past surveys (e.g. Steyn et al., 1996) have revealed that the Maloti minnow was the only fish species inhabiting the rivers flowing into the Mohale Reservoir. Situated 4 km below the Reservoir, the 20 m high Semongkoaneng waterfall has historically prevented larger fish species from moving upstream into the upper catchment. Following the filling of the Mohale Reservoir in 2003, an inter-basin transfer (IBT) tunnel linking it to Katse Reservoir was opened. Biologists working in the catchment subsequently expressed concern that non-native fishes might colonise the Mohale Reservoir via the IBT tunnel, and from there invade the influent rivers (Rall and Sephaka, 2008). Because the Maloti minnow evolved in the absence of large-bodied fishes, it would not have had an opportunity to evolve

Figure 8.C The Maloti minnow, the only freshwater fish species endemic to the highlands of Lesotho, faces extinction due to habitat degradation and invasive species.

adaptations to cope with competition from and predation by larger species and may, therefore, be particularly sensitive to the arrival of other fish.

In 2006, the smallmouth yellowfish (*Labeobarbus aeneus*, LC), a larger, more aggressive cyprinid, was recorded in Mohale Reservoir (Rall and Sephaka, 2008), suggesting that it had dispersed from Katse Reservoir through the IBT tunnel. By 2013, it had spread into the major influent rivers in that system and coinciding with this was a virtual disappearance of the Maloti minnow from this former stronghold for the Mohale lineage. To illustrate this, surveys in previous decades described healthy populations of several thousand fish (e.g. Steyn et al., 1996), while only five individuals were recorded from the same sites in 2013 (Shelton et al., 2017).

Interestingly, the saving grace for this lineage may have originated from the same source that landed them in this predicament in the first place: human intervention. Prompted by the opening of the Kaste-Mohale IBT, a small team of passionate conservation scientists translocated several Maloti minnows to sections of stream above tall waterfalls, upstream of their natural distribution range (Rall and Sephaka, 2008). These sections, they knew, would be unreachable by larger species swimming upstream from Mohale Reservoir. This assisted colonisation approach has been viewed as controversial, but it may also have saved a tiny minnow from almost certain extinction in the wild. The prospect of losing a charismatic species like the Maloti minnow showcases how projects like the Lesotho Highlands Water Project can easily damage sensitive ecosystems that were not consider in development plans. In order to save the Maloti minnow from extinction, the next step will be to assess the success of translocation efforts and develop a rescue plan for the species.

Figure 8.6 A cheetah mother and her cubs in Tanzania's Tarangire National Park. Once found across much of Africa, cheetahs are now extirpated in 90% of their historic range.

8.5 Which Species are at Risk of Extinction?

An important task for conservation biologists is to identify and prioritise those species in greatest danger of extinction. Accomplishing this task requires biologists to collect and review all the information we have on each species. To facilitate this major undertaking, the IUCN has formalised the evaluation and reporting of threatened species assessments using an internationally accepted standard of conservation categories to reflect a taxon's risk of extinction. These nine categories (Figure 8.7), known as **Red List** Assessments (IUCN, 2017), are:

> The IUCN has formalised the evaluation of threatened species using an internationally accepted standard of conservation categories describing a taxon's risk of extinction.

- *Extinct* (*EX*). These species are no longer known to exist. As of mid-2019, the IUCN has listed 84 Sub-Saharan African species as *Extinct*.
- *Extinct in the Wild* (*EW*). These species exist only in cultivation, in captivity, or other human-managed situations. As of mid-2019, the IUCN has listed nine Sub-Saharan African species as *Extinct in the Wild*.
- *Critically Endangered* (*CR*). These species have an extremely high risk of going extinct in the wild. As of mid-2019, the IUCN has listed 880 Sub-Saharan African species as *Critically Endangered*. Also included in this category are the 202 Sub-Saharan African species that the IUCN considered *possibly Extinct*.
- *Endangered* (*EN*). These species have a very high risk of extinction in the wild. As of mid-2019, the IUCN has listed 1,600 Sub-Saharan African species as *Endangered*.

- *Vulnerable* (*VU*). These species have a moderately high risk of extinction in the wild. As of mid-2019, the IUCN has listed 2,153 Sub-Saharan African species as *Vulnerable*.
- *Near Threatened* (*NT*). These species are close to qualifying for a threatened category but are not currently considered threatened. As of mid-2019, the IUCN has listed 1,034 Sub-Saharan African species as *Near Threatened*.
- *Data Deficient* (*DD*). Inadequate information exists to determine the risk of extinction for these species. As of mid-2019, the IUCN has listed 2,441 Sub-Saharan African species as *Data Deficient*.
- *Least Concern* (*LC*). These species are not considered *Near Threatened* or threatened. (Widespread and abundant species are included in this category.) As of mid-2019, the IUCN has listed 11,776 Sub-Saharan African species as *Least Concern*.
- *Not Evaluated* (*NE*). Species that have not yet been evaluated. Most species fall in this category.

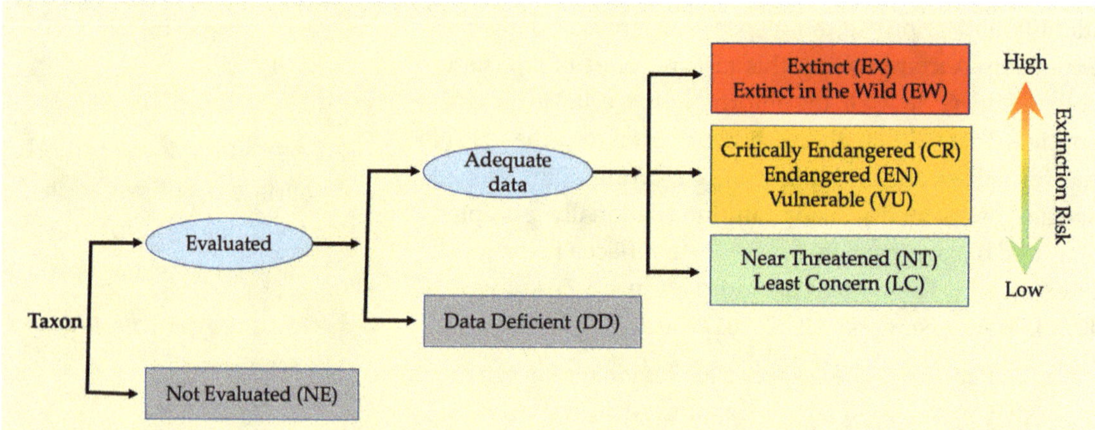

Figure 8.7 Flow diagram illustrating the structure of the IUCN categories of conservation status. An evaluated species can be considered at lower risk of extinction, at high risk of extinction (i.e. threatened), or extinct. A species for which not enough data are available for evaluation is considered *Data Deficient* (DD).

These categories, and the **Red List Criteria** (Table 8.1) used to classify each species, are broadly based on population viability analysis (Section 9.2), and consider population size, population trends, and habitat availability. Species that are *Extinct in the Wild, Critically Endangered, Endangered,* and *Vulnerable* categories are officially considered "threatened with extinction". The advantage of this system is that it provides a standard protocol by which decisions can be reviewed and evaluated according to widely accepted yet flexible criteria. Consequently, species, subspecies, varieties, populations, and subpopulations can be assessed on a global or regional level, all under a unified set of standards. The resultant threat status assessment forms the basis of Red Data Books and Red Lists: detailed lists of threatened wildlife by group and/or by region compiled by the IUCN and its affiliate organisations. All global (and many regional) Red List assessments are freely available at http://www.iucnredlist.org, with feedback links provided from which anyone can alert the IUCN if they find errors or have suggestions for improvements.

Table 8.1 The IUCN's Red List criteria for evaluating a taxon's threat status. A species that meet any one of criteria A–E could be classified as *Critically Endangered*.

Red List criteria A–E	Summary criteria used to evaluate a taxon as *Critically Endangered*[a]
A. Population size declining	The population size has declined by 90% (or more) over last 10 years or 3 generations (whichever is longer).
B. Geographical range declining	The species is restricted to < 100 km^2 and it occurs at a single location *and* its distribution range is observed/ expected to decline.
C. Small and declining populations	There are less than 250 mature individuals left *and* population has declined by 25% (or more) over last 3 years or 1 generation (whichever is longer).
D. Small populations	There are less than 50 mature individuals left.
E. Population viability analysis	There is a 50% (or greater) chance of extinction within 10 years or 3 generations.

[a] *Additional criteria for Critically Endangered, as well as criteria for Endangered and Vulnerable listings can be found at http://www.iucnredlist.org.*

While nearly 20,000 Sub-Saharan African species have been evaluated as of mid-2019 (IUCN, 2019), these assessments only cover a small proportion of the region's overall biodiversity. Consider for example that as of mid-2019, just over 4,900 Sub-Saharan Africa's plants have been listed on the IUCN Red List website. Yet, the Cape Floristic Region alone hosts over 6,200 endemic plant species. The assessment gaps are even more conspicuous for lesser-known taxa; for example, only seven species of bryophytes (a group of non-vascular plants that includes mosses) have been assessed as of mid-2019; some readers of this textbook will have more bryophyte species in their gardens. The reasons for such assessment gaps are many, but most boil down to manpower and funding limitations, which restrict our ability to obtain the data needed for comprehensive assessments. It is thus important to understand that the lack of information on these and other poorly known groups does not mean there is no threat. For example, as of mid-2019, no African abalone (*Haliotis* spp.) have been assessed, even though these highly valued molluscs are some of Africa's most heavily exploited (and heavily poached) marine organisms (Minnaar et al., 2018). A lack of information about a species' threats and populations trends is thus a good argument that more studies are needed, sometimes urgently. Similarly, continued monitoring of species thought to be common is also important, as it can shed light on how new threats may emerge or escalate over time.

8.5.1 Course-filter assessments

To fill Red List species assessment gaps, conservation biologists are increasingly relying on broader metrics, or **coarse-filter assessments**, to identify groups of species that are threatened with extinction. One such method, which reduces the need to evaluate every individual species, is to identify ecosystems that are threatened. This premise rests on the assumption that any threatened ecosystem will contain many threatened species. Hence, protecting and restoring threatened ecosystems will simultaneously allow many populations living in those ecosystems to recover. To facilitate this type of coarse-filter assessment, the IUCN recently established a Red List of Ecosystems (RLE, http://iucnrle.org). The RLE assesses ecosystem status against five criteria: (1) distribution declines, (2) distribution restrictions, (3) environmental degradation, (4) disruption of ecological processes and interactions, and (5) quantitative estimates for risk of ecosystem collapse (Keith et al., 2013). While the ecosystem assessment protocol was only recently developed—only three African ecosystems have been assessed as of mid-2019—its holistic strategy promises a more comprehensive accounting of local biodiversity which could be more informative than an accumulation of single species assessments.

8.6 Characteristics of Threatened Species

While a great number of factors may make a species vulnerable to extinction, conservation biologists have observed that species most vulnerable to extinction generally fall under one of six main groups:

- *Species with small populations*: Some species have very small populations, consisting of just a few individuals. Such small populations are highly vulnerable to random variations in demography or environmental conditions, and to the loss of genetic diversity—all factors that increase the risk of extinction (Section 8.7). Species whose population sizes naturally fluctuate between large and small populations also fall in this category, as they are at an increased risk of extinction during the small population phases of those fluctuations.

- *Species with declining populations*: Trends in population sizes tend to persist, so populations that are declining in abundance face a high risk of extinction (Caughley, 1994) unless conservation managers identify and address the causes of decline. Species impacted by the threats discussed in Chapters 5–7 generally also have declining populations.

- *Species with restricted distribution ranges*: Some species, such as those that are restricted to oceanic islands; mountains peaks; or isolated lakes, can be found only in a limited geographic range. A major disturbance, such as a cyclone/hurricane or drought, could easily affect that entire species' range, potentially driving the species to extinction.

- *Species with only one or a few populations*: A sufficiently large disturbance—such as a wildfire, storm, or disease outbreak—can wipe out a single population of a species. For a species with only one population, that means its extinction, while the loss of even a single population leaves species with only a few populations more vulnerable to the next disturbance. Species in this category (few populations) overlap with those in the previous category (restricted distribution ranges) because species with few populations tend to have restricted ranges.

- *Species that are exploited by people*: Overharvesting can easily reduce a population to the point of extinction (Section 7.2). Even if overharvesting is stopped just before the point of extinction, it may still have reduced a population to a size where it becomes susceptible to one or more of the three additional pressures faced by small populations (Section 8.7).

- *Species with critical symbiotic relationships*: Species that are members of obligate **symbiotic relationships** (where one species cannot survive without another) will go extinct if its host disappears. For instance, larvae of the rhinoceros stomach botfly (*Gyrostigma rhinocerontis*) mature in the stomach lining of African rhinoceros, and no other species (Barraclough, 2006). Thus, if the host species (the rhinoceros) were to go extinct, so would the botfly, Africa's largest fly species. This phenomenon in which one species' extinction leads to the extinction of other is called a coextinction (Koh et al., 2004), while a series of linked coextinctions is called an extinction cascade (Section 4.2.1).

The following characteristics are also linked with extinction, although the links are not as strong as is the case with the previous six categories:

- *Animal species with large body sizes*: Large animals generally require large ranges and more food, have lower rates of reproduction, and have smaller population sizes relative to smaller animals. Often, they are harvested by humans for material benefits (see Box 8.1). Consequently, within groups of related species, the largest are generally also the most vulnerable to extinction—that is, a larger species of carnivore, ungulate, or whale is more likely to go extinct than a smaller carnivore, ungulate, or whale.

- *Species that require a large home range*: Individuals or social groups of some species must forage over wide areas to fulfil their needs. When portions of their range are being degraded or fragmented, the remaining area will eventually be too small to support a viable population.

- *Species that are poor dispersers*: Moving to more suitable habitat is a common survival response following altered environmental conditions. But species with poor dispersal abilities may be doomed to extinction if they are unable to move to more suitable areas elsewhere (see e.g. discussion on range-shift gaps, Section 6.3.5).

- *Seasonal migrants*: A migratory species depends on intact ecosystems at two or more locations to complete its life cycle (see Box 5.3). If those ecosystems, either at stop-over sites along migration routes and/or at migratory endpoints, are damaged, the species may be at risk of extinction.
- *Species with low genetic diversity*: Because genetic diversity (Section 3.2) enables species to adapt to changing environmental conditions, species with low genetic diversity are more vulnerable to extinction because they have less ability to adapt to new diseases, new predators, or recent changes in their ecosystems.
- *Species that evolved in stable ecosystems*: Species that evolved in relatively stable environments (e.g. tropical ecosystems) are often threatened with extinction because under stabile conditions, a species is unlikely to retain the ability to adapt to environmental changes such as altered microclimates.
- *Species with specialised requirements*: Specialist species are often threatened with extinction because they are unable to adapt to altered ecosystems.
- *Group-living species*: A range of factors leaves group-living species at risk of extinction. For example, a herd of ungulates, a flock of birds at their night-time roost, or a school of fish can be harvested in its entirely by people using highly effective techniques. Even if some individuals remain, the harvesting may still leave the population below a critical threshold needed for effective foraging, mating, or territorial defence. This link between population size/density and individual fitness is termed the **Allee effect** (Section 8.7.2).
- *Species that have had no prior contact with people*: Species that encounter people for the first time are **ecologically naïve**—they lack avoidance strategies that promote survival during these encounters. Ecologically naïve species thus have a higher chance of extinction than species that have already survived human contact.
- *Species closely related to species that recently went extinct*: Groups of closely-related taxa, where some members are threatened or already extinct, often share characteristics that elevate their threat of extinction. Groups of related taxa that include many threatened species include apes, cranes, sea turtles, and cycads.
- *Species that live on islands*: Island species generally exhibit many of the characteristics mentioned above. In addition, the mere fact that an island is surrounded by ocean means that species that are unable to swim or fly have nowhere to go when they need to escape a threat.

8.7 Problems of Small Populations

While some small populations have persisted against the odds, sufficiently large populations are generally needed to prevent eventual extinction (Halley et al., 2016, see also Section 9.2). Small populations—which include species that have always had small populations and previously large populations that have been reduced to a few individuals—face three additional inherent and unavoidable pressures beyond the threats discussed in Chapters 5–7. These three additional pressures are: (1) loss of genetic diversity; (2) demographic stochasticity; and (3) environmental stochasticity and natural catastrophes. We will now examine how each of these pressures can lead a small population to eventual extinction. Much of this discussion is based on a ground-breaking manuscript by New Zealand ecologist Graeme Caughley, which discusses at length the threats faced by small and declining wildlife populations (Caughley, 1994).

8.7.1 Loss of genetic diversity

> Small populations are at risk of losing genetic variation much faster than large populations.

Species with high genetic diversity are generally more able to adapt to and reproduce under new conditions such as those brought by environmental changes (Section 3.2). These adaptations can occur at both individual and population levels. For example, under climate change, some genes may allow some populations to adapt their ranges faster or better tolerate warmer and wetter environments, while **phenotypic plasticity**—the ability of one gene to express itself differently under different conditions—may allow certain individuals to better adapt to a changing environment. One species that displays remarkable phenotypic plasticity is the crystalline iceplant (*Mesembryanthemum crystallinum*); by regulating its photosynthetic pathways, an individual plant can adjust its water needs based on the amount of salt and moisture available in the environment (Tallman et al., 1997). Such flexibility may explain why this species, native to southwestern Africa, North Africa, and Europe, has been a successful invader in environments as diverse as those in South America, North America, and Australia.

While populations with many individuals usually also have high levels of genetic diversity, small populations regularly suffer from low levels of genetic diversity. This low genetic diversity not only leaves those populations unable to adapt to changing conditions, but also makes them more susceptible to a variety of deleterious genetic effects (Caughley, 1994). Each of these effects leads to even greater loss of fitness and genetic diversity, hence even larger population declines, and eventually extinction. In the next sections, we discuss further why these deleterious genetic effects are so harmful to small populations.

Genetic drift

In wildlife populations, there are always some alleles that are relatively common, and others that are relatively rare. The relative abundance of any of these alleles may however change from one generation to another purely by chance. While common alleles generally tend to stay common, rare alleles have a high chance of being randomly lost in subsequent generations. Consider how each parent only passes on half of their genetic code to each offspring; this means that the ability of a rare allele to persist is dependent on how many individuals carry it, which individuals produce offspring, and how many offspring those individuals produce. Another important factor is population size (Figure 8.8): in any small population, only a limited number of individuals can carry any single allele, so the smaller the population, the higher the likelihood that alleles are lost to the next generation. This loss of alleles is called **genetic drift.**

While genetic drift equates to a loss of genetic diversity, there are some cases where populations show no obvious ill effects. Such may have been the case for female elephants in South Africa's Addo Elephant National Park. Hunting once nearly killed off this entire population; by the time they were adequately protected in 1931, only 11 animals remained, eight of which were female. Of those eight females, at least four were tuskless, while only two, maybe three, females carried both tusks. Over the next decades, Addo's female elephants have shown increasing degrees of tusklessness; by 2002, only 2% of females had tusks (by comparison, 96–98% of elephant females are normally expected to develop tusks, Maron, 2018). One can therefore postulate that the allele responsible for the tusk development in female elephants became rare, and that the progressive loss of tusked females is a sign of genetic drift (Whitehouse, 2002). While Addo's female elephants do not show any known limitations from being tuskless, the loss of alleles can also be devastating to the population suffering from genetic drift if, for example, the lost allele(s) coded for traits that would have allowed a species to adapt to a changing environmental condition.

It is important to note that genetic drift is distinct from natural selection. That is, genetic drift involves random changes in the frequency of alleles, whereas natural selection involves changes in traits in response to sexual selection or specific environmental conditions. For example, reduced tusk size in some heavily-hunted elephants in Africa (e.g. Chiyo et al., 2015) is a selective pressure in response to hunting that favour large tusks—this is distinct from Addo's female elephants that have lost their tusks even in the absence of selective hunting pressure.

Inbreeding depression

> Mating among closely related individuals, which occurs in small populations, often results in lower reproductive success and weaker offspring.

In large populations, a variety of instinctive mechanisms are in place to promote **heterosis**, which occur when offspring have a level of genetic variation that improves their individual evolutionary fitness. Some species are predisposed to disperse from their place of birth to prevent sibling–sibling or parent–offspring mating, while others are restrained from mating with close relatives through

Genetic Variation Worksheet

Small and isolated populations are expected to experience significant losses of genetic variation over time. To illustrate this point, consider an isolated heterozygous population that is not subjected to mutation. The proportion of original heterozygosity (H) that remains after one generation can be estimated using the formula (Wright 1931):

$$H = 1 - 1/[2N_e]$$

where (N_e) is effective population size. A population with $N_e = 2$ (two breeding individuals) would thus retain 75% of its original heterozygosity after one generation:

$$H = 1 - 1/4 = 1.00 - 0.25 = 0.75$$

But without a source for new genetic material, this population's heterozygosity will continue to decrease. After t generations (H_t):

$$H_t = H^t$$

The heterozygosity remaining in our population with two breeding individuals would thus be 56% after two generations (0.75 x 0.75), 24% after five generations, and 6% after ten generations. In contrast, a population with one hundred breeding individuals would retain 99.5% of its original heterozygosity after one generation, 98% after five generations, 95% after ten generations.

The migration of only a few individuals each generation or so can be enough to counter genetic drift in small populations. Mutation can theoretically also help, but natural mutation rates—estimated to be between 1 in 10,000 and 1 in 1,000,000 per gene per generation—are too rare to have an impact.

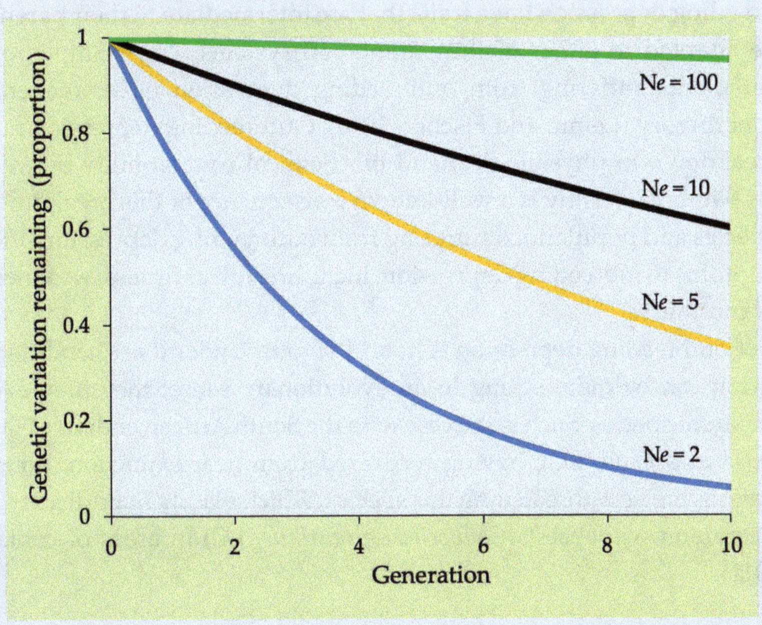

Figure 8.8 The amount of genetic diversity that is randomly lost over time due to genetic drift is highly dependent on a population's effective population size (*Ne*). A theoretical population with *Ne* = 2 may lose approximately 95% of its genetic diversity over 10 generations, while a population with *Ne* = 100 may lose only 5%. After Meffe and Carroll, 1997.

sensory cues such as individual odours. Many plants have morphological and physiological traits that facilitate cross-pollination and reduce self-pollination.

However, in small populations with few unrelated mates, the urge to breed might be stronger than the mechanisms that promote heterosis. Under these conditions, rather than forgoing reproduction, breeding among closely-related individuals (or **inbreeding**) can occur. This breeding among close relatives might result in **inbreeding depression**, which can occur when closely-related parents give their offspring two copies of a deleterious allele. Individuals suffering from inbreeding depression typically have fewer offspring or have offspring that are weak or fail to reproduce. Such is the case for some mountain gorillas (*Gorilla beringei beringei*, EN): genetic studies have shown how birth defects in several small populations can be attributed to inbreeding depression (Xue et al., 2015). Inbreeding depression has also been identified as the reason why some small lion populations are more susceptible to diseases (Trinkel et al., 2011). Inbreeding depression can result in a vicious cycle for declining population sizes, where such declines can lead to even more inbreeding depression, and eventually extinction (see Section 8.7.4).

Outbreeding depression

Large populations have many ecological, behavioural, and physiological mechanisms that prevent hybridisation, the production of offspring among genetically distant taxa, whether they be individuals of different species, or individuals of the same species but with different adaptations (the latter being intraspecific hybridisation). As with inbreeding depression, these mechanisms may fail in small populations, leading to **outbreeding depression** (Frankham et al., 2011). Because offspring that result from outbreeding depression have traits that are intermediate to their parents, they may not be adapted to either of the parents' ecosystems. For example, one study found that plants suffering from outbreeding depression have weakened defences against herbivory (Leimu and Fischer, 2010). Outbreeding depression may also lead to a breakdown in physiological and biochemical compatibility between would-be parents—hybrid sterility is a well-known consequence of this breakdown. Consequently, species and populations suffering from outbreeding depression often show similar symptoms to inbreeding depression, including lower fitness, weakness, and high rates of mortality.

The opposite of outbreeding depression is hybrid vigour. Under these conditions, the hybrid offspring can be quite strong in an evolutionary sense; they may even outcompete their parent species. Such is the case with the South African endemic black wildebeest (*Connochaetes gnou*, LC); having recovered from near-extinction, poorly planned translocations are now threatening this species, which readily hybridises with the widespread common wildebeest (*Connochaetes taurinus*, LC) in areas of contact (Grobler et al., 2011).

Population bottlenecks

In some taxa, such as butterflies, annual plants, and amphibians, population size varies dramatically from generation to generation. During some years, populations can be so large that they appear to face little risk of extinction. However, abundant years can be misleading when followed by successive years of low abundance. Generally, in a population that undergoes extreme size fluctuations, the population size required to ensure continued persistence (i.e., the **minimum viable population** (MVP), Section 9.2) is in effect much nearer the lowest than the highest number of individuals in any given year. However, during years with low abundance, a phenomenon known as a **population bottleneck** may occur—that is, the small population size may lead to the loss of rare alleles from one generation to the next. Population bottlenecks may lead to more inbreeding depression which, in turn, reduces reproductive success (Heber and Briskie, 2010) and increases vulnerability to diseases (Dalton et al., 2016). Low genetic diversity in great white sharks (*Carcharodon carcharias*, VU) living in South Africa's Indian Ocean is thought to be the result of a population bottleneck (Andreotti et al., 2015).

New populations founded by only a few individuals are vulnerable to a special type of population bottleneck, the **founder effect**. The founding individuals of a new population by definition start off with low genetic diversity, much less than the original population that the founders left behind. This low genetic diversity puts the new population at risk of further genetic diversity declines, which have lasting effects through time. This situation can occur naturally when only a small number of individuals disperse to establish a new population or when founder individuals come from a small population that already suffered from low genetic diversity. Being mindful of these concerns is especially important for translocation (Section 11.2) or captive breeding (Section 11.5) projects. For example, to prevent extinction of the world's smallest gazelle, the Speke's gazelle (*Gazella spekei*, EN), a captive population of this species, almost entirely restricted to Somalia, was established in the USA. The founder population for this captive breeding project consisted of only one male and three females, leading to severe levels of inbreeding depression and high mortality rates in offspring (Kalinowski et al., 2000). Understanding the importance of managing for genetic diversity can help avoid these and other challenges that can threaten the success of translocation projects.

> Populations founded by only a few individuals by definition start off with low genetic diversity, having lasting effects in the population through time.

8.7.2 Demographic stochasticity

Demographic stochasticity (also known as demographic variation) refers to random variations in a population's demographic traits (e.g. sex ratios, birth rates, death rates), the cumulative effect of variation in individual organisms' fitness. In any natural population, some individuals will produce fewer offspring than average, while others will produce more than average; some individuals will produce no offspring at all. Similarly, some individuals die younger than average, while others live longer than average. For populations that are sufficiently large, average birth and death rates provide relatively stable descriptions of key aspects of that population's demography. However, when a population's size decreases to below a certain threshold, variations in fitness of a small number of individuals can have a large impact on the overall populations' demographic parameters, causing population size and other characters to fluctuate up or down unpredictably (Schleuning and Matthies, 2009). Consider, for example, an isolated population of crocodiles with only a few females. As with many other reptiles, offspring sex ratios of crocodiles are determined by the environmental temperature during incubation (Hutton 1987). If, by chance, the population experiences two years of high temperatures, which favour male offspring, and the few females die by chance, the all-male population may be doomed for extinction unless some female crocodiles immigrate from elsewhere.

Small population sizes or low densities can also disrupt social interactions among individuals—especially interactions that affect reproduction—which can cause populations to become demographically unstable. This situation, referred to as the Allee effect, can result in further declines in population size, population density, and population growth rate. Obligate **cooperative breeders,** such as African wild dogs (*Lycaon pictus*, EN), are especially vulnerable to the Allee effect (Courchamp et al., 2000) since they need a certain number of individuals to protect their territories and obtain enough food for their offspring (Figure 8.9). Allee effects might also prevent impact group-living species that are not cooperative breeders—recalling the "safety in numbers" mantra, Allee effects seem to prevent the recovery of locally-rare sable antelope (*Hippotragus niger*, LC) populations in South Africa's Kruger National Park, as reduced herd sizes increases their exposure to predation (Owen-Smith et al., 2012). But even solitary species that live at low densities are susceptible to Allee effects, since they may find it hard to locate mates once the population density drops below a certain level.

> The social systems of group-living animals can easily be disrupted when their population size or density falls below a critical level.

8.7.3 Environmental stochasticity and catastrophes

Environmental stochasticity, the unpredictable variation in environmental conditions, can cause dramatic population size fluctuations over time, and hence, substantially increase the risk of extinction. Consider, for example, how the development rate of many insects is strongly temperature-dependent (e.g. Rebaudo and Rabhi, 2018). In an average or warm year, young insects that hatch on time and feed well may result in ecologically fit adults that produce many young, whereas unusually cold years might reduce hatching success and larval activity, which could also reduce adult fitness

Figure 8.9 A pack of African wild dogs on a hunt in Madikwe Game Reserve, South Africa. Due to their vulnerability to Allee effects, African wild dog populations can only be sustained if packs are above a certain threshold that allows them to hunt, feed their young, and protect themselves effectively.

(Gibert et al., 2001). So, highly unfavourable conditions in any one year can cause dramatic population declines, or even push a species to extinction if conditions persist over successive years across its range.

> Even though a small population may appear to be stable or increasing, an environmental catastrophe can severely reduce population size or even cause extirpation or extinction.

The increased risk of extinction from environmental stochasticity also applies to natural catastrophes that can occur at unpredictable intervals (e.g. droughts, storms, earthquakes, and fires). Range-restricted species are particularly vulnerable to this kind of threat. For example, the biodiversity living in and around several African crater lakes are vulnerable to a rather unique natural phenomenon called "lake burping". Volcanic chambers underneath some of these lakes are rich in CO_2. Small amounts of CO_2 may sometimes (or constantly, in some cases) seep up through the lake bed into the surrounding water. Because these lakes are thermally stratified—layers of cold, dense water settle near the bottom while warm, less dense water floats near the top—the CO_2-saturated water remains near the bottom of the lake. However, when there is a geologic disturbance, such as a landslide or earthquake, massive amounts of CO_2 may suddenly be released, first saturating the warmer water at higher levels with CO_2 (killing fish and other oxygen-dependent species in the process), before displacing the breathable surface air in and around the lake. In 1986, one such CO_2 eruption killed 1,800 people and 3,500 heads of livestock near Cameroon's Lake Nyos (Krajick, 2003). Some scientists fear that increased deforestation (which may trigger erosion and landslides) and hydraulic fracturing (which may trigger earthquakes, Section 7.1.1) could trigger similar events at other crater lakes in the region.

Environmental stochasticity tends to increase the probability of extinction more than does demographic stochasticity. As discussed, this is especially true for small populations and range-restricted species.

8.7.4 The extinction vortex

As populations decline in size, they become increasingly vulnerable to the combined impacts from the loss of genetic diversity, inbreeding depression, Allee effects, environmental stochasticity, and demographic stochasticity. All these factors tend to lower reproduction, increase mortality rates, and reduce population size even more, in turn driving populations to extinction at increasingly faster rates over time (Fagan and Holmes, 2006). Conservationists sometimes compare this phenomenon to a vortex, spiralling inward, moving faster (or declining faster in the case of a population) as it gets closer to the centre. At the centre of this **extinction vortex** (Gilpin and Soulé, 1986) is oblivion—the extinction of the species (Figure 8.10).

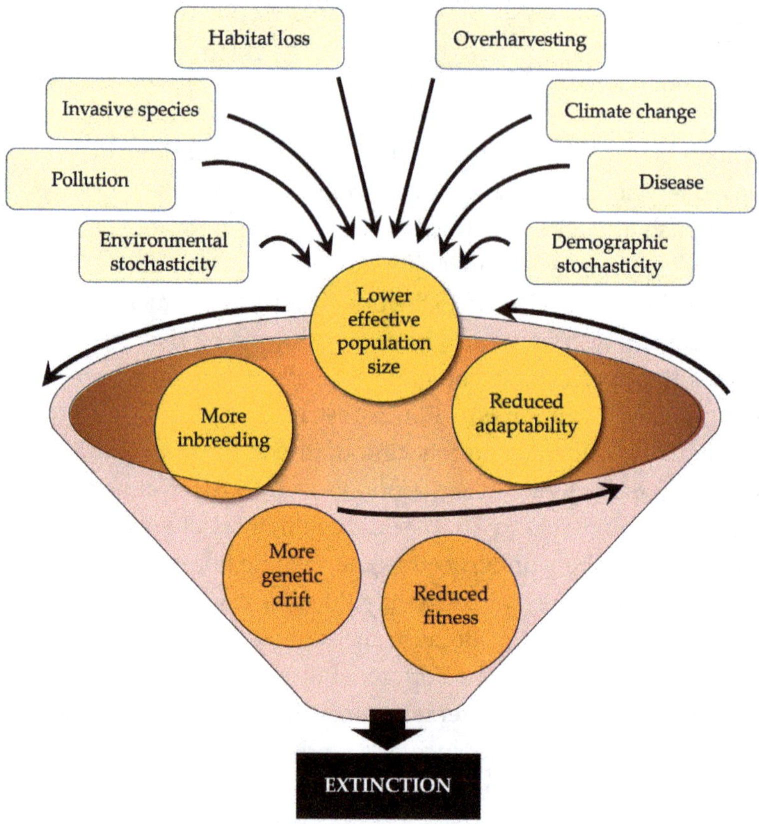

Figure 8.10 The extinction vortex describes a process whereby the factors that affect small populations can drive its size progressively downward towards extinction.

The demise of the bluebuck—the first large mammal of Africa to face this fate after European colonisation—may have been the result of an extinction vortex. When European colonists first arrived in South Africa, this ungulate already persisted as a single, small population of an estimated 370 individuals (**effective population size** at 100 individuals) and a highly restricted (4,300km^2) distribution. Considering this small and restricted population's vulnerable to deleterious genetic factors and demographic stochasticity, a recent study showed that this species was probably caught in an extinction vortex by the time the first colonist shot the first bluebuck (Kerley et al., 2009). This species would thus likely have gone extinct even in the absence of hunting and habitat loss, which only hastened its departure.

8.7.5 Is there any hope for small populations?

Despite the odds and the many threats facing Africa's wildlife, many species that were once on the brink of extinction have clawed their way back from the abyss towards stable, and sometimes even growing populations. Prime examples include the Pemba flying fox (*Pteropus voeltzkowi*, VU); considered *Critically Endangered* in 1996, conservation education programmes raised awareness of this unique bat, which now has considered *Vulnerable*, having recovered to more than 28,000 individuals (Entwistle and Juma, 2016). Similarly, because of habitat destruction and introduced predators, the future of the Seychelles magpie-robin (*Copsychus sechellarum*, EN) looked rather bleak in 1970, when only 16 individuals remained, all on one island. Today, thanks to habitat restoration efforts, supplemental feeding, invasive species eradication, provisioning of nest boxes, and a translocation programme, there are more than 280 Seychelles magpie-robins scattered across five islands (Burt et al., 2016). Another remarkable conservation success story involves the rescue of the southern white rhinoceros (*Ceratotherium simum simum*, NT), which was reduced to about 20 individuals in a single protected area in the late 1880s. Dedicated conservation efforts since then have seen this iconic species recover to more than 20,000 individuals, with individuals introduced and reintroduced all over Africa and zoos throughout the world. None of these species would have been alive today if it wasn't for intensive multi-year efforts by dedicated conservation biologists to pull them out of their individual extinction vortices.

Bringing species with small populations back from the edge of extinction requires dedication, careful planning, and significant amounts of resources. It also requires careful population management to mitigate the negative impacts of founder effects and both demographic and environmental stochasticity (Box 8.4; see also Chapter 11). As these examples show, it can be done. But, given the challenges, it should always be a priority to prevent a species from declining to very low numbers in the first place.

Bringing species with small populations back from the edge of extinction requires dedication, careful planning, and significant amounts of resources.

8.8 Is De-extinction a Solution?

One of the more interesting conservation debates to have emerged in recent years involve efforts to reverse extinction. This field, known as **de-extinction** or resurrection biology aims to revive extinct species, and eventually to reintroduce viable populations to their original locations (Seddon, 2017). One possible method, called "breeding back", aims to produce individuals genetically similar to an extinct species by selective

Box 8.3 Fenced Reserves Conserving Cheetahs and African Wild Dogs in South Africa

Kelly Marnewick[1,2]

[1]*Carnivore Conservation Programme, Endangered Wildlife Trust, Johannesburg, South Africa.*

[2]*Current address: Department of Nature Conservation, Tshwane University of Technology, Pretoria, South Africa.*

✉ *marnewickKA@tut.ac.za*

South Africa is one of the few countries in Africa where numbers of many large carnivore species are stable and, in some cases, increasing. Much of this success can be attributed to the managed metapopulation approach, which involves the reintroduction and subsequent translocation and management of populations in geographically isolated fenced reserves, between which natural dispersal is highly unlikely. As of 2016, more than 300 cheetahs are being managed in 51 reserves encompassing 10,995 km^2 (mean: 195 km^2 range: 20–1,000 km^2) and nearly 250 African wild dogs in 11 reserves encompassing 5,086 km^2 (mean: 216 km^2 range: 19–1,000 km^2). The reserves are situated across the country within a variety of land tenure systems including state and provincial protected areas and privately owned and community-run game reserves. Most reserves derive income primarily from ecotourism.

Each reserve forms part of the national network. Animals are moved between reserves to maintain the genetic integrity and demographic balance of individual subpopulations, but also to minimise direct management in the long term. Translocations are planned to mimic natural processes as far as possible but, due to the intricacies involved in managing animals between several reserves, this is not always possible. For wild dogs, small groups of unrelated adult males and females are artificially bonded to form packs, which mimics natural pack formation in the wild. For cheetahs, sub-adults are removed once they disperse from their maternal range. The animals are generally immobilised in the field and transported awake in crates on vehicles to their new reserves. Soft releases (Section 11.2.1) are preferred: these involve the animals being kept in temporary holding bomas of approximately 1 ha in size for about three months. The formation of artificial social groups is also done during this period. Intensive post-release monitoring is done at intervals reliant on reserve resources, but daily monitoring is recommended. The success rate of reintroductions has been high and, for wild dogs, has been strongly linked to the social cohesion of released groups (Marneweck et al., 2019), and the integrity of perimeter fences (Gusset et al., 2008).

This highly collaborative process involves multiple stakeholders, including conservation NGOs, provincial government conservation departments, private reserve owners and managers, researchers, local communities, and tourists. Effective and responsible population management tools help to prevent local populations growing too large or too small, and best practice guidelines ensure the ethical handling and management of animals. Individual reserves are responsible for providing infrastructure and other requirements including managing sustainable prey populations, perimeter fences, bomas and post release monitoring, as well as ensuring that a management plan is in place and adhered to. In many cases, students or volunteer organisations conduct post-release monitoring. National, high-level management is coordinated by the Endangered Wildlife Trust (EWT) and is funded through donations from corporations, individual philanthropists, conservation trusts, and foundations.

The managed metapopulation approach to carnivore conservation has increased the number and distribution of both cheetahs and African wild dogs in South Africa and built technical capacity in the country for metapopulation management (Davies-Mostert and Gusset, 2013), which has also been applied to species, such as lions, elephants, and black rhinoceros (*Diceros bicornis*, CR). Opportunities abound in other countries to use lessons learned in South Africa for the recolonisation of other areas where large mammals have been locally or regionally extirpated. Additionally, projected human population expansion, and the habitat fragmentation that comes with it, means that this approach is likely to become an indispensable tool in maintaining the viability of populations in disconnected landscapes.

breeding of extant species that carry genetic material of their extinct relatives. This is the main method currently being used to revive the aurochs (*Bos primigenius*, EX), the ancestor of today's domestic cattle (Stokstad, 2015). Other "breeding back" projects place less emphasis on genetics and more on morphology, by selectively breeding individuals with certain traits to produce individuals that visually appear similar to the extinct species. Such is the case at The Quagga Project, where selectively breeding of plains zebras (*Equus quagga*, NT) with quagga-like characteristics (reduced striping and brown hues) are resulting in animals (Figure 8.11) that look increasingly like extinct quaggas (Harley et al., 2009).

The second popular method used for de-extinction is **cloning**. This involves the transfer of viable genetic material from an extinct species to the eggs (or embryo) of a closely related surrogate mother, who will hopefully give birth to an individual of the extinct species. Cloning has been used in selective breeding of livestock for many years, and plans are also currently underway to use cloning to prevent the extinction of highly threatened species such as the northern white rhinoceros (see Box 11.4). Despite the promise that cloning offers for reviving extant and recently extinct species,

Figure 8.11 Not extinct anymore? A selective breeding programme in South Africa has raised several plain's zebras that closely resemble the extinct quagga. The progress from one generation to the next can be seen in this photo, with the adults showing reduced striping, and the foal showing brown hues.

cloning species that went extinct many years ago has been more challenging. So far, attempts to clone Spain's Pyrenean ibex (*Capra pyrenaica pyrenaica,* EX) and Australia's gastric-brooding frog (*Rheobatrachus silus,* EX) have produced individuals that lived for only a few minutes (Ogden, 2014).

Despite the progress made, de-extinction is one of the most controversial and polarising debates to emerge among conservation biologists in recent years. Proponents of de-extinction hope that the early work described above paves the way for the resurrection of extinct species once the threats that drove them to extinction have been managed. Many resurrection biologists have even started establishing banks where genetic material of threatened species is **cryopreserved** for future use. They also hope that their work will inspire more people to be interested in science in general and especially in conservation. Protected areas with extinct species may even draw tourists that can fund conservation projects, while reintroductions of once-extinct species can revive lost ecosystem services.

Bringing a species back from extinction is, however, highly controversial for several reasons. First, there is the argument that the limited funds available for conservation are better spent on species currently facing extinction rather than on projects with possibly insurmountable technical challenges. Others argue that there is no point in spending millions of dollars to bring back an extinct species if we cannot even solve the extinctions drivers that caused the demise of the extinct species in the first place. Conservationists also wonder how the issues facing small populations will be managed, especially early in the process. Many believe that these small compromised populations will simply occupy valuable space in zoos and protected areas that can be better used for protecting extant species. There are also major misgivings about whether the resurrected species will fill the same ecosystem function as before since they may behave differently; in fact, some worry that unpredictable behaviours may introduce new harmful threats to ecosystems. Many conservationists are also worried that the public's concern for species currently threatened may fade if there is a perception that we can simply revive the species after the last individual died.

Lastly, ethical questions are frequently raised about humans essentially trying to "play God" with these "vanity projects", and the possibility that this entire field will undermine one of the most important foundations of conservation biology—that we need to act now because extinction is forever. Clearly there are some advantages, but also disadvantages, to de-extinction. Most importantly, much research still needs to happen for this to be a viable idea.

8.9 Summary

1. The rates of species extinction are currently 1,000 times greater than natural background levels; this may soon increase to 10,000 times. Over 99% of modern extinctions can be attributed to human activity. These extinctions are leading to the rapid loss of ecosystem services.
2. The IUCN has developed quantitative criteria that assign species to nine conservation categories based on their risk of extinction. Species that are *Extinct in the Wild* (EW), *Critically Endangered* (CR), *Endangered* (EN), and *Vulnerable* (VU) are officially considered "threatened with extinction". The five other categories are *Extinct* (EX), *Near Threatened* (NT), *Least Concern* (LC), *Data Deficient* (DD), and *Not Evaluated* (NE).
3. Species with the following characteristics are particularly vulnerable to extinction: species with small populations, species with declining populations, species with restricted distribution ranges, species with one or only a few small populations, species that are exploited by people, and species with critical symbiotic relationships.
4. Small populations are at high risk of extinction because they are vulnerable to several deleterious genetic factors, as well as demographic and environmental stochasticity. Such populations often require intensive management to prevent them from becoming a victim of an extinction vortex.
5. De-extinction as a scientific field aims to revive extinct species using methods such as selective breeding and cloning. But this practice is controversial, and not practical with current technology.

8.10 Topics for Discussion

1. Why should you, or anyone else, be concerned if a species becomes extirpated (also known as locally extinct)? How does this concern compare to when a species becomes globally extinct?
2. Use the IUCN Red List (http://www.iucnredlist.org) to identify one species in your country that is currently threatened with extinction. How might this species be affected by the various challenges facing small populations?

Consider genetic, physiological, behavioural, and ecological factors, as appropriate.

3. Think of an imaginary animal that was recently discovered. Imagine this animal is also threatened with extinction. Name three characteristics that make your imaginary animal vulnerable to its threats. Now discuss some steps that can be implemented to ensure that your animal will continue to survive.
4. A herd of 80 rhinoceros have been moved from South Africa to Australia to "save the species" because "there is no safe place in Africa for rhinos today" (see Hayward et al., 2017). What do you think of this plan? Do you think the project will be successful? What are the main opportunities and challenges? Once you're done answering the question read Lundgren et al. (2017) and decide if you still feel the same.

8.11 Suggested Readings

Bonebrake, T.C., F. Guo, C. Dingle, et al. 2019. Integrating proximal and horizon threats to biodiversity for conservation. *Trends in Ecology and Evolution* 34: *in press*. https://doi.org/10.1016/j.tree.2019.04.001 Coordination is critical when combatting multiple threats.

Caughley, G. 1994. Directions in conservation biology. *Journal of Animal Ecology* 63: 215–24. https://doi.org/10.2307/5542 The classic overview of the challenges faced by small and declining populations.

Ceballos, G., P.R. Ehrlich, and R. Dirzo. 2017. Biological annihilation via the ongoing sixth mass extinction signaled by vertebrate population losses and declines. *Proceedings of the National Academy of Sciences* 114: E6089–E6096. https://doi.org/10.1073/pnas.1704949114 Extinctions by the numbers.

IBPES. 2019. Nature's dangerous decline 'unprecedented': Species extinction rates accelerating. *IBPES media release*. https://www.ipbes.net/news/Media-Release-Global-Assessment We are in the midst of a biodiversity crisis.

IUCN. 2012. *IUCN Red List Categories and Criteria*: v. 3.1 (Gland: IUCN). https://portals.iucn.org/library/sites/library/files/documents/RL-2001-001-2nd.pdf A summary of the IUCN Red List classifications.

Jones, H.P. 2010. Seabird islands take mere decades to recover following rat eradication. *Ecological Applications* 20: 2075–80. https://doi.org/10.1890/10-0118.1 Control of invasive species can be an effective method to achieve recovery of threatened species.

Koh, L.P., R.R. Dunn, N.S. Sodhi, et al. 2004. Species coextinctions and the biodiversity crisis. *Science* 305: 1632–34. https://doi.org/10.1126/science.1101101 Thousands of species face extinction due to the decoupling of important symbiotic relationships.

McClenachan, L., A.B. Cooper, K.E. Carpenter, et al. 2012. Extinction risk and bottlenecks in the conservation of charismatic marine species. *Conservation Letters* 5: 73–80. https://doi.org/10.1111/j.1755-263X.2011.00206.x Most marine species have not been evaluated for their risk of extinction.

Stearns, B.P., and S.C. Stearns. 2010. Still watching, from the edge of extinction. *BioScience* 60: 141–46. https://doi.org/10.1525/bio.2010.60.2.8 Many threatened species increasingly rely on human actions to avoid extinction.

Tranquilli, S., M. Abedi-Lartey, F. Amsini, et al. 2012. Lack of conservation effort rapidly increases African great ape extinction risk. *Conservation Letters* 5: 48–55. https://doi.org/10.1111/j.1755-263X.2011.00211.x Neglecting species in conservation need increases extinction risk.

Bibliography

Andreotti, S., S. Heyden, R. Henriques, et al. 2016. New insights into the evolutionary history of white sharks, *Carcharodon carcharias*. *Journal of Biogeography* 43: 328–39. https://doi.org/10.1111/jbi.12641

Balon, E.K., M.N. Bruton, and H. Fricke. 1988. A fiftieth anniversary reflection on the living coelacanth, *Latimeria chalumnae*: Some new interpretations of its natural history and conservation status. *Environmental Biology of Fishes* 23: 241–80. https://doi.org/10.1007/BF00005238

Barnosky, A.D., N. Matzke, S. Tomiya, et al. 2011. Has the Earth's sixth mass extinction already arrived? *Nature* 471: 51–57. https://doi.org/10.1038/nature09678

Barnosky, A.D., P.L. Koch, R.S. Feranec, et al. 2004. Assessing the causes of late Pleistocene extinctions on the continents. *Science* 306: 70–75. https://doi.org/10.1126/science.1101476

Barraclough, D.A. 2006. Bushels of bots. *Natural History* 115: 18–21.

Bartlett, L.J., D.R. Williams, G.W. Prescott, et al. 2015. Robustness despite uncertainty: Regional climate data reveal the dominant role of humans in explaining global extinctions of Late Quaternary megafauna. *Ecography* 39: 152–61. https://doi.org/10.1111/ecog.01566

Bauer, H., C. Packer, P.F. Funston, et al. 2015. *Panthera leo*. *The IUCN Red List of Threatened Species* 2015: e.T15951A79929984. https://doi.org/10.2305/IUCN.UK.2016-3.RLTS.T15951A107265605.en

Bazelet, C., and P. Naskrecki. 2014. *Aroegas nigroornatus*. *The IUCN Red List of Threatened Species 2014*: e.T20639917A56180093. https://doi.org/10.2305/IUCN.UK.2014-1.RLTS.T20639917A56180093.en

BirdLife International 2018a. *Crithagra concolor*. *The IUCN Red List of Threatened Species* 2018: e.T22720310A128249895. https://doi.org/10.2305/IUCN.UK.2018-2.RLTS.T22720310A128249895.en

BirdLife International 2018b. *Lanius newtoni*. *The IUCN Red List of Threatened Species* 2018: e.T22705080A131390093. https://doi.org/10.2305/IUCN.UK.2018-2.RLTS.T22705080A131390093.en

Blackburn, D.C., C. Boix, E. Greenbaum, et al. 2016. The distribution of the Bururi Long-fingered Frog (*Cardioglossa cyaneospila*, family Arthroleptidae), a poorly known Albertine Rift endemic. *Zootaxa* 4170: 355–64. http://doi.org/10.11646/zootaxa.4170.2.8

Boschian, G., D. Caramella, D. Saccà, et al. 2019. Are there marrow cavities in Pleistocene elephant limb bones, and was marrow available to early humans? New CT scan results from the site of Castel di Guido (Italy). *Quaternary Science Reviews 215* 86–97. https://doi.org/10.1016/j.quascirev.2019.05.010

Brito, J.C., S.M. Durant, N. Pettorelli, et al. 2018. Armed conflicts and wildlife decline: Challenges and recommendations for effective conservation policy in the Sahara-Sahel. *Conservation Letters* 11: e12446. http://doi.org/10.1111/conl.12446

Brook, B.W., and M.J.S. Bowman. 2005. One equation fits overkill: Why allometry underpins both prehistoric and modern body-sized extinctions. *Population Ecology* 47: 137–41. https://doi.org/10.1007/s10144-005-0213-4

Brooks, T.M., S.L. Pimm, and J.O. Oyugi. 1999. Time lag between deforestation and bird extinction in tropical forest fragments. *Conservation Biology* 13: 1140–50. https://doi.org/10.1046/j.1523-1739.1999.98341.x

Burt, A.J., J. Gane, I. Olivier, et al. 2016. The history, status and trends of the Endangered Seychelles Magpie-robin *Copsychus sechellarum*. *Bird Conservation International* 26: 505–23. https://doi.org/10.1017/S0959270915000404

Callaway, E. 2017. Oldest *Homo sapiens* fossil claim rewrites our species' history. *Nature News*. https://doi.org/10.1038/nature.2017.22114

Caughley, G. 1994. Directions in conservation biology. *Journal of Animal Ecology* 63: 215–24. https://doi.org/10.2307/5542

Ceballos, G., P.R. Ehrlich, A.D. Barnosky, et al. 2015. Accelerated modern human-induced species losses: Entering the sixth mass extinction. *Science Advances* 1: e1400253. https://doi.org/10.1126/sciadv.1400253

Ceballos, G., P.R. Ehrlich, and R. Dirzo. 2017. Biological annihilation via the ongoing sixth mass extinction signaled by vertebrate population losses and declines. *Proceedings of the National Academy of Sciences* 114: E6089–E6096. https://doi.org/10.1073/pnas.1704949114

Chakona, A, and S. Kubheka. 2018. *Pseudobarbus quathlambae*. *The IUCN Red List of Threatened Species* 2018: e.T18475A100171498. http://doi.org/10.2305/IUCN.UK.2018-2.RLTS.T18475A100171498.en

Channing, A., K.S. Finlow-Bates, S.E. Haarklau, et al. 2006. The biology and recent history of the Critically Endangered Kihansi Spray Toad *Nectophrynoides asperginis* in Tanzania. *Journal of East African Natural History* 95: 117–38. https://doi.org/10.2982/0012-8317(2006)95[117:TBARHO]2.0.CO;2

Chiyo, P.I., V. Obanda, and D.K. Korir. 2015. Illegal tusk harvest and the decline of tusk size in the African elephant. *Ecology and Evolution* 5: 5216–29. https://doi.org/10.1002/ece3.1769

Clarke, G.P., N.D. Burgess, F.M. Mbago, et al. 2011. Two 'extinct' trees rediscovered near Kilwa, Tanzania. *Journal of East African Natural History* 100: 133–40. https://doi.org/10.2982/028.100.0109

Contu, S. 2013. *Cyperus chionocephalus*. *The IUCN Red List of Threatened Species* 2013: e.T44393328A44490119. http://doi.org/10.2305/IUCN.UK.2013-1.RLTS.T44393328A44490119.en

Courchamp, F., T. Clutton-Brock, and B. Grenfell. 2000. Multipack dynamics and the Allee effect in the African wild dog, *Lycaon pictus*. *Animal Conservation* 3: 277–85. https://doi.org/10.1111/j.1469-1795.2000.tb00113.x

Cowlishaw, G. 1999. Predicting the pattern of decline of African primate diversity: An extinction debt from historical deforestation. *Conservation Biology* 13: 1183–93. https://doi.org/10.1046/j.1523-1739.1999.98433.x

Cronk, Q. 2016. Plant extinctions take time. *Science* 353: 446–47. https://doi.org/10.1126/science.aag1794

Cumming, D.H.M. 2007. Of elephants, predators, and plants in protected areas: A case of classic trophic cascades. Paper presented in Symposium: *Sharing the range: Elephants, people and biological conservation in Africa.* SCB Annual Meeting, 1–5 July, Port Elizabeth, South Africa.

Dalton, D.L., E. Vermaak, H.A. Smit-Robinson, et al. 2016. Lack of diversity at innate immunity Toll-like receptor genes in the Critically Endangered White-winged Flufftail (*Sarothrura ayresi*). *Scientific Reports* 6: 36757. https://doi.org/10.1038/srep36757

Davies-Mostert H.T., and M. Gusset. 2013. Restoring African wild dogs in South Africa: A managed metapopulation approach. *WAZA Magazine* 14: 41–44

de Vos, J.M., L.N. Joppa, J.L. Gittleman, P.R. Stephens, et al. 2015. Estimating the normal background rate of species extinction. *Conservation Biology* 29: 452–62. https://doi.org/10.1111/cobi.12380

Durant, S.M., T. Wacher, S. Bashir, et al. 2013. Fiddling in biodiversity hotspots while deserts burn? Collapse of the Sahara's megafauna. *Diversity and Distributions* 20: 114–22. https://doi.org/10.1111/ddi.12157

Durant, S., N. Mitchell, A. Ipavec, et al. 2017. The global decline of cheetah *Acinonyx jubatus* and what it means for conservation. *Proceedings of the National Academy of Sciences* 114: 528–33. https://doi.org/10.1073/pnas.1611122114

Entwistle, A.C., and J. Juma. 2016. *Pteropus voeltzkowi. The IUCN Red List of Threatened Species* 2016: e.T18768A22089205. http://doi.org/10.2305/IUCN.UK.2016-1.RLTS.T18768A22089205.en

Fagan, W.F., and E.E. Holmes. 2006. Quantifying the extinction vortex. *Ecology Letters* 9: 51–60. https://doi.org/10.1111/j.1461-0248.2005.00845.x

Faith, J.T., J. Rowan, A. Du, et al. 2018. Plio-Pleistocene decline of Africa's megaherbivores: No evidence for ancient hominin impacts. *Science* 362: 938–41. https://doi.org/10.1126/science.aau2728

Feranec, R.S. 2004. Geographic variation in the diet of hypsodont herbivores from the Rancholabrean of Florida. *Palaeogeography, Palaeoclimatology, Palaeoecology* 207: 359369. https://doi.org/10.1016/j.palaeo.2003.09.031

Frankham, R., J.D. Ballou, M.D.B. Eldridge, et al. 2011. Predicting the probability of outbreeding depression. *Conservation Biology* 25: 465–75. https://doi.org/10.1111/j.1523-1739.2011.01662.x

Gibert, P., R.B. Huey, and G.W. Gilchrist. 2001. Locomotor performance of *Drosophila melanogaster*: interactions among developmental and adult temperatures, age, and geography. *Evolution* 55: 205–09. https://doi.org/10.1111/j.0014-3820.2001.tb01286.x

Gilpin, M.E., and M.E. Soulé. 1986. Minimum viable populations: Processes of species extinction. In: *The Science of Scarcity and Diversity*, ed. by M.E. Soulé (Sunderland: Sinauer).

Goldschmidt, T., F. Witte, and J. Wanink. 1993. Cascading effects of the introduced Nile perch on the detritivorous/phytoplanktivorous species in the sublittoral areas of Lake Victoria. *Conservation Biology* 7: 686–700. https://doi.org/10.1046/j.1523-1739.1993.07030686.x

Grobler, J.P., I. Rushworth, J.S. Brink, et al. 2011. Management of hybridization in an endemic species: Decision making in the face of imperfect information in the case of the black wildebeest—*Connochaetes gnou*. *European Journal of Wildlife Research* 57: 997–1006. https://doi.org/10.1007/s10344-011-0567-1

Guerrant, E.O. 1992. Genetic and demographic considerations in the sampling and reintroduction of rare plants. In: *Conservation Biology: The Theory and Practice of Nature Conservation, Preservation and Management*, ed. by P.L. Fiedler and S.K. Jain (New York: Springer). https://doi.org/10.1007/978-1-4684-6426-9

Gusset, M., S.J. Ryan, M. Hofmeyr, et al. 2008. Efforts going to the dogs? Evaluating attempts to re-introduce endangered wild dogs in South Africa. *Journal of Applied Ecology* 45: 100–08. https://doi.org/10.1111/j.1365-2664.2007.01357.x

Halley, J.M., N. Monokrousos, A.D. Mazaris, et al. 2016. Dynamics of extinction debt across five taxonomic groups. *Nature Communications* 7: 12283. https://doi.org/10.1038/ncomms12283

Harley, E.H., M.H. Knight, C. Lardner, et al. 2009. The Quagga project: Progress over 20 years of selective breeding. *South African Journal of Wildlife Research* 39: 155–63. https://doi.org/10.3957/056.039.0206

Haynes G. 2018. The evidence for human agency in the Late Pleistocene megafaunal extinctions. In *Encyclopedia of the Anthropocene v. 1*, ed. by D.A. DellaSala, and M.I. Goldstein (Oxford: Elsevier).

Hayward, M.W., W.J. Ripple, G.I.H. Kerley, et al. 2017. Neocolonial conservation: Is moving rhinos to Australia conservation or intellectual property loss? *Conservation Letters* 11: e12354. https://doi.org/10.1111/conl.12354

Heber, S., and J.V. Briskie. 2010. Population bottlenecks and increased hatching failure in endangered birds. *Conservation Biology* 24: 1674–78. https://doi.org/10.1111/j.1523-1739.2010.01553.x

Hutton, J.M. 1987. Incubation temperatures, sex ratios and sex determination in a population of Nile crocodiles (*Crocodylus niloticus*). *Journal of Zoology* 211: 143–55. http://doi.org/10.1111/j.1469-7998.1987.tb07458.x

IUCN. 2012. *IUCN Red List categories and criteria*: v. 3.1 (Gland: IUCN). https://portals.iucn.org/library/sites/library/files/documents/RL-2001-001-2nd.pdf

IUCN. 2017. *Guidelines for using the IUCN Red List categories and criteria*, v. 13 (Gland: IUCN). http://nc.iucnredlist.org/redlist/content/attachment_files/RedListGuidelines.pdf

IUCN. 2019. *The IUCN Red List of Threatened Species*. http://www.iucnredlist.org

Janzen, D.H. 1983. The Pleistocene hunters had help. *American Naturalist* 121: 598–99. https://doi.org/10.1086/284088

Johnson, C.N. 2009. Ecological consequences of Late Quaternary extinctions of megafauna. *Proceedings of the Royal Society of London B* 276: 2509–19. https://doi.org/10.1098/rspb.2008.1921

Kalinowski, S.T., P.W. Hedrick, and P.S. Miller. 2000. Inbreeding depression in the Speke's gazelle captive breeding program. *Conservation Biology* 14: 1375–84. https://doi.org/10.1046/j.1523-1739.2000.98209.x

Keith, D.A., J.P. Rodríguez, K.M. Rodríguez-Clark, et al. 2013. Scientific foundations for an IUCN Red List of Ecosystems. *PLoS ONE* 8: e62111. https://doi.org/10.1371/journal.pone.0062111

Kerley, H.I.H., R. Sims-Castley, A.F. Boshoff, et al. 2009. Extinction of the blue antelope *Hippotragus leucophaeus*: Modelling predicts non-viable global population size as the primary driver. *Biodiversity and Conservation* 18: 3235. https://doi.org/10.1007/s10531-009-9639-x

Koh, L.P., R.R. Dunn, N.S. Sodhi, et al. 2004. Species coextinctions and the biodiversity crisis. *Science* 305: 1632–34. https://doi.org/10.1126/science.1101101

Krajick, K. 2003. Defusing Africa's killer lakes. *Smithsonian Magazine* 34: 46–55. https://www.smithsonianmag.com/science-nature/defusing-africas-killer-lakes-88765263

Leimu, R., and M. Fischer. 2010. Between-population outbreeding affects plant defence. *PLoS ONE* 5: e12614. https://doi.org/10.1371%2Fjournal.pone.0012614

Lombardo, M.P., and R.O Deaner. 2018. Born to throw: The ecological causes that shaped the evolution of throwing in humans. *Quarterly Review of Biology* 93: 1–16. https://doi.org/10.1086/696721

Lundgren, E.J., D. Ramp, W.J. Ripple, et al. 2017. Introduced megafauna are rewilding the Anthropocene. *Ecography* 41: 857–66. https://doi.org/10.1111/ecog.03430

Marneweck, C., P.A. Becker, G. Beverley, et al. 2019. Factors affecting the success of artificial pack formation in an endangered, social carnivore: The African wild dog. *Animal Conservation* 22: *in press*. https://doi.org/10.1111/acv.12490

Maron, D.F. 2018. Under poaching pressure, elephants are evolving to lose their tusks. *National Geographic*. https://on.natgeo.com/2z9mE1x

Meffe, G.C., and C.R. Carroll. 1997. *Principles of Conservation Biology* (Sunderland: Sinauer).

Minnaar, A., L. van Schalkwyk, and S. Kader. 2018. The difficulties in policing and combatting of a maritime crime: The case of Abalone poaching along South Africa's coastline. *Journal of the Indian Ocean Region* 14: 71–87. https://doi.org/10.1080/19480881.2018.1421448

Ogden, L.E. 2014. Extinction is forever… or is it? *BioScience* 64: 469–75. https://doi.org/10.1093/biosci/biu063

Okubamichael, D.Y., S. Jack, J. de Wet Bösenberg, et al. 2016. Repeat photography confirms alarming decline in South African cycads. *Biodiversity and Conservation* 25: 2153–70. http://doi.org/10.1007/s10531-016-1183-x

OpenStax. 2019. *Biology 2nd ed.* OpenStax CNX. https://openstax.org/details/books/biology-2e

Owen-Smith, N., G.J. Chirima, V. Macandza, et al. 2012. Shrinking sable antelope numbers in Kruger National Park: What is suppressing population recovery? *Animal Conservation* 15: 195–204. https://doi.org/10.1111/j.1469-1795.2011.00504.x

Pimm, S.L., C.N. Jenkins, R. Abell, et al. 2014. The biodiversity of species and their rates of extinction, distribution, and protection. *Science* 344: 1246752. https://doi.org/10.1126/science.1246752

Pringle, R.M. 2005. The origins of the Nile perch in Lake Victoria. *BioScience* 55: 780–87. https://doi.org/10.1641/0006-3568(2005)055[0780:TOOTNP]2.0.CO;2

Rall, J.L., and T. Sephaka. 2008. *Re-evaluation of the relevance to construct barriers as in-situ conservation measures for the protection of the Maloti minnow in the Senqunyane Catchment* (Florida: ECOSUN Environmental Consultants).

Rebaudo, F., and V.-B. Rabhi. 2018. Modeling temperature-dependent development rate and phenology in insects: Review of major developments, challenges, and future directions. *Entomologia Experimentalis et Applicata* 166: 607–17. https://doi.org/10.1111/eea.12693

Rebelo, A.G. 1992. Red Data Book species in the Cape Floristic Region: Threats, priorities and target species. *Transactions of the Royal Society of South Africa* 48: 55–86. https://doi.org/10.1080/00359199209520256

Ripple, W.J., and B. Van Valkenburgh. 2010. Linking top-down forces to the Pleistocene megafaunal extinctions. *BioScience* 60: 516–26. https://doi.org/10.1525/bio.2010.60.7.7

Schleuning, M., and D. Matthies. 2009. Habitat change and plant demography: Assessing the extinction risk of a formerly common grassland perennial. *Conservation Biology* 23: 174–83. https://doi.org/10.1111/j.1523-1739.2008.01054.x

Seddon, P.J. 2017. The ecology of de-extinction. *Functional Ecology* 31: 992–95. https://doi.org/10.1111/1365-2435.12856

Shelton, J.M., B.M. Clark, T. Sephaka, et al. 2017. Population crash in Lesotho's endemic Maloti minnow *Pseudobarbus quathlambae* following invasion by translocated smallmouth yellowfish *Labeobarbus aeneus*. *Aquatic Conservation* 65–77. https://doi.org/10.1002/aqc.2633

Skelton, P.H., J.L. Rall, E.R Swartz, et al. 2001. Maloti minnow conservation project, *LHDA Report*. 1041 (Grahamstown: JLB Smith Institute of Ichthyology).

Smith, F.A., R.E. Elliott Smith, S.K. Lyons, et al. 2019. The accelerating influence of humans on mammalian macroecological patterns over the late Quaternary. *Quaternary Science Reviews* 211: 1–16. https://doi.org/10.1016/j.quascirev.2019.02.031

Steyn, G., J.L. Rall, V. Rall, et al. 1996. Fish. In: Baseline biology survey and reserve development: Phase 1B. v. 3-Fauna Lesotho, *LHDA Report* 1008, ed. by AfriDev Consultants (Maseru: Lesotho Highlands Development Authority).

Stokstad, E. 2015. Bringing back the aurochs. *Science* 350: 1144–47. https://doi.org/10.1126/science.350.6265.1144

Surovell, T., N. Waguespack, and P.J. Brintingham. 2005. Global archaeological evidence for proboscidians overkill. *Proceedings of the National Academy of Science* 102: 6321–26. https://doi.org/10.1073/pnas.0501947102

Tallman, G., J. Zhu, B.T. Mawson, et al. 1997. Induction of CAM in *Mesembryanthemum crystallinum* abolishes the stomatal response to blue light and light-dependent zeaxanthin formation in guard cell chloroplasts. *Plant and Cell Physiology* 38: 236–42. https://doi.org/10.1093/oxfordjournals.pcp.a029158

Trinkel, M., D. Cooper, C. Packer, et al. 2011. Inbreeding depression increases susceptibility to bovine tuberculosis in lions: An experimental test using an inbred-outbred contrast through translocation. *Journal of Wildlife Diseases* 47: 494–500. https://doi.org/10.7589/0090-3558-47.3.494

Van Valkenburgh, B., M.W. Hayward, W.J. Ripple, et al. 2016. The impact of large terrestrial carnivores on Pleistocene ecosystems. *Proceedings of the National Academy of Sciences* 113: 862–67. https://doi.org/10.1073/pnas.1502554112

Waters, C.N., J. Zalasiewicz, C. Summerhayes, et al. 2016. The Anthropocene is functionally and stratigraphically distinct from the Holocene. *Science* 351: aad2622. https://doi.org/10.1126/science.aad2622

Werdelin, L., and M.E. Lewis. 2013. Temporal change in functional richness and evenness in the eastern African Plio-Pleistocene carnivoran guild. *PLoS ONE* 8: e57944. https://doi.org/10.1371/journal.pone.0057944

Whitehouse, A.M. 2002. Tusklessness in the elephant population of the Addo Elephant National Park, South Africa. *Journal of Zoology* 257: 249–54. https://doi.org/10.1017/S0952836902000845

Witte, F., T. Goldschmidt, P.C. Goudswaard, et al. 1991. Species extinction and concomitant ecological changes in Lake Victoria. *Netherlands Journal of Zoology* 42: 214–32. https://doi.org/10.1163/156854291X00298

Wright, S. 1931. Evolution in Mendelian populations. *Genetics* 16: 97–159. http://www.ncbi.nlm.nih.gov/pubmed/17246615

Xue, Y., J. Prado-Martinez, P.H. Sudmant, et al. 2015. Mountain gorilla genomes reveal the impact of long-term population decline and inbreeding. *Science* 348: 242–45. https://doi.org/10.1126/science.aaa3952

9

Population Biology and its Applications

Staff from the Frankfurt Zoological Society (FZS) conducting an aerial survey over Selous Game Reserve, Tanzania.

Even without human influences, the size of any wildlife population may be stable, increasing, decreasing, or even fluctuating. These population changes, combined with occasional natural perturbations, can and have driven some species and populations to extinction. Such natural extinction events generally occur at local scales, and are interspersed by long periods of little change, so that overall ecosystem stability is not compromised. Moreover, as explained by the intermediate disturbance hypothesis (e.g. Bongers et al., 2009), localised disturbances and subsequent local extinctions play an important role in maintaining regional biodiversity, as they increase opportunities for a greater variety of species to live in an area (Figure 9.1), at least until succession drives them out again. Some species that colonise the empty niches left by extinctions or extirpations may even evolve to become new species over time.

Figure 9.1 A treefall gap allowing sunshine to penetrate the canopy in the sacred Bubi Forest on Bioko Island, Equatorial Guinea. Treefall gaps and other localised natural disturbances benefit regional biodiversity because they provide opportunities for a greater variety of species to eke out an existence. Responses do vary, however, from ecosystem to ecosystems: while fire disturbance maintains most grassland and savannah ecosystems, it has an overall negative impact on tropical forests.

Human-driven disturbances often occur at larger scales and more frequently than natural perturbations. Consider, for example, the large amount of natural forests that are converted to agricultural land every year, or climate change impacts that are affecting every ecosystem on Earth. Because these disturbances are so widespread and occur with such regularity, they are causing a wholesale destabilisation of the natural environment. Many species and populations are unable to cope with these fast and vast changes and are consequently undergoing sharp declines. The human-driven extinctions that follow are leaving compromised ecosystems more vulnerable to invasions by widespread generalist species and exotic species. What remains is an environment dominated by only a few species unable to offer many of the ecosystem services we depend upon. To prevent further harm, we need to identify the most vulnerable species and ecosystems and develop strategies that can slow or even reverse current extinction rates. But how can we identify the species most likely to go extinctions soon, and how can we determine which actions should be taken to save them? The field of population biology, defined as the study of population dynamics over time and space, provides us the tools to answer many of these questions.

9.1 Monitoring Population Size

The primary aim of population monitoring is to detect changes in the environment, population size, and species distribution over time. Such monitoring efforts frequently focus on a particular area or a population of concern, but it can also target more common but sensitive species, such as butterflies and macroinvertebrates, which can function as indicator species to assess ecosystem condition (Section 4.2.6). The great number of methods (which are all types of surveys) used to monitor populations usually fall into one of three different categories: biodiversity inventories, population censuses, and demographic studies.

9.1.1 Biodiversity inventories

A biodiversity inventory is an attempt to document which species are present in some defined locality. Such an effort can focus on one specific taxa (e.g. a bird survey) or several taxa, on a small area (e.g. a city park) or large area (e.g. a large national park), over a short period of time (e.g. a few hours) or long period of time (e.g. several years, Box 9.1). There are many methods to compile a biodiversity inventory, ranging from uncomplicated to highly organised, performed by a single person or a large team of experts. Some of the most popular methods for biodiversity inventories include site visits by professional naturalists and questionnaires distributed among local people. To tap into the knowledge and eagerness of amateur naturalists, conservation biologists are also increasingly compiling biodiversity inventories using citizen science surveys (see Box 15.3). Rapid biodiversity assessments (RAP) are sometimes used to compile an inventory under tight deadlines to answer urgent questions and inform urgent decisions. A bioblitz is a special type of biodiversity inventory during which experts on a range of taxa come together to record all the living species within a designated area over a brief period (usually over 24 hours).

The primary aim of population monitoring is to detect changes in the environment, population size, and species' distributions over time.

Box 9.1 The Role of Biodiversity Inventories in the Management of Gorongosa National Park

Marc Stalmans[1] and Piotr Naskrecki[2]

[1] *Scientific Services, Gorongosa National Park, Mozambique.*

[2] *E.O. Wilson Biodiversity Laboratory, Gorongosa National Park, Mozambique.*

✉ *stalmans@gorongosa.net and pnaskrec@oeb.harvard.edu*

The 4,000 km^2 Gorongosa National Park in central Mozambique was proclaimed in 1960 to protect one of the highest densities of large herbivores at the southern end of Africa's Great Rift Valley (Tinley, 1977). National Parks are often victims of war and political instability and Gorongosa National Park is no exception. It suffered grievously during the protracted period of civil war from the early 1970s to early 1990s. During this time the park lost 90–99% of its elephants, common hippopotamuses (*Hippopotamus amphibious*, VU), African buffalo (*Syncerus caffer*, NT), plains zebras, and common wildebeest (*Connochaetes taurinus*, LC) through poaching by warring parties and hunters from nearby cities and rural communities.

Since then, restoration efforts that started in earnest in 2004 have brought about a spectacular recovery of several affected large mammal populations (Bouley et al., 2018; Stalmans et al., 2019). But conservation management cannot only focus on these flagship species. Considering, amongst others, the impact of climate change and the importance of agriculture (with its associated pests and pollinators) to rural communities, it is vital that conservationists understand the breadth of biodiversity and its relationship to ecosystem functioning. To accomplish this, a programme of systematic biodiversity surveys is currently being undertaken in Gorongosa. Each year, a group of international and national specialists team up with park technicians and rangers to conduct a three-week long bioblitz in a subsection of the park. These surveys also serve as training opportunities to prepare young Mozambican scientists to apply modern biological survey methods and technologies.

By the beginning of 2019, a total of nearly 5,900 species represented by some 44,000 observations have been entered into the park's biodiversity database. Based on these data, initial projections suggest that Gorongosa protects 37,500–76,500 different species. Vertebrates are likely to number 850–1,000 species, while plants are estimated to number 2,000–3,000 species. Single orders of insects far exceed those numbers; for example, there may be 3,000–5,000 species of wasps, and 4,000–6,000 species of moths of which 15–25% may be new to science. Local ecosystems are also particularly rich. For the surveys around the Bunga inselbergs (Figure 9.A) in 2015, at least 580 species of butterflies and moths were collected, most of them never before recorded from the Park. Forty species of katydids were recorded, with two species of significance. A large population of *Debrona cervina,* a large arboreal katydid was discovered, until now known only from two type specimens collected in 1890. Also collected was the predaceous katydid *Peringueyella macrocephala,* Mozambique's largest katydid, previously known only from a handful of specimens collected between 1850 and 1965. About 100 species of grasshoppers were recorded, including two species new to science. Additionally, about 30 species of mantids were recorded, including *Rhomboderella thorectes,* a species previously known from the single holotype collected in the early 1900s. It is expected that the full inventory of the park's biodiversity will span a period of 20 years.

Figure 9.A Surveys in little-explored corners of Africa often yield biological discoveries. (Top) A recently described gecko species new to science, *Afroedura gorongosa,* discovered in 2015. (Bottom) The Mozambique girdled lizard (*Smaug mossambicus*) was previously known only from a small population on Mount Gorongosa and a single record in Manica province. Surveys in 2015 found a new population on Bunga inselberg.

Biodiversity inventories play an important role in the management of Gorongosa and other national parks, especially in long-term conservation planning. Amongst others, baseline data obtained from our surveys will be used in future to measure overall biodiversity responses to large mammal population changes, evolving patterns of land use around the park, and the impact of climate change. Future biodiversity surveys will also target little known areas adjacent to the park to provide information required for corridor planning.

While biodiversity inventories seldom offer the kinds of detailed data required to predict likelihood of a species' persistence, they have several uses in conservation. First, a biodiversity inventory can be a comparatively inexpensive and straightforward method to broadly monitor an area's species and populations. Biodiversity inventories conducted over a wide area can also help determine the distribution of a species, while a comparison with follow-up inventories can highlight distribution changes (which often correspond to population changes). This was well illustrated in a study that used repeated citizen scientist surveys to investigate how songbird distributions have changed across South Africa, Lesotho, and eSwatini between 1987 and 2013 (Péron and Altwegg, 2015).

9.1.2 Population censuses

A population **census** (also called a count) uses a repeatable sampling protocol to estimate the abundance or density of a population or species which, in turn, can tell us whether a population is doing well or not. When a species is easy to detect, relatively sedentary, and the sampling area is small, a comprehensive census of all individuals may be possible. However, comprehensive censuses are generally very difficult, if not impossible, to conduct when implemented on large or highly mobile populations, or over large areas. In these cases, it may be better to restrict the census to a more manageable subsection of the population, by dividing the area of interest into sampling units, and randomly censusing only some of the units. Population estimates that capture only a fraction of the overall population can then serve as an index for broader trends, or it can be used to estimate the total population size through **extrapolation**, if the researcher knows which fraction of the population or area was counted.

Some popular methods for censusing subsections of wildlife populations are, sampling plots, distance sampling, and mark-recapture surveys. Sampling plots are popular in studies focussing on plants and invertebrates, allowing biologists to systematically count each individual observed in a small area (Figure 9.2). Birds and mammals are often censused using distance sampling, during which all observed individuals on predetermined transects or from points are tallied. The number of individuals observed in the count area can then be extrapolated to obtain population size (or density) estimates for individual (or multiple) species observed across the entire area of interest. Aerial censuses are often used to conduct distance sampling transects over large and open areas, while point counts and walked line-transects are more popular for small areas or closed-canopy ecosystems (White and Edward, 2000). Mark-recapture surveys, mark-resight surveys, and sight-resight surveys are popular for species that are easy to catch, trap, or individually recognised. In this case, captured (and thus counted) individuals would be marked for future identification, after which the total population in an area is estimated by accounting for the proportion of marked and unmarked individuals seen on subsequent visits. The marking of animals can be done with a variety of procedures, including using highly visible tags, paint approved for animal use, or unique marks on the animal itself. One creative study used tourists' photographs to generate a mark-recapture dataset, which was used to estimate the size of cheetah and African wild dog (*Lycaon pictus*, EN) populations in South Africa's Kruger National Park (Marnewick et al., 2014). Like inventories, population censuses can sometimes also lead to unexpected yet important findings: the first comprehensive population survey of sea turtles breeding on Africa's Atlantic coast recently alerted marine biologists to the fact that Gabon hosts several globally important rookeries (Box 9.2).

Box 9.2 Sea Turtle Conservation along Africa's Atlantic Coast

Angela Formia

Wildlife Conservation Society, Global Conservation Program, New York, NY, USA.

✉ *aformia@wcs.org*

Virtually all the characteristics of sea turtles' life histories make them difficult to study and conserve. They are long-lived, slow growing, migratory, and almost entirely ocean-dwelling. Although they return to their natal beaches to reproduce, these are usually thousands of kilometres from their developmental and adult foraging grounds. In addition, sea turtle habitat often overlaps with areas of high human use such as developed coastlines and intensive fisheries. Describing population ranges and assessing interaction with human threats is thus critical to their survival.

Over recent decades, we have learnt much about sea turtles along the coastline of Africa (Figure 9.B) thanks to extensive research efforts. For instance, we know that these coasts host globally important populations of green turtles (*Chelonia mydas*, EN) in Mauritania, Guinea Bissau, Equatorial Guinea and Republic of the Congo; loggerheads (*Caretta caretta*, VU) on Cabo Verde;

hawksbills (*Eretmochelys imbricata*, CR), on São Tomé and Principe; leatherbacks (*Dermochelys coriacea*, VU) in Equatorial Guinea and Gabon; and olive ridleys (*Lepidochelys olivacea*, VU) in Gabon and Angola.

Figure 9.B (Top) One of thousands of leatherback sea turtle females nesting in Gabon every year. Photograph by M.J. Witt. (Bottom) An olive ridley turtle hatchling makes its way to sea on a northern Angolan beach where the local community ensures its protection.

One of Africa's most remarkable sea turtle populations is Gabon's leatherback rookery, the biggest in the world with as many as 15,000 to 41,000 nesting females (Witt et al., 2009). Gabon also hosts the largest olive ridley rookery in the Atlantic (Metcalfe et al., 2015), and foraging grounds for green and hawksbill turtles. Until the late 1990s, virtually nothing was known about these populations, other than the fact that eggs and adults were frequently collected for human consumption. Since then, a multi-pronged approach has been adopted to describe and protect Gabon's sea turtles. Intensive coastal monitoring has allowed scientists to assess spatio-temporal trends in nesting frequency and abundance, and levels of nest-site fidelity and reproductive success. Using techniques, such as satellite telemetry, flipper tagging, oceanic modelling, and dispersal simulations, and genetic and isotopic analyses, researchers have been able to map sea turtle behaviour at sea, in Gabon's coastal waters, and during post-nesting migrations to foraging grounds off South America and South Africa (i.e. Formia et al., 2006, Maxwell et al., 2011, Witt et al., 2011, Pikesley et al., 2018).

Building upon this knowledge, measures have been established to quantify and reduce the impact of threats to Gabon's sea turtles. In 2002, the Gabonese government created a system of national parks and protected areas encompassing approximately 80% of Gabon's sea turtle nests; in 2017, a new network of 20 marine protected areas (MPA) was officially created, covering 26% of Gabon's territorial waters (Parker, 2017). Laws enacted in 2011 prohibit all hunting, capture, and commercialisation of sea turtles. Trained observers on-board industrial fishing vessels quantify sea turtle bycatch from bottom trawling and tuna seiners and reduce mortality by treating and releasing captured turtles. In addition, the Gabonese government now requires that all shrimp trawlers use turtle excluder devices (TED), aluminium grids sewn into the nets allowing sea turtles and other large bycatch to escape, while conserving shrimp catch; similar devices are being developed for fish trawlers. Ongoing efforts are shifting traditional turtle hunting and other destructive practices toward more sustainable fisheries. Turtle-watching ecotourism also represents a growing potential to increase awareness and incentivize conservation efforts.

Nevertheless, African sea turtle conservation remains a formidable challenge. Although the economic context is changing rapidly, impoverished coastal villagers in many countries continue to collect turtles and eggs for local consumption or market sale, and many wealthier urbanites continue to consider them delicacies. These problems are often compounded by corruption, political instability, inadequate law enforcement, and development priorities focused on destructive exploitation. With funding deficits, combating these challenges sometimes seems like a losing battle, but public attitudes are slowly shifting. Even in remote beach villages, the idea that a turtle alive is worth more than dead is no longer such a bizarre concept.

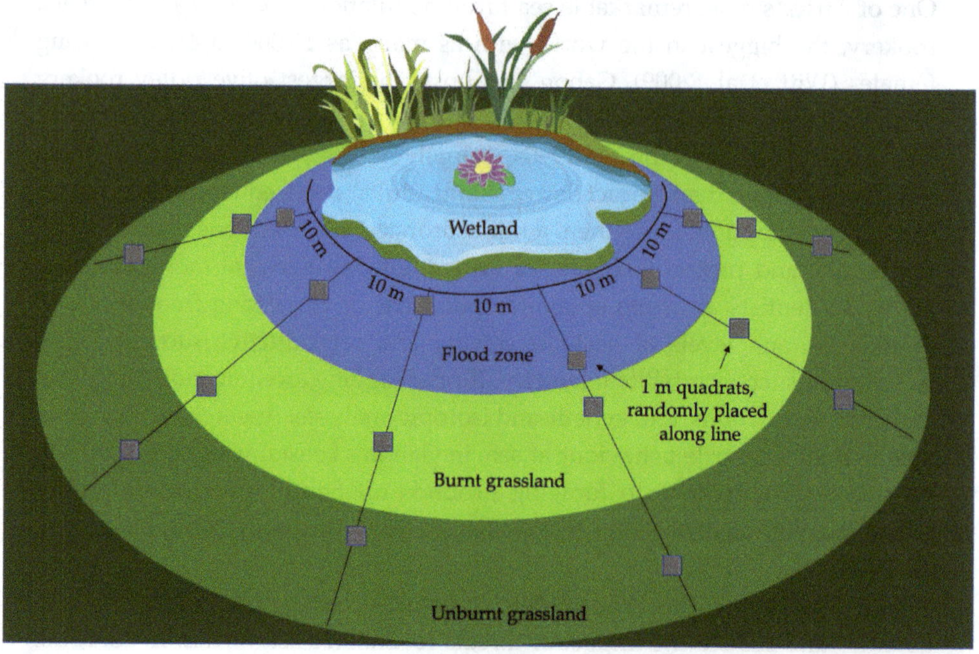

Figure 9.2 (Top) A schematic of a systematic sampling protocol using quadrat frames. Dividing a large area into smaller sampling units makes the survey task much more feasible. The survey can be performed in the field, or photos such as these can be taken for analysis once back at the office. (Bottom) A quadrat frame divided into 10x10 cm squares, set out to monitor the species richness and abundance of plants in a grassland recovering from a fire.

9.1.3 Demographic studies

Demographic studies monitor individuals of different ages and sizes over time (Figure 9.3) to obtain a more comprehensive dataset than would be produced by population censuses. Most demographic studies use the same methods that what would be used for a population census; however, in addition to counting and marking, individuals would also be aged, measured for size and body condition, and sexed, when possible. The best demographic studies involve collecting these data from the same individuals over time, which is easiest when working with sedentary species (e.g. plants), populations in an enclosed space (e.g. in a small fenced reserve), animals that are fairly resident and/or habituated to human presence, or individuals carrying **biologging devices** (Kays et al., 2015). This may not always be possible, in which case biologists may obtain data from different individuals during each field session, to serve as an index for larger population trends.

Mark-recapture survey worksheet

Mark–recapture survey, basic formula (Caughley 1977):

$$N = \frac{M \times n}{m}$$

where
N = Population size;
M = Number of individuals marked (first visit);
n = Number of individuals seen (second visit);
m = Number of marked individuals seen (second visit).

Assume 21 individuals were marked with ear tags on the first visit. With 13 marked individuals recaptured out of a total of 30 individuals (both marked and unmarked) captured on a second visit, the estimated population size is:

$$N = \frac{21 \times 30}{13} = 48 \text{ individuals}$$

Figure 9.3 A biologist gathering biometric data from a juvenile central African slender-snouted crocodile (*Mecistops leptorhynchus*, CR) in the DRC. The crocodile will be tagged with a permanent marker before release so it can be recognised when caught again. Accompanying the photo is an example of mark-recapture survey worksheet to estimate population size.

The data obtained from demographic studies are often used in combination with mathematical modelling to guide and refine conservation strategies. For example, researchers frequently compare the age structure (i.e. the percentage of juveniles, reproductively active adults, and older post-reproductive-age adults) of a declining population to that of a stable population to identify causes of decline, and the population parameters that are most sensitive to disturbances. This information can then be used to predict population sizes at different points in the future, and how those populations may respond to different management scenarios. The aim of many demographic studies is to predict, and identify strategies to reduce, extinction risk (see Section 9.2).

9.1.4 Recent progress in collecting survey data

Conservation activities are regularly impeded by insufficient information. This is especially true in tropical regions of the world, where most threatened species lack demographic data, and some species lack reliable data altogether. Faced with these gaps, biologists have started using several innovative methods to fill data gaps. Prominent examples include using market surveys (e.g. Kümpel et al., 2010, Ingram et al., 2015) and interviews with local people (e.g. Edwards and Plagányi, 2008) to obtain much-needed baseline survey data. It is important to note that such datasets, obtained second-hand rather than directly, can be unreliable and biased, especially if data are collected from harvesters unwilling to report on their own illegal activities. It is thus important to combine potentially unreliable datasets with reliable datasets, or obtain independent verification, before using such data to make important decisions. One such example comes from West Africa, where researchers wanted to quantify extinction risk for the Nigeria-Cameroon chimpanzee (*Pan troglodytes ellioti*, EN). Here, biologists related unreliable market survey data to two reliable datasets—orphan intake rate at wildlife sanctuaries and the number of young in wild groups—to estimate that the region's chimpanzees might be extinct within the next 20 years because hunting was two to 13 times higher than the population could sustain (Hughes et al., 2011).

> Camera traps, hair snares, and faecal samples all provide non-invasive sampling techniques to obtain baseline data needed for conservation assessments.

Collecting genetic material on elusive and rarely-seen animals with **non-invasive techniques** such as hair snares and faecal sampling are also becoming increasingly popular means of collecting survey data. Researchers in Gabon did just that, by using genetic material obtained from dung to estimate the population size, gender ratio, age distribution, breeding status, relatedness, and dispersal patterns of the region's forest elephant (*Loxodonta cyclotis*) population (Eggert et al., 2013). These non-invasive techniques reduce the need for researchers to be in the field, thereby reducing both the researchers' exposure to dangerous conditions and disturbances to the populations they are trying to monitor.

Camera traps represent another non-invasive survey technique whose popularity has greatly increased in recent years. These special cameras, often placed at supplemental food or next to wildlife paths, are activated automatically when an animal passes into the area covered by the camera's motion sensors (Figure 9.4). This photographic record of movement can then be used to obtain biodiversity inventories, population size estimations, or even to compile demographic datasets (Steenweg et al., 2017). Creative researchers at South Africa's Robben Island even successfully combined camera trapping with human facial recognition technology—more generally associated with law enforcement—to automate monitoring of individual African penguins (*Spheniscus demersus*, EN) (Sherley et al., 2010).

Figure 9.4 (Left) A nature conservation student sets a camera trap in northern South Africa to monitor leopard (*Panthera pardus*, VU) and brown hyena (Parahyaena brunnea, NT) populations on a privately protected area. Photograph by Kelly Marnewick. (Right) Congo peafowl (*Afropavo congensis*, VU)—a highly elusive species—investigating a camera trap in the DRC.

9.2 Estimating Extinction Risk

Biologists often use the positive relationship between population size and likelihood of persistence (Section 8.7) to predict the probability that a population may go extinct at some point in the future. One of the most popular tools for making such predictions is **population viability analysis (PVA).** A PVA can be thought of as a type of extinction risk assessment; it uses demographic data and mathematical methods to predict at what point in the future a population or species is likely to perish. In addition, by considering a species' resource requirements and the availability of limiting resources, biologists can use the results of a PVA to identify a species' most vulnerable life stages, and to estimate how management techniques may influence population size and extinction risk. In this way, PVAs can guide conservation decisions by highlighting the need to, for example, modify harvesting regulations, perform translocations (Section 11.2), or provide and protect a greater amount of suitable habitat. Even the IUCN's Red List Criteria (Section 8.5) uses PVA as a criterion to help prioritise conservation targets: populations with low extinction risk may not require immediate attention, while those approaching extinction thresholds will gain higher priority.

9.2.1 A word of warning

The purpose of this chapter is to provide a brief introduction on the usefulness of quantitative population biology methods such as PVA in conservation. While the methods for studying population sizes, fluctuations, and demographics are very powerful, they are also highly technical, and require specialist knowledge of mathematical procedures. Erroneous predictions from using incorrect methods, violating assumptions, and/or using inadequate data would run counter to well-intentioned objectives; and so, the increased popularity and use of PVA by insufficiently trained conservation scientists is of serious concern. For many people, the methods highlighted in this chapter are best learned by studying under the supervision of an expert, to better understand each model's assumptions and the newest developments in the field. For people with advanced mathematical skills who might want to study more on their own, texts such as *Quantitative Conservation Biology* (Morris and Doak, 2002) and *Bayesian Methods for Ecology* (McCarthy, 2007) may help. The development of user-friendly software packages, such as VORTEX and RAMAS (reviewed in Brook et al., 2000), have also expanded the PVA user-group in recent years. Nonetheless, when obtaining results—even from seasoned demographic modellers—it is important to remember that we cannot account for all future possibilities. Interpreting the results of a PVA, as any other model predicting the future, requires a great deal of caution and a healthy dose of common sense.

9.2.2 Probability of extinction

> Population viability analysis (PVA) uses demographic data and mathematical methods to predict if a population or species is likely to persist or perish.

The main purpose of a PVA is to estimate the viability (or time to extinction) of a species or population from observed population sizes and growth rates. Consider a population with 100 individuals that loses 50% of its individuals each year. A simple model will suggest that this population will lose 50 individuals the first year, 25 individuals the second year, and so on, until no individuals are left in the seventh year. The probability of extinction for this population is thus 100%, and the time to extinction is seven years. But how do we deal with the more realistic complex variations in population sizes we see in nature?

A more realistic PVA begins by constructing a mathematical model representing the population of interest using data obtained from a demographic study, which may include the current age (or size) structure of the population, average birth rates, and average survival rates of each age class. This dataset would be organised in a format suitable for PVA modelling using a database package, and then analysed using the methods of matrix algebra. Because results from this initial model have only one outcome—a population that is either stable or growing/declining at a fixed rate—it is called a **deterministic model**. Typically, deterministic models are then tailored to include a variety of independent environmental parameters, such as food availability, storm frequency, or invasive competitors. Variability can also be added into the model by allowing some or all the model elements (e.g. survival rate or habitat availability) to vary within their observed ranges of values. Catastrophic events, such as a fire that kills a large proportion of the population, can also be programmed to occur at random points in time. Hundreds or even thousands of simulations of this complex model can then be run to determine changes in population size over time, the probability of population extinction within a certain period, and the median time to extinction. Because of the variability built into this more complex model, each iteration's output will vary from the next; for that reason, it is called a **stochastic model**. The choice of models and the parameters included depend on the goals of the analysis and the management options under consideration.

9.2.3 Minimum viable population

When a PVA shows that a population has a relatively high risk of extinction, a logical next step would be to determine what could be done to prevent the extinction from happening. In general, protecting larger populations reduces extinction probability (Figure 9.5). To understand exactly how large is large enough, a PVA can also be used to estimate a **minimum viable population** (MVP). As the name implies, an MVP is the smallest number of individuals necessary for a population to have a chance of long-term persistence, despite the potential effects of demographic, environmental, and genetic stochasticity, and natural catastrophes faced by small populations (Section 8.7). This is well illustrated in the influential paper by Shaffer (1981), who compared setting MVP targets to planning for floods; engineers cannot rely on the average annual rainfall when designing flood control systems near rivers and wetlands. Instead, they must design systems that can also handle extreme rainfall and flooding events. These extreme events may occur rarely, perhaps once every 50 years, but they will likely occur during the lifetime of a flood control system. Similarly, to maximise the long-term protection of a threatened species, we must take actions that

> A minimum viable population (MVP) is an estimate of the smallest number of individuals necessary for a population to have a good chance of long-term persistence.

protect them in both average and extreme years characterised by catastrophic events such as cyclones/hurricanes, forest fires, and disease epidemics (Anderson et al., 2017). This is especially true considering future climate change scenarios, where every year may be uncharacteristically harsh, in effect a 50-year event.

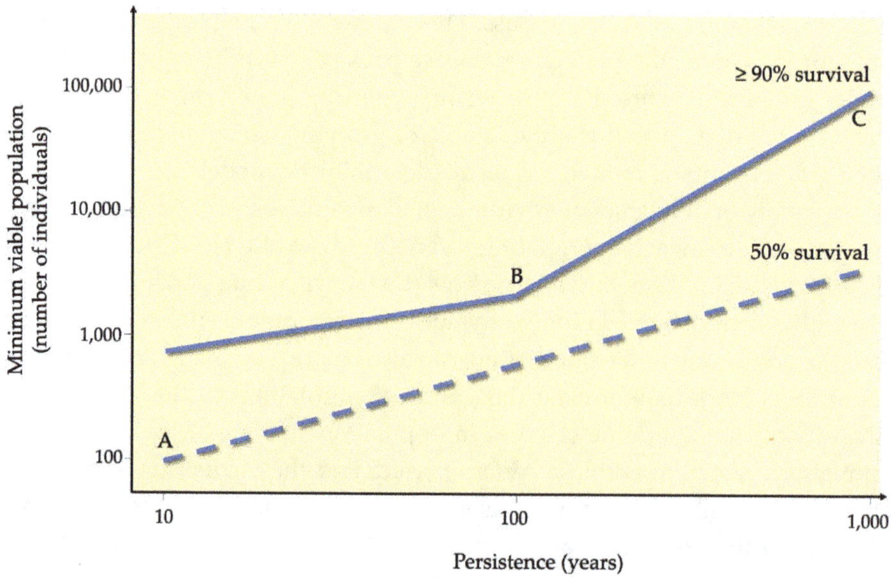

Figure 9.5 A graph (both axes on log scales) derived from a meta-analysis including 1,198 species showing how a larger minimum viable population (MVP) size translates to a higher likelihood of persistence over time. (A) If the goal is for 50% chance of persistence after 10 years, 100 individuals are required; (B) If the goal is for 90% chance of persistence after 100 years, 3,000 individuals are required; (C) If the goal is for 90% chance of persistence after 1,000 years, 100,000 individuals are required.

Several studies have attempted to come up with a "universal" MVP value that could ensure that a population of any species has a reasonable chance of persistence. The estimates vary greatly. For example, a universal MVP estimate from the 1980s, the "50/500 rule", suggested that at least 50 individuals are necessary to prevent inbreeding, and 500 to prevent genetic drift (Frankham et al., 2014). While this 50/500 rule is currently used to guide the IUCN Red List Criteria for small populations (see e.g. Table 8.1, Criteria D), more recent studies suggested that this estimate is much too low. For example, one study that considered over 1,000 species calculated that 1,377 individuals must be protected to ensure the survival of the population and species (Brooke et al., 2006). Another study argued that 4,169 adults needed to be protected (Traill et al., 2007), while a third study identified 7,316 adults as the universal MVP (Reed et al., 2003). The reason why these estimates are highly variable is because MVPs are context specific, with the results varying greatly by species, location, and degree of threat (Flather et al., 2011). For some species, it might be necessary to protect large numbers of individuals—maybe thousands or tens of thousands for invertebrates and annual plants with that can experience large population size fluctuations. For other species, such as those that are long-lived and reproduce regularly, protecting only a few hundred individuals may suffice. Unfortunately, many threatened species have population sizes much smaller than any of these recommended minimums. For example, half of the 23 surveyed elephant populations remaining in West Africa have fewer than 200 individuals (Bouché et al., 2011), a number considered to be vastly inadequate for their long-term survival, especially in the absence of strong conservation management.

While a universal MVP value will probably never be agreed upon, species and location specific MVP estimates have great value for guiding conservation efforts. For example, it can suggest the minimum number of individuals that need to be released to improve chances of reintroduction success (Section 11.2). MVP estimates can also be combined with a species' home range requirements to determine a **minimum dynamic area (MDA)**, which is the smallest area of suitable habitat required to sustain the MVP. The use of MVP and MDA, and factors influencing it, were well illustrated in several studies on South Africa's fragmented cheetah (*Acinonyx jubatus*, VU) population. Here, researchers originally found that translocations every 1–5 years can greatly improve the likelihood of persistence for 20 subpopulations with at least 10 cheetahs each, or for 10 subpopulations with at least 15 cheetahs each (Lindsey et al., 2009). But a follow-up study then showed that these results were context specific, and highly dependent on the presence of other predators that compete for the same prey (Lindsey et al., 2011). With no competitors, a minimum dynamic area of 200 km^2 would be sufficient to support 10 cheetahs. However, a reserve of at least 700 km^2 would be needed for 15 cheetahs and 15 lions, and even more if other competitor carnivores are present.

Because of the close relationship between population viability and habitat availability, these two factors are often considered together in **population and habitat viability assessments (PHVA**, http://www.cpsg.org/our-approach/workshop-processes/phva-workshop-process). Such an assessment was recently performed for Sierra Leone's western chimpanzees (*Pan troglodytes verus*, CR), where 53 conservation partners came together to develop a recovery plan for this highly threatened species (Carlsen et al., 2012). As an illustration of how conservation projects can bring people from different walks of life together, the participants for this PHVA came from universities, government, NGOs, and the private sector, and included Paramount Chiefs, representatives from the UN and Sierra Leone's government ministries, and well as experts in tourism, communications, population modelling, and wildlife rehabilitation.

Because of the close relationship between population viability and habitat availability, these two factors are often considered together in population and habitat viability assessments (PHVA).

9.2.4 Effective population size

One of the most important considerations when estimating MVPs is deciding which individuals to include in the calculations. Because population viability depends greatly on a population's ability to produce young to increase in size (or at least balance out mortality), it makes sense that reproductive status is important in MVP estimations. For that reason, biologists often calculate MVPs using the **effective population size (N_e)**, an estimate of how many individuals or pairs in a population are actively breeding. Consider, for example, a school of 1,000 dolphins; it might have 990 immature individuals and only 10 mature dolphins (five males and five females) that are actively breeding. Even though the full population consists of 1,000 dolphins, the effective population size is only 10—just the mature breeding dolphins.

It is worth noting that the effective population size may sometimes be even smaller than the number of individuals capable of breeding at any one time. Factors that cause such a scenario include unequal sex ratios, variation in reproductive output, or an inability to find mates. Health status may also play a role; for example, many long-lived seabird species will forego breeding in years where adults did not attain a necessarily healthy body condition, or years when food is scarce (Crawford et al., 2008). Such reduced effective population sizes can lead to drastic population declines, especially when unsuitable conditions persist over consecutive years.

> A population's effective size is often much smaller than the total population size because not all individuals are capable of breeding at any one time.

It is also important to remember that the individuals included in effective population size are not the only ones deserving conservation attention. For example, while young animals may not immediately contribute to population growth and stability, they remain a conservation priority for their potential to contribute to population viability in future. Protecting non-reproductive individuals is also important to avoid having cooperative breeders such as African wild dogs (*Lycaon pictus*, EN) succumb to Allee effects (Section 8.7.2). Individuals that forego reproduction because of poor body condition (e.g. malnourished individuals) can easily become reproductive, and contribute to population viability, if their stressors are mitigated. Lastly, for many species (e.g. many plants, fungi, bacteria, and protists), many (sometimes all) individuals may be dormant for long periods in the soil as seeds, spores, tubers, or other structures. While these dormant individuals may not be part of the effective breeding population, they still contribute to population viability in the long term.

9.2.5 Maximum sustainable yield

An important but under-utilised benefit of PVAs is the ability to help conservation managers estimate sustainable harvest rates for wildlife populations at risk of overharvesting (Milner-Gulland and Rowcliffe, 2007). Many threatened species can withstand some level of harvesting, so long as harvest rates are lower than **recruitment** rates. To estimate the sustainable level of harvesting, biologists may use PVA to estimate a

> A population's maximum sustainable yield provide an estimate of the greatest number of individuals that can be harvested without detriment to the population.

population's **maximum sustainable yield**—the greatest number of individuals that can be harvested without detriment to the population (Box 9.3). When estimating maximum sustainable yields for overharvested taxa, it is important to consider not only the total population size (or effective population size), but also harvesting biases produced by harvester preferences and techniques. For example, when estimating hunting quotas, hunter preferring larger animals (Lindsey et al., 2013; Barthold et al., 2016) and animal behaviour (Caro et al., 2009) can significantly influence model output. Also, in fisheries management, it is important to consider the outsized role older and larger fish play in recruitment rates, or the indirect damage fishing does the environment or to juvenile individuals (De Leo and Micheli, 2015). Lastly, it is important to consider how harvesting right at maximum sustainable yield levels may leave those populations less buffered to future disturbances (Cumming and Cumming, 2015)—it is thus advisable to maintain harvest quotas well below maximum levels.

Box 9.3 Sustainably Harvesting Fruit Bats Through Better Understanding of Life Histories

David T. S. Hayman

Molecular Epidemiology and Public Health Laboratory, Hopkirk Research Institute, Massey University, Palmerston North, New Zealand.

✉ *d.t.s.hayman@massey.ac.nz*

> "Full-time hunters are employed to shoot them [...] Nothing is known about the natural factors that encourage or repress population growth in the straw-coloured fruit bat, or on what age category these factors have maximum effects. [...] No laws, customs or taboos protect the straw-coloured fruit bat from exploitation [...].
>
> Funmilayo, 1978

Funmilayo's comments from the 1970s still ring true about the problems currently facing straw-coloured fruit bats (*Eidolon helvum*, NT) throughout their African distribution range. The species is hunted widely in West and Central Africa (Figure 9.C), with scientists estimating that over 128,000 and up to 306,000 individuals are killed annually in Ghana (Kamins et al., 2011) and Côte D'Ivoire (Niamien et al., 2015). In Ghana, the population "is hunted far beyond maximum sustainable yield", concluded an initial study that predicted maximum sustainable yield based on population sizes and estimated intrinsic rate of increase (Kamins et al., 2011). This overhunting has been going on for a long time. Notes from a 1909 field trip to DRC reported them hunted in the "hundreds" (Allen et al., 1917).

Figure 9.C (Top) Smoked straw-coloured fruit bats, an important source of protein in many parts of Africa, for sale at a local market in Ghana. (Bottom) Straw-coloured fruit bats at their daytime roost.

Despite these reports of intensive harvesting, straw-coloured fruit bats remain abundant with colonies comprised of several million individuals often reported. The species is also highly mobile, migratory, and panmictic, breeding freely across its continental distribution (Peel et al., 2017). These life history traits make it difficult to determine how hunting is impacting the population because presence and size of colonies are highly variable in space and time (Hayman and Peel, 2016).

What can the natural history of the species tell us about their possible vulnerability to the pressures inherent of being hunted? Straw-coloured fruit bats exhibit classic life history traits of long-lived species. These bats invest time and energy into single, well-developed pups that they nurse and carry, as Funmilayo noted, "until they are capable of independent existence, which gives [the pup] a high chance of survival". This investment in individual young and single annual breeding events means that straw-coloured fruit bats are susceptible to over-harvesting.

Good information on birth and death rates are required to accurately assess the impact of harvesting. Hayman et al. (2012) estimated birth rate and survival probability parameters in a single colony of up to 1 million straw-coloured fruit bats that roost in trees in Accra, Ghana, demonstrating the feasibility of obtaining such information. Histological examination of tooth growth layers allowed age estimation and life-table analyses to estimate an annual survival probability for juveniles of 43% and adults of 83%. Mark-recapture data using radio-collar telemetry and multi-state models to address confounding emigration estimated lower annual adult survival probability, c. 63%. True survival probabilities likely exist between these estimates, as follow up studies from four further locations suggest (Hayman and Peel, 2016), because permanent emigration may underestimate capture–recapture estimates and population decline may bias life table estimates. Birth rates for the species are high (0.96 young per female per year). Improved estimation of these key parameters will allow for critical analyses of harvest sustainability of straw-coloured fruit bat populations in future.

9.2.6 Sensitivity analysis

A particularly useful feature of PVA—and models in general—is that model parameters can be individually evaluated to better understand the implications of different management strategies. This is usually accomplished with a **sensitivity analysis**, a method that determines which parameter or combination of parameters has the biggest influence on population viability. Obviously, parameters that greatly influence population viability should become the focus of conservation efforts, whereas parameters that have a minimal effect can be given less attention. Some of the most popular model parameters to investigate are demographic parameters by age class, which can identify which life stages are most sensitive to conservation management. Such a sensitivity analysis might reveal that slight changes in adult mortality rates greatly affect population viability, whereas relatively large changes in juvenile recruitment rates have a minimal impact. Crouse et al. (1987) obtained such a result in their classic study on loggerhead turtles (*Caretta caretta* VU) living off the USA's Atlantic coast. At the time, great effort was invested in improving hatching success and ensuring that hatchlings to reach the sea. However, Crouse's study showed that, even if 100% egg and hatchling success was achieved, sea turtles will remain threatened unless adult survival were also improved. Results from this study subsequently played a significant role in initiating global efforts to reduce sea turtle bycatch during fisheries operations (see e.g. Fennessy and Isaksen, 2007; Ayinla et al., 2011).

9.3 Challenges to PVA Implementation

9.3.1 Lack of adequate data

Population biologists often require several years of survey data to distinguish long-term population trends from "model noise"—short-term population fluctuations caused by weather and other unpredictable events (Figure 9.6). For that reason, general guidelines suggest that at a minimum, six (Morris and Doak, 2002) to 10 (McCarthy et al., 2003) years' worth of population data are required before a PVA is attempted.

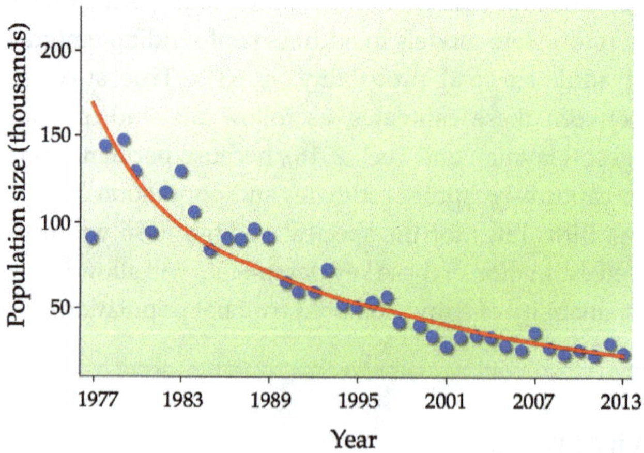

Figure 9.6 It often takes several years of data to distinguish long-term population trends from the "noise" caused by short-term fluctuations. In this example, it appears as if Kenya's topi (*Damaliscus lunatus jimela*, VU) population size is relatively stable, and sometimes even increasing, between 1977 and 1989. However, the 82% decline is unmistakable when long-term trends are considered.

In recent years, considerable effort has been invested in collating, summarising, and making available demographic datasets. One example is the Demographic Species Knowledge Index (Conde et al., 2019) meant to summarise demographic data obtained from ex situ conservation facilities (Section 11.5). Nevertheless, most African species continue to lack multi-year datasets, while many threatened species lack reliable survey data altogether. Because the enormous task of filling these data gaps is impractical, there is a need to be strategic as to which populations to consider for PVA purposes. For example, it does not make sense to conduct a PVA on each species in a threatened ecosystem when a few carefully selected indicator species will suffice to monitor ecosystem health (McGeoch et al., 2002). Other priorities for PVA efforts include (1) species harvested by humans, (2) species most sensitive to ecosystem changes, (3) species with the greatest uncertainty regarding viability, and (4) species that are the focus of current management efforts (Wilson et al. 2015).

Population biologists often require several years of survey data to distinguish long-term population trends from short-term population fluctuations.

But even in the absence of reliable and complete datasets, PVAs can still be useful. For example, sensitivity analysis can inform future data collection efforts, particularly to fill gaps that lead to high levels of uncertainty, or to verify data accuracy for particularly sensitive parameters.

9.3.2 Data reliability

While strategically filling data gaps should be a priority, it should not come at the expense of data quality and reliability. Many—perhaps most—population monitoring programmes are poorly designed (Buckland and Johnston, 2017), leading to biased data, poor survey precision, and misleading results. Poorly designed surveys not only waste valuable time and resources, but the erroneous results also seriously hamper conservation efforts.

To overcome these shortcomings, there are five criteria that a well-designed monitoring programme should satisfy (Buckland and Johnston, 2017). First, survey sites should represent the region or species of interest. Second, a sufficiently large number of monitoring sites should be chosen. Third, monitoring programmes should be set up that every target species—whether common or rare—is adequately counted. Fourth, species selected for monitoring should represent the community of interest, rather than charismatic species that are easily detected. Fifth, multiple surveys need to be conducted over time to detect long-term population trends. Given resource constraints, some compromises in survey design may at times be required. It may also be worth considering the use of citizen scientists and new technologies such as camera traps (Section 9.1.4) to improve data collection efficiency and to provide back-up evidence of reported species for follow-up expert review, if needed.

9.3.3 Model reliability

While PVAs can provide reasonably accurate predictions when based on reliable data (Brook et al., 2000; McCarthy et al., 2003), many conservationists continue to be sceptical of PVA results and their ability to predict future population changes over time (Crone et al., 2013). Part of the reason is our inability to accurately account for unanticipated future events, such as unusual weather events or the arrival of a new invasive species. There are also mechanistic challenges to PVA modelling, including their sensitivity to model assumptions and slight changes in model parameters i.e. slight changes in model input generate vastly different results. For this reason, some biologists have started to discourage the use of PVAs in conservation management, especially when faced with inadequate data (Ellner et al., 2002).

While this scepticism is important and model interrogation should always be welcomed (both aspects usually lead to model improvements), PVA will continue to play a crucial role in conservation in the foreseeable future. It is however important for biologists using PVA to be familiar with the challenges associated with model reliability, as well as the assumptions and limitations of each PVA model. It always helps to begin any PVA model with a clear understanding of the ecology of the target population, the threats it faces, and its demographic characteristics, which in turn enables the modellers to better evaluate model results.

9.4 Summary

1. Protecting a threatened species requires a firm grasp of its population biology. Long-term monitoring using biodiversity inventories, population censuses, and demographic studies can reveal temporal changes in population size and distribution and help to distinguish short-term fluctuations from long-term decline.
2. Biologists are increasingly relying on innovative methods to track wildlife populations and demographics. Among the most popular are market surveys, hair snares and faecal sampling, while photos taken by tourists and camera traps have also been used to obtain population-level data.
3. Population viability analysis (PVA) uses demographic, genetic, and environmental data to predict changes in population sizes and extinction risk over time. Sensitivity analysis can be used to guide conservation action by estimating how different management actions will affect a population's extinction probability.
4. Minimum viable population estimates can be used to determine how many individuals are needed to reduce the threat of extinction, while maximum sustainable harvest estimates can be used to set harvest limits on species threatened by overharvesting.
5. Many surveys are poorly designed, leading to biased data, poor survey precision, and misleading results, which hamper our ability to halt biodiversity losses. To overcome these challenges, surveys should be representative, sufficiently large, and conducted repeatedly over time.

9.5 Topics for Discussion

1. Read the manuscript by Pfab and Witkowski, (2000), which is a PVA study that is relatively easy to understand. Can you identify some strengths and weaknesses of this PVA? Which assumptions did this study make? What parameters were used? Are there any other model parameters you think could have been useful?
2. For this exercise, you are going to construct a simple PVA for a threatened frog species on a sheet of paper. This frog formerly occupied an expansive lowland forest, which over time was disturbed and degraded. A recent survey was able to find only ten frogs (five males and five females), all in

one small, isolated forest patch that can accommodate up to 20 frogs. In the spring, males and females form mating pairs; each pair typically produce zero, one, two, three, or four, offspring that survive to breeding age the following year (to create this demographic dataset, flip four coins for each mated pair; the number of heads is the number of offspring). The sex of the offspring is assigned at random (flip a coin for each young animal, with heads for males and tails for females. Individuals not mated because of uneven sex ratios do not breed. After the breeding season, all the adult frogs die. (A) Run five different population simulations for five generations each, and chart population size over time. What percentage of populations would go extinct within the 10 generations? (B) Perform a sensitivity analysis by making the frogs' living conditions more severe. For example, lower the number of frogs found during the survey to six, or impose 50% mortality on offspring every year due to introduced rats. (C) Perform another sensitivity analysis by making the frogs' living conditions more accommodating. For example, examine the impact of supplying extra food to the frogs, which would allow more offspring to be produced each year. Examine the results of all your different models to determine which factor is most important to address to ensure the frog species does not go extinct.

9.6 Suggested Readings

Anderson, S.C., T.A. Branch, A.B. Cooper, et al. 2017. Black-swan events in animal populations. *Proceedings of the National Academy of Sciences* 114: 3252–57. https://doi.org/10.1073/pnas.1611525114 Ignoring extreme weather events may severely underestimate extinction risk.

Buckland, S.T., and A. Johnston. 2017. Monitoring the biodiversity of regions: Key principles and possible pitfalls. *Biological Conservation* 214: 23–34. https://doi.org/10.1016/j.biocon.2017.07.034 Five principles for reliable surveys.

Danielsen, F., N.D. Burgess, P.M. Jensen, et al. 2010. Environmental monitoring: The scale and speed of implementation varies according to the degree of peoples' involvement. *Journal of Applied Ecology* 47: 1166–68. https://doi.org/10.1111/j.1365-2664.2010.01874.x Involving the local community in environmental monitoring increases the speed of conservation actions.

Guschanski, K., L. Vigilant, A. McNeilage, et al. 2009. Counting elusive animals: Comparing field and genetic census of the entire mountain gorilla population of Bwindi Impenetrable National Park, Uganda. *Biological Conservation* 142: 290–300. https://doi.org/10.1016/j.biocon.2008.10.024 Genetic techniques are providing new opportunities for studying populations.

Jewell, A. 2013. Effect of monitoring technique on quality of conservation science. *Conservation Biology* 27: 501–08. https://doi.org/10.1111/cobi.12066 The methods that researchers use to tag and monitor species can affect and sometimes even harm the species being studied.

Mascia, M.B., S. Pailler, M.L. Thieme, et al. 2014. Commonalities and complementarities among approaches to conservation monitoring and evaluation. *Biological Conservation* 169: 258–67.

https://doi.org/10.1016/j.biocon.2013.11.017 Describes different objectives in monitoring, with a goal of developing standard procedures for evaluating projects.

Sebastián-González, E., J.A. Sánchez-Zapata, F. Botella, et al. 2011. Linking cost efficiency evaluation with population viability analysis to prioritize wetland bird conservation actions. *Biological Conservation* 144: 2354–61. http://doi.org/10.1016/j.biocon.2011.06.015 Different management approaches are evaluated for their cost effectiveness on bird populations in Spain.

One of the following two texts:

Bibby, C., M. Jones, and S. Marsden. 1998. *Expedition Field Techniques: Bird Surveys* (London: Royal Geographic Society). http://www.conservationleadershipprogramme.org/media/2014/09/Bird_Surveying_Manual.pdf Methods for conducting biological surveys. Written on birds, but applicable to other taxa.

White, L., and A. Edwards. 2000. *Conservation Research in the African Rain Forests: A Technical Handbook* (New York: WCS). http://apes.eva.mpg.de/eng/pdf/documentation/WhiteEdwards2000 Methods for obtaining data on animals and their environment. Written for forest work, but also applicable in other ecosystems.

Bibliography

Allen, J.A., H. Lang, and J.P. Chapin. 1917. *The American Museum Congo Expedition Collection of Bats* (New York: Order of the Trustees, American Museum of Natural History). http://digitallibrary.amnh.org/handle/2246/1068

Anderson, S.C., T.A. Branch, A.B. Cooper, et al. 2017. Black-swan events in animal populations. *Proceedings of the National Academy of Sciences* 114: 3252–57. https://doi.org/10.1073/pnas.1611525114

Ayinla, O.A., A.B. Williams, D.A. Bolaji, et al. 2011. *Development of turtle excluder device (TED) and its adoption in Nigeria* (Lagos: Nigerian Institute for Oceanography and Marine Research). http://hdl.handle.net/1834/5337

Barthold, J.A., A.J. Loveridge, D.W. Macdonald, et al. 2016. Bayesian estimates of male and female African lion mortality for future use in population management. *Journal of Applied Ecology* 53: 295–304. https://doi.org/10.1111/1365-2664.12594

Bongers, F., L. Poorter, W.D. Hawthorne, et al. 2009. The intermediate disturbance hypothesis applies to tropical forests, but disturbance contributes little to tree diversity. *Ecology Letters* 12: 798–805. https://doi.org/10.1111/j.1461-0248.2009.01329.x

Bouché, P., I. Douglas-Hamilton, G. Wittemyer, et al. 2011. Will elephants soon disappear from West African savannahs? *PLoS ONE* 6: e20619. https://doi.org/10.1371/journal.pone.0020619

Bouley P., M. Poulos, R. Branco, et al. 2018. Post-war recovery of the African lion in response to large-scale ecosystem restoration. *Biological Conservation* 227: 233–42. https://doi.org/10.1016/j.biocon.2018.08.024

Brook B.W., J.J. O'Grady, A.P. Chapman, et al. 2000. Predictive accuracy of population viability analysis in conservation biology. *Nature* 329: 512–19. https://doi.org/10.1038/35006050

Brook, B., M. Burgman, and R. Frankham. 2000. Differences and congruencies between PVA packages: The importance of sex ratio for predictions of extinction risk. *Conservation Ecology* 4: 6.

Brook, B.W., L.W. Traill, and C.J.A. Bradshaw. 2006. Minimum viable population sizes and global extinction risk are unrelated. *Ecology Letters* 9: 375–82. https://doi.org/10.1111/j.1461-0248.2006.00883.x

Buckland, S.T., and A. Johnston. 2017. Monitoring the biodiversity of regions: Key principles and possible pitfalls. *Biological Conservation* 214: 23–34. https://doi.org/10.1016/j.biocon.2017.07.034

Carlsen, F., K. Leus, K. Traylor-Holzer, et al. 2012. *Western chimpanzee population and habitat viability assessment for Sierra Leone: Final report.* IUCN/SSC CBSG—Europe (Copenhagen: CBSG Europe). http://www.cpsg.org/sites/cbsg.org/files/documents/Sierra%20Leone%20Chimpanzee%20PHVA%20Final%20Report.pdf

Caro, T.M., C.R. Young, A.E. Cauldwell, et al. 2009. Animal breeding systems and big game hunting: Models and application. *Biological Conservation* 142: 909–29. https://doi.org/10.1016/j.biocon.2008.12.018

Caughley, G. 1977. *Analysis of Vertebrate Populations* (New York: Wiley).

Conde, D.A., J. Staerk, F. Colchero, et al. 2019. Data gaps and opportunities for comparative and conservation biology. *Proceedings of the National Academy of Sciences* 116: 9658–64. https://doi.org/10.1073/pnas.1816367116

Crawford, R.J.M., L.G. Underhill, J.C. Coetzee, et al. 2008. Influences of the abundance and distribution of prey on African penguins *Spheniscus demersus* off western South Africa. *African Journal of Marine Science* 30: 167–75. https://doi.org/10.2989/AJMS.2008.30.1.17.467

Crone, E.E., M.M. Ellis, W.F. Morris, et al. 2013. Ability of matrix models to explain the past and predict the future of plant populations. *Conservation Biology* 27: 968–78. https://doi.org/10.1111/cobi.12049

Crouse, D.T., L.B. Crowder, and H. Caswell. 1987. A stage-based population model for loggerhead sea turtles and implications for conservation. *Ecology* 68: 1412–23. https://doi.org/10.2307/1939225

Cumming, D.H.M., and G.S. Cumming. 2015. One Health: An ecological and conservation perspective. In: *One Health: The Theory and Practice of Integrated Health Approaches*, ed. by J. Zinsstag, et al. (Wallingford: CAB International).

De Leo, G.A., and F. Micheli. 2015. The good, the bad and the ugly of marine reserves for fishery yields. *Philosophical Transactions of the Royal Society B* 370: 20140276. https://doi.org/10.1098/rstb.2014.0276

Eggert, L.S., R. Buij, M.E. Lee, et al. 2014. Using genetic profiles of African forest elephants to infer population structure, movements, and habitat use in a conservation and development landscape in Gabon. *Conservation Biology* 28: 107–18. https://doi.org/10.1111/cobi.12161

Ellner, S.P., J. Fieberg, D. Ludwig, et al. 2002. Precision of population viability analysis. *Conservation Biology* 16: 258–61. https://doi.org/10.1046/j.1523-1739.2002.00553.x

Fennessy, S.T., and B. Isaksen. 2007. Can bycatch reduction devices be implemented successfully on prawn trawlers in the Western Indian Ocean? *African Journal of Marine Science* 29: 453–63. https://doi.org/10.2989/AJMS.2007.29.3.12.342

Flather, C.H., G.D. Hayward, S.R. Beissinger, et al. 2011. Minimum viable populations: Is there a 'magic number' for conservation practitioners? *Trends in Ecology and Ecolution* 26: 307–16. https://doi.org/10.1016/j.tree.2011.03.001

Formia, A., B.J. Godley, J.F. Dontaine, et al. 2006. Mitochondrial DNA diversity and phylogeography in West and Central African green turtles (*Chelonia mydas*). *Conservation Genetics* 7: 353–69. https://doi.org/10.1007/s10592-005-9047-z

Frankham, R., C.J.A. Bradshaw, and B.W. Brook. 2014. Genetics in conservation management: Revised recommendations for the 50/500 rules, Red List criteria and population viability analyses. *Biological Conservation* 170: 56–63. https://doi.org/10.1016/j.biocon.2013.12.036

Funmilayo, O. 1978. Fruit bats for meat: are too many taken? *Oryx* 14: 377–78. https://doi.org/10.1017/S0030605300016008

Hayman, D.T.S., and A.J. Peel. 2016. Can survival analyses detect hunting pressure in a highly connected species? Lessons from straw-coloured fruit bats. *Biological Conservation* 200: 131–39. https://doi.org/10.1016/j.biocon.2016.06.003

Hayman, D.T.S., R. McCrea, O. Restif, et al. 2012. Demography of straw-colored fruit bats in Ghana. *Journal of Mammalogy* 93: 1393–404. https://doi.org/10.1644/11-MAMM-A-270.1

Hughes, N., N. Rosen, N. Gretsky, et al. 2011. Will the Nigeria-Cameroon chimpanzee go extinct? Models derived from intake rates of ape sanctuaries. In: *Primates of Gashaka*, ed. by V. Sommer and C. Ross (New York: Springer). http://doi.org/10.1007/978-1-4419-7403-7

Ingram, D.J., L. Coad, B. Collen, et al. 2015. Indicators for wild animal offtake: Methods and case study for African mammals and birds. *Ecology and Society* 20: 40. http://doi.org/10.5751/ES-07823-200340

Kamins, A.O., O. Restif, Y. Ntiamoa-Baidu, et al. 2011. Uncovering the fruit bat bushmeat commodity chain and the true extent of fruit bat hunting in Ghana, West Africa. *Biological Conservation* 144: 3000–08. https://doi.org/10.1016/j.biocon.2011.09.003

Kays, R., M.C. Crofoot, W. Jetz, et al. 2015. Terrestrial animal tracking as an eye on life and planet. *Science* 348: aaa2478. http://doi.org/10.1126/science.aaa2478

Kümpel, N.F., E.J. Milner-Gulland, G. Cowlishaw, et al. 2010. Assessing sustainability at multiple scales in a rotational bushmeat hunting system. *Conservation Biology* 24: 861–71. https://doi.org/10.1111/j.1523-1739.2010.01505.x

Lindsey, P., C.J. Tambling, R. Brummer, et al. 2011. Minimum prey and area requirements of the vulnerable cheetah *Acinonyx jubatus*: Implications for reintroduction and management of the species in South Africa. *Oryx* 45: 587–99. https://doi.org/10.1017/S003060531000150X

Lindsey, P., K. Marnewick, H. Davies-Mostert, et al. 2009. *Cheetah (*Acinonyx *jubatus) population habitat viability assessment workshop report* (Johannesburg: IUCN CBSG and EWT). http://www.cbsg.org/sites/cbsg.org/files/documents/South%20African%20Cheetah%20PHVA%202009.pdf

Lindsey, P.A., G.A. Balme, P. Funston, et al. 2013. The trophy hunting of African lions: Scale, current management practices and factors undermining sustainability. *PLoS ONE* 8: e73808. https://doi.org/10.1371/journal.pone.0073808

Marnewick, K., S.M. Ferreira, S. Grange, et al. 2014. Evaluating the status of and African wild dogs *Lycaon pictus* and cheetahs *Acinonyx jubatus* through tourist-based photographic surveys in the Kruger National Park. *PloS ONE* 9: e86265. https://doi.org/10.1371/journal.pone.0086265

Maxwell, S.M., G.A. Breed, B.A. Nickel, et al. 2011. Using satellite tracking to optimize protection of long-lived marine species: Olive ridley sea turtle conservation in Central Africa. *PloS ONE* 6: e19905. https://doi.org/10.1371/journal.pone.0019905

McCarthy, M.A. 2007. *Bayesian Methods for Ecology* (Cambridge: Cambridge University Press). https://doi.org/10.1017/CBO9780511802454

McCarthy, M.A., S.J. Andelman, and H.P. Possingham. 2003. Reliability of relative predictions in population viability analysis. *Conservation Biology* 17: 982–89. https://doi.org/10.1046/j.1523-1739.2003.01570.x

McGeoch, M.A., B.J. van Rensburg, and A. Botes. 2002. The verification and application of bioindicators: A case study of dung beetles in a savanna ecosystem. *Journal of Applied Ecology* 39: 661–72. https://doi.org/10.1046/j.1365-2664.2002.00743.x

Metcalfe, K., P.D. Agamboué, E. Augowet, et al. 2015. Going the extra mile: Ground-based monitoring of olive ridley turtles reveals Gabon hosts the largest rookery in the Atlantic. *Biological Conservation* 190: 14–22. https://doi.org/10.1016/j.biocon.2015.05.008

Milner-Gulland, E.J., and M.J. Rowcliffe. 2007. *Conservation and Sustainable Use: A Handbook of Techniques* (Oxford: Oxford University Press).

Morris, W.F., and D.F. Doak. 2002. *Quantitative Conservation Biology* (Sunderland: Sinauer).

Niamien, M., J. Coffi, B. Kadjo, et al. 2015. Initial data on poaching of *Eidolon helvum* (Kerr, 1792) near-threatened species in Côte D'ivoire, West Africa. *European Journal of Scientific Research* 35: 219–27.

Ogutu, J.O., H.-P. Piepho, M.Y. Said, et al. 2016. Extreme wildlife declines and concurrent increase in livestock numbers in Kenya: What are the causes? *PLoS ONE* 11: e0163249. https://doi.org/10.1371/journal.pone.0163249

Parker, L. 2017. New ocean reserve, largest in Africa, protects whales and turtles. *National Geographic.* http://on.natgeo.com/2samx3a

Peel, A.J., J.L.N. Wood, K.S. Baker, et al. 2017. How does Africa's most hunted bat vary across the continent? Population traits of the straw-coloured fruit bat (*Eidolon helvum*) and its interactions with humans. *Acta Chiropterologica* 19: 77–92. https://doi.org/10.3161/15081109 ACC2017.19.1.006

Péron, G., and R. Altwegg. 2015. Twenty-five years of change in southern African passerine diversity: Nonclimatic factors of change. *Global Change Biology* 21: 3347–55. https://doi.org/10.1111/gcb.12909

Pfab, M.F., and E.T.F. Witkowski. 2000. A simple population viability analysis of the critically endangered *Euphorbia clivicola* R.A. Dyer under four management scenarios. *Biological Conservation* 96: 263–70. http://doi.org/10.1016/S0006-3207(00)00088-4

Pikesley S.K., P.D. Agamboue, J.P. Bayet, et al. 2018. A novel approach to estimate the distribution, density and at-sea risks of a centrally-placed mobile marine vertebrate. *Biological Conservation* 221:246256. https://doi.org/10.1016/j.biocon.2018.03.011

Reed, D.H., J.J. O'Grady, B.W. Brook, et al. 2003. Estimates of minimum viable population sizes for vertebrates and factors influencing those estimates. *Biological Conservation* 113: 23–34. https://doi.org/10.1016/S0006-3207(02)00346-4

Shaffer, M.L. 1981. Minimum population sizes for species conservation. *BioScience* 31: 131–34. https://doi.org/10.2307/1308256

Sherley, R.B., T. Burghardt, P.J. Barham, et al. 2010. Spotting the difference: Towards fully-automated population monitoring of African penguins *Spheniscus demersus*. *Endangered Species Research* 11: 101–11. https://doi.org/10.3354/esr00267

Stalmans M., T.J. Massad, M.J.S. Peel, et al. 2019. War-induced collapse and asymmetric recovery of large-mammal populations in Gorongosa National Park, Mozambique. *PLoS ONE* 14: e0212864. https://doi.org/10.1371/journal.pone.0212864

Steenweg, R., M. Hebblewhite, R. Kays, et al. 2017. Scaling-up camera traps: Monitoring the planet's biodiversity with networks of remote sensors. *Frontiers in Ecology and the Environment* 15: 26–34. https://doi.org/10.1002/fee.1448

Tinley, K.L. 1977. *Framework of the Gorongosa ecosystem*. Ph.D. thesis (Pretoria: University of Pretoria). http://hdl.handle.net/2263/24526

Traill, L.W., B.W. Brook, R.R. Frankham, et al. 2010. Pragmatic population viability targets in a rapidly changing world. *Biological Conservation* 143: 28–34. https://doi.org/10.1016/j.biocon.2009.09.001

Traill, L.W., C.J.A. Bradshaw, and B.W. Brook. 2007. Minimum viable population size: A meta-analysis of 30 years of published estimates. *Biological Conservation* 139: 159–66. https://doi.org/10.1016/j.biocon.2007.06.011

White, L., and A. Edwards. 2000. *Conservation Research in the African Rain Forests: A Technical Handbook* (New York: WCS). http://apes.eva.mpg.de/eng/pdf/documentation/WhiteEdwards2000.pdf

Wilson, H.B., J.R. Rhodes, and H.P. Possingham. 2015. Two additional principles for determining which species to monitor. *Ecology* 96: 3016–22. https://doi.org/10.1890/14-1511.1

Witt, M.J., B. Baert, A.C. Broderick, et al. 2009. Aerial surveying of the world's largest leatherback turtle rookery: A more effective methodology for large-scale monitoring. *Biological Conservation* 142: 1719–27. https://doi.org/10.1016/j.biocon.2009.03.009

Witt, M.J., E.B. Augowet, A.C. Broderick, et al. 2011. Tracking leatherback turtles from the world's largest rookery: Assessing threats across the South Atlantic. *Proceedings of the Royal Society B* 278: 2338–47. https://doi.org/10.1098/rspb.2010.2467

10

Ecosystem Conservation and Management

Rising 500 m above the Sahelian plains of Mali, the sandstone cliffs of the Bandiagara Escarpment are home to the Dogon people, whose unique homes are carved into the cliff's walls. The Escarpment is a World Heritage Site, known for its outstanding cultural and natural value. However, both nature and humans are suffering from environmental degradation due to climate change and unsustainable land use.

Habitat loss (and its associated degradation) is currently the most important threat facing Africa's wildlife (Figure 10.1). When an ecosystem is destroyed or degraded, its ability to sustain wildlife is compromised, and the individuals that depend on that ecosystem for survival either need to adapt or move elsewhere, or they will die. Conversely, preventing ecosystem degradation and destruction is one of the single most important actions we can take to protect biodiversity. In the process, we also improve our own well-being, given that natural ecosystems are our first line of defence against natural disasters, and provide us with food, clean water, and other ecosystem services.

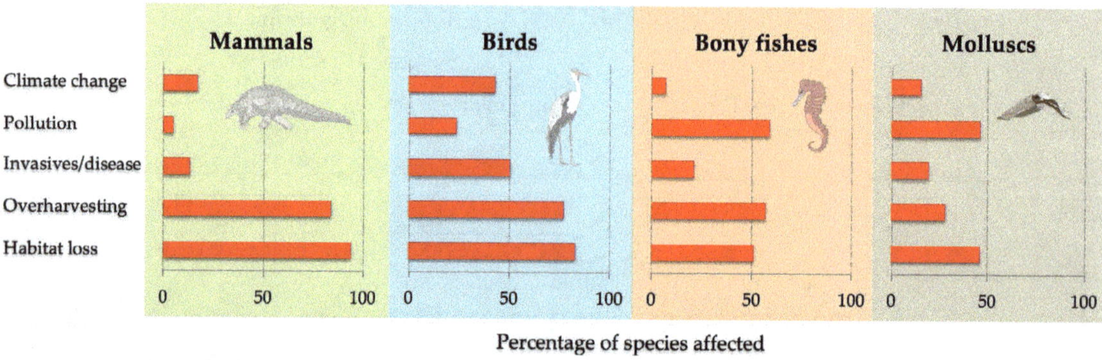

Figure 10.1 Habitat loss and degradation, much of which are driven by agriculture, are the most important threats to Africa's wildlife, followed by overharvesting, invasive species and disease, and pollution. Groups of species often face similar threats: mammals and birds are more likely to be threatened by habitat loss, while fish and molluscs are more likely to be threatened by pollution. Percentages add up to more than 100% because many species face multiple threats. The influence of climate change is under-estimated because its impact on most species still need to be assessed.

Broadly speaking, ecosystem conservation involves three different activities: (1) monitoring ecosystems, (2) maintaining ecosystems, and (3) restoring damaged ecosystems. While many books have been written on each of these three activities, the broad overview this chapter provides will hopefully enable readers to gain a basic understanding of the tools and methods used in ecosystem conservation.

10.1 Ecosystem Monitoring

A complex and adaptive ecosystem in which all the chemical, physical, and biological components, functions, and processes are intact and functioning normally is considered a **healthy ecosystem** (but see Cumming and Cumming (2015), for a discussion on this value-based term). In contrast, disturbing any of an ecosystem's components, functions, and/or processes will, by definition, alter them to some degree (Table 10.1). In many cases, ecosystems that have been exposed to certain forms and levels of disturbances remain healthy because there is redundancy in the roles performed by different ecosystem components (Section 4.2.1). This ability of an ecosystem to withstand certain forms and levels of disturbances is referred to as ecosystem stability. Ecosystem stability could be the result of one or both of two qualities: resistance and resilience. **Resistance** is the ability of an ecosystem to retain the same characteristic communities and natural cycles throughout and after a disturbance event, while **resilience** is the ability of an ecosystem to rapidly recover or adapt after a disturbance event. For example, if the number of native aquatic insect species decline after non-native fishes are introduced to previously fish-free ponds, the pond's ecosystem has low resistance. But if the native insect community recovers rapidly after the non-native fishes were removed, the ecosystem is resilient.

Table 10.1 Three ways how humans have changed the natural world.

Natural function	Changes attributed to human activities
Land surface	As much as half of the world's ice-free land surface has been transformed to cater to people's need for natural resources. Much of these changes are driven by agricultural activities.
Nitrogen cycle	Human activities release massive amounts of nitrogen into natural ecosystems on a daily basis. Much of this occurs through the use of nitrogen fertilisers, burning fossil fuels, and cultivating nitrogen-fixing crops.
Atmospheric carbon cycle	Scientists estimate that humans would have doubled levels of carbon dioxide in the Earth's atmosphere by the middle of this century. This is primarily the result of fossil fuel use and deforestation.
Wildlife populations	Between 1970 and 2014, Sub-Saharan Africa have lost three quarters of its freshwater vertebrates; the rate of these declines shows no sign of reducing.
Pollutants	Pollution from human activities have become so omnipresent that it is hard to escape its impacts. Microplastics have been found in drinking water and the food we eat (Chapter 7).

Sources: MEA, 2005; Kulkarni et al., 2008; http://www.livingplanetindex.org

Many forms of ecosystem disturbances are easy to observe. Consequently, monitoring these visible forms of disturbances—such as the outright destruction of a forest or plastic pollution on a beach—focuses less on detection and more on developing systematic survey protocols (Section 9.1) that can provide information on whether a disturbance is spreading and increasing in intensity, or whether conservation action is successful in containing the threat. However, some disturbances are subtler, unobtrusive, and thus difficult to detect; examples include pesticide drift and agricultural runoff (Section 7.1). Adopting a "wait and see" approach to detecting these invisible forms of disturbances can be particularly damaging, since that approach generally ends at a point where the harm will either be impossible to reverse or will require significantly more resources and time than would have been the case if the problem was addressed earlier. In this way, there are many similarities between monitoring ecosystem health and human health—some ailments are easier to diagnose than others, but we avoid the worst-case scenarios by screening regularly for diseases and treating the threatening ones promptly.

Figure 10.2 Biologists sampling aquatic macroinvertebrates in the Okavango Delta, Botswana, as part of a biomonitoring project of the Freshwater Research Centre.

Perhaps the most popular method conservation biologists use to monitor ecosystem health is known as **biomonitoring**. By monitoring the abundance and/or fitness of sensitive species (Box 10.1), biologists can sometimes detect ecosystem degradation before it becomes apparent to the human eye or escalates to a point where it starts impacting human lives (Bornman and Bouwman, 2012). Monitoring environmental indicators such as macroinvertebrates (Figure 10.2) is particularly popular when examining the ecological condition of aquatic ecosystems; mayflies, caddisflies, and stoneflies—specialists of undisturbed streams—are often replaced by flies and midges in polluted and disturbed environments. Sometimes however, when plants or animals are not easily monitored, certain aspects of those species can still be monitored. One example is monitoring total plant biomass as a proxy for soil nutrients or intensity of herbivory. Another option is to perform a **bioassay**, during which a sensitive organism (typically water fleas or plankton) is released into a potentially contaminated environment to see if death or declining health occurs.

By monitoring the abundance and/or fitness of sensitive species, biologists can detect threats to biodiversity before it becomes apparent to the human eye.

Box 10.1 Using Insects to Monitor Environmental Health

Rosina Kyerematen

Department of Animal Biology and Conservation Science,
University of Ghana,
Legon, Ghana.

✉ *rkyerematen@ug.edu.gh*

Insects are important to nearly every terrestrial food web in the world and serve a multitude of different purposes: some insects are responsible for pollination of plants while others are scavengers that clean up dead plant and animal material. In some cases, our understanding of an insect species' ecological role can make it suitable as an indicator of environmental health. Biomonitoring looks at the presence and abundance of organisms within their natural communities to assess the impact of environmental disturbances; this knowledge can then be used to guide **ecosystem management**. An indicator taxon is one whose impact can be specifically and precisely measured; its abundance serves as a measure of the overall health of an ecosystem. Understanding how the presence and abundance of indicator species, and the relative abundance of tolerant and intolerant species, reflects the relative health of an environment can allow for rapid surveys of impaired ecosystems to assess trends as well as to track changes following remediation and restoration efforts.

Over the past few years, biomonitoring with insects as indicator taxa has become increasingly popular in Ghana. Butterflies are especially popular because they show varying relative sensitivities to environmental change; the abundance of certain butterfly species can for example be used to study the impact of habitat loss, fragmentation, and climate change (Kyerematen et al., 2018). The presence and abundance of butterflies more characteristic of open and disturbed ecosystems (Figure 10.A) can, for example, be used as an indicator of forest degradation.

Aquatic insects, particularly benthic macroinvertebrates, are also useful bioindicators. Freshwater resources, such as lakes and rivers, provide water for drinking and washing to local people, and a home for economically important taxa, such as fish and shellfish. Protecting these water sources is therefore important for safeguarding people's health and livelihoods. The presence, absence, and diversity of certain benthic macroinvertebrates, even at the order level, can provide valuable information about whether a waterbody is being degraded or not (Kyerematen et al., 2014; Nnoli et al., 2019). A recent study showed that dragonfly and damselfly diversities and populations along the coastal Densu River in Ghana vary widely depending on the physical condition of the river and surrounding area (Acquah-Lamptey et al., 2013).

Figure 10.A Because the green-banded swallowtail (*Papilio nireus*) prefers open woodlands, researchers in Ghana are using their abundances in forests as a measure of habitat degradation.

With their high diversity and varying tolerances for ecosystem conditions, insects are extraordinarily suited as ecological indicators in environmental monitoring. Each insect species is also part of a wider biological community with important ecological roles. If lost, not only will an abundance of other life be affected, such a loss may also hint at a looming crisis facing people living in those compromised ecosystems.

At times, conservation biologists may need to measure the physical environment to assess environmental health. This approach is particularly common when tracking pollution, for example by monitoring for changes in **biochemical indicators**. For example, measuring total phosphorus, nitrogen, and dissolved oxygen load in streams and other surface water can help scientists track eutrophication (Section 7.1.1). Measuring these and other biochemical indicators is usually accomplished directly via chemical analysis of environmental samples, such as soil and water. Sometimes however, biochemicals indicators are tracked indirectly via biological samples obtained from plants and animals. Because they bio-accumulate heavy metals and other pollutants, filter feeders such as clams and mussels (e.g. Bodin et al., 2013) are particularly useful in this regard as they can be used to detect very low concentrations of harmful chemicals in the environment.

10.1.1 Monitoring ecosystems with geospatial analysis

A persistent challenge facing biologists who monitor ecosystems—and other aspects of biodiversity—is achieving consistency across space and time. Consider a survey of a sensitive bird community to track ecosystem change; not only will different observers have varying levels of experience, but they will almost certainly see different birds during an early morning census compared to one later in the afternoon due to differences in biology and behaviour between species. These factors introduce error into monitoring data, which in turn can mask the effect a biologist tries to measure (Buckland and Johnston, 2017). Laboratory scientists' control for these **confounding factors** by making multiple measurements under strictly controlled conditions. But for conservation biologists working outside in the wind and rain, repeated observations under similar conditions can be near impossible.

Geospatial analysis offers a variety of tools that allow biologists to overcome some of these traditional field monitoring challenges. These tools use **geographic information systems (GIS)** computer software packages to store, display, and manipulate a wide variety of data representing the natural environment, biodiversity, and human land-use patterns as they relate to one another on Earth's surface. GIS thereby allows biologists to easily visualise and analyse spatial relationships between mapped data, which may include aspects such as vegetation types, climate, soils, topography, geology, water availability, species distributions, existing protected areas, human settlements, and human resource use (Figure 10.3). Understanding such relationships helps conservation biologists to prioritise their actions, for example by identifying areas where data are lacking, where an environmental change requires further investigation, or where gaps in regional protected areas network exist.

Remote sensing is a special branch of geospatial analysis directed at obtaining ecosystem data without making physical contact (i.e. boots on the ground) with the observation site. Before the turn of the 20th century, the most popular form of remote sensing was aerial photography from airplanes. These aerial photographs facilitated geographers' ability to draw maps of landscape features, including human infrastructure and natural vegetation patterns. Remote sensing opportunities greatly expanded from 1960 onward, with the launch of the National Aeronautical Space Administration's (NASA) first **Earth observation satellites**, to take photographs of Earth from space for weather forecasting. Subsequent satellite programmes expanded their scope to also collect additional data of Earth's surface and atmosphere. While much of this data would have been useful to conservation, early satellite data products were very expensive and thus largely out of reach of the larger conservation community. This all changed in 2008 when NASA started distributing their Earth observation products for free to the public, heralding an era in which remote sensing became a standard tool in the conservation field.

> Remote sensing offers a variety of tools that allow biologists to monitor biodiversity beyond the abilities of traditional field monitoring techniques.

Today, hundreds of Earth observation satellites circle the planet, offering near real-time access to unbiased and consistent environmental datasets of nearly all terrestrial surfaces, oceanic surfaces and floor depths, and the atmosphere, all from the comfort of a computer connected to the internet (Wilson et al., 2013). Scientists use these products in ecosystem monitoring efforts, including monitoring water quality (Dube et al. 2015), forest loss (Laporte et al.,

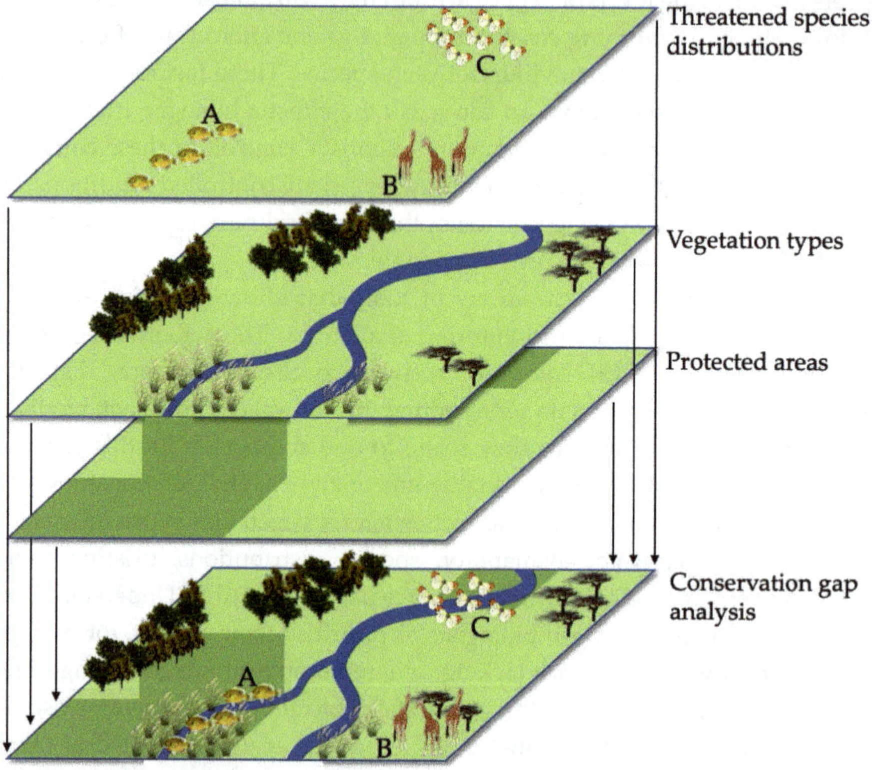

Figure 10.3 Distribution maps for three threatened species are overlaid onto maps of protected areas and vegetation types to identify potential conservation gaps (discussed in Chapter 13). This GIS analysis shows that Species A is well protected, Species B is protected to some extent, and Species C is not protected at all. Species C would thus be considered a high conservation priority.

2007), coral reef health (McClanahan et al., 2011), desertification (Symeonakis et al., 2004), and fire regimes (Archbald et al., 2010). Linking the information obtained by Earth observation satellites to biological information collected on the ground has proved invaluable in monitoring species' threat statuses (Di Marco et al., 2014), **ecosystem connectivity** (Wegmann et al., 2014), and habitat suitability (Torres et al., 2010), as well as understanding how biodiversity responds to environmental changes (Box 10.2).

> Conservation biologists are often faced with the shifting baseline syndrome, where the reference points they use to measure their progress may be vastly different from earlier states.

The popularity and utility of these products have preceded and facilitated the expansion of other remote sensing applications in ecosystem monitoring. Among the most popular are radar products (Figure 10.4), which have become the standard method for obtaining elevation and other terrain data (NASA, 2009, 2013), as well as estimates of carbon stocks (Carreiras et al., 2012). Advances have also been made in using hyper-spectral imagery to monitor soil properties (Mashimbye et al., 2012) and even individual trees (Naidoo et al., 2012). LiDAR has enabled biologists to

Box 10.2 Remote Sensing and Spatial Analysis for African Conservation

Barend F. N. Erasmus

Global Change Institute (GCI), University of the Witwatersrand, Johannesburg, South Africa.

✉ *Barend.Erasmus@wits.ac.za*

Remote sensing is the art and science of observing objects or landscapes from a distance, without being in direct contact with the environment. Although you can think of wildlife photography as a type of remote sensing, the term usually refers to aerial photography (Figure 10.B), or images taken via satellite. For both cases, there is a trade-off between the area covered by each photo (the footprint), how much digital storage space is available, and how often a satellite takes a picture of the same area. For satellites that take pictures of the earth systematically, along a pre-defined path, cloud cover determines how often you can get a usable image. Recent improvements in technology, now allow for the deployment of constellations of satellites that have a collective point-and-track capability to observe an area almost continuosly.

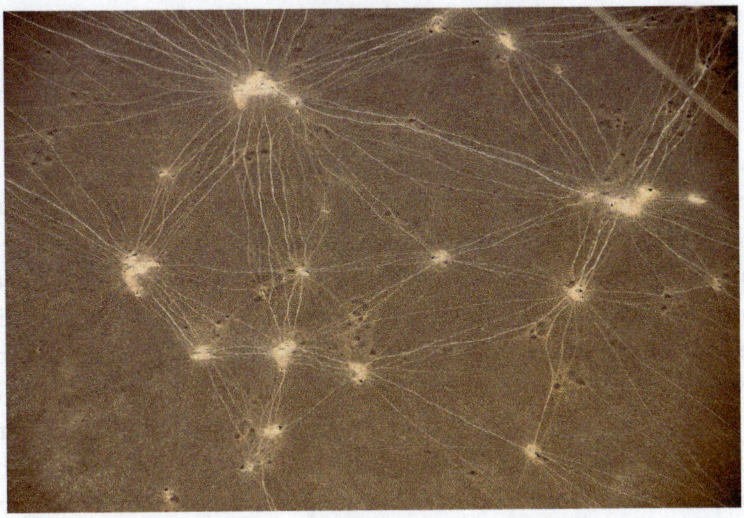

Figure 10.B Aerial photograph of Kaa pan in the southwestern Kalahari region of Botswana. Gemsbok (*Oryx gazella*, LC), red hartebeest (*Alcelaphus buselaphus caama*, LC), and eland (*Tragelaphus oryx*, LC) excavate holes for lekking (eating soil with high salt content), and the footpaths between the different lekking sites clearly show preferences for certain sites. In the same way, on a much broader scales, ungulates move across landscapes to access other resources, such as water and grass, whilst avoiding human hunters and predators.

Our eyes are sensitive to the colours red, green, and blue, together called the visible part of the electromagnetic spectrum. This is actually a very small part of the entire spectrum, and scientists have found, for example, that vegetation seen as uniformly green shows a lot of variation in the infrared part of the spectrum. For this reason, many satellites carry cameras that can "see" infrared light, and by proxy, measure vegetation health, biomass, and sometimes even structure. This capability, together with frequent revisit rates, allows for a unique view of how African landscapes change, whether through habitat loss, seasonal changes, or drought. Analyses of 13 years of remotely sensed data show that the most arid parts of southwest Botswana now experience typical summer vegetation conditions later in the year (Dubovyk et al., 2015), so herbivores must cope with a much longer dry season now than they experienced in 2000.

African landscapes are always changing, and sometimes in unpredictable ways—localised thunderstorms at the beginning of the rainy season can rapidly change a dry dustbowl landscape into green grazing. These "wet footprints" can cover areas as small as 1 km × 3 km; in contrast, a large frontal weather system can cover dozens or even hundreds of kilometres. An ungulate looking for green grazing not too far from drinking water, while trying to avoid predators and hunters, needs the ability to detect such green patches, and the strength and knowledge to move there. Obtaining this knowledge from an ungulate's perspective of the landscape is no small task. Hopcraft et al. (2014) show how common wildebeest and plains zebra in the Serengeti have different migration strategies: wildebeest move to green grass as quickly as they can, with little effort to avoid predators, whereas zebra gauge predation risk and forage quality concurrent to their trek.

Our ability to understand ungulate movements and other ecosystem patterns has been greatly enhanced over the last few years, as animal-tracking technology (where GPS positions are logged and stored using radio-frequency tracking, mobile phone networks, satellite systems, or any combination) and the resulting analyses became more sophisticated. It is now possible to distinguish between locations where animals often spend a little time (for example, a preferred shady tree for resting during the heat of the day), or the same location where they infrequently spend a lot of time (for example, once during an oestrus cycle, a lactating lioness will spend a lot of time at her den, with cubs). It is also possible to "see" when such an animal changes "mode" of movement. For example, researchers have found that springbok (*Antidorcas marsupialis*, LC) rams around the Etosha pan in Namibia show sedentary behaviour (small movements around a specific area) when grazing is good, which transitions to searching behaviour during dry seasons (long, relatively fast movements in a straight line) as they move to areas that had water or grass during previous drought periods (Lyons et al., 2013).

If we combine this animal tracking capability with regular remotely sensed images of vegetation quality, then we can start to answer questions about why certain animals move to certain areas. It also highlights the fact that it is very seldom good enough to put a fence around an area and call it preserved. Due to the changing nature of Africa's savannahs, animals need to be able to move to areas with water or forage, often outside reserves, when they become available. In the face of a changing climate and changing rainfall patterns, this ability to move long distance to reach vital resources remains one of the best adaptation responses that African ungulates may have to cope with climate change. However, fences, roads, and farmland may block these migrations across the landscape, putting those populations at risk of extinction (Section 5.1.1).

African conservation areas need to make provision for these animal movements, or risk conservation areas without sustainable animal populations. This presents a problem—how do we investigate options for large animals to move across a transformed rural landscape and minimise human-wildlife conflict while, on the other hand, still providing access to green grass or drinking water at a specific protected area? Both resources change in location and time of year, and only regular, detailed remote sensing of vegetation, combined with detailed animal movement studies, will provide the necessary picture in time and space.

map three-dimensional vegetation, which can be used to explain animal movements (Loarie et al., 2013; Davies et al., 2016) and measure carbon stocks and forest loss (Burton et al., 2017).

Despite the opportunities presented by remote sensing, it is critical to remember that it is not a substitute for traditional field monitoring methods. Most importantly, remote sensing applications cannot be considered reliable without verification using field data (see Burton et al., 2017). Most remote sensing products are also relatively new, which does not allow for enough opportunities to compare across time. In the absence of historical remotely sensed data, geospatial analysts usually choose the best **reference site** currently available; this may expose those analysts to **shifting baseline syndrome**, because the chosen reference site may be vastly different from earlier states the scientists are actually interested in studying (Bunce et al., 2008; Papworth et al., 2009). Remote sensing is, therefore, not a cure-all for ecosystem monitoring challenges; it is simply a powerful tool to supplement traditional field-based monitoring.

10.2 Maintaining Complex and Adaptive Ecosystems

Even when monitoring data show that an ecosystem is healthy, management is often required to maintain those desired conditions. That is because very few ecosystems are completely free of human influences. For example, rivers and streams carry

Figure 10.4 A radar composite of equatorial Africa obtained in 1996 by Japan's Earth Resources Satellite. The area shown covers about 7.4 million km^2. Due to the filters applied to the image, yellow represents flooded forests, palm plantations, and urban areas; green represents forest, and black represents surface water. Savannahs may be black, blue, purple, or green, depending on the ecoregion type. Displays such as these allow researchers to map ecosystems, and ecosystem loss at a much larger scale than if only field observations were used. Image courtesy of NASA.

pollutants far beyond the point of contamination (Section 7.1) and roads acting as firebreaks suppress natural fire regimes. Today, even the most isolated patches of habitats may not be completely protected from the influences of global processes such as climate change. To maintain complex and adaptive ecosystems, conservation biology is guided by four complementary management principles: (1) maintain ecosystem processes, (2) minimise external threats, (3) be adaptive, and (4) be minimally intrusive.

10.2.1 Maintaining critical ecosystem processes

Ecologists generally divide **ecosystem processes** into four disparate yet interdependent categories: water cycling, nutrient cycling (which include the carbon and nitrogen cycle), energy flow, and community dynamics. The linkages between these processes create feedback loops, where changes in one factor may be amplified elsewhere. Maintaining ecosystem processes is thus very important because small, seemingly small, changes can have major impacts on biological communities.

The water cycle

The water cycle refers to the distribution of water through an ecosystem, and includes the absorption and distribution of water vapour, rainwater, and surface water in lakes, rivers, and oceans. Since much of the water cycle happens out of sight and is generally associated with large-scale phenomena, such as weather patterns and anthropogenic climate change, land managers sometimes fail to recognise how local factors influence the water cycle. This is a grave mistake; many deadly ecological disasters (e.g. desertification, flooding, and landslides) can be attributed to disturbances to the water cycle at the local scale.

Outside of ensuring sustainable use of water resources, maintaining vegetation cover arguably plays the most important role in preserving the water cycle at local scales. Plants and their roots enable soil to store and release water, and make these water reserves available for soil organisms, which in turn aid in decomposition of dead plants and animals (Section 4.2.2). In contrast, a loss of vegetation cover increases surface runoff, which leads to deteriorating soil conditions through nutrient **leaching** and erosion of fertile topsoil. An increasing number of studies have also shown how forest loss can change a region's climate by reducing rainfall which in turn exacerbates drought conditions (Lawrence and Vandecar, 2015). For example, forest clearing for agriculture has reduced rainfall by 50% over much of West Africa (Garcia-Carreras and Parker, 2011). Many forest restoration programmes thus focus on reversing these losses.

Complex and adaptive ecosystems provide more opportunities for people to benefit from ecosystem services than uniform plantations with single species

When restoring degraded forests and other ecosystems to repair the water cycle and other ecosystem services, it is important to remember that complex ecosystems with locally-adapted plants are generally the most effective in maintaining the water cycle and other ecosystem services (Burton et al., 2017). There have been cases across Africa where well-intended restoration efforts used fast-growing timber species such as gum (*Eucalyptus* spp.) and pine (*Pinus* spp.). While these single-crop plantations may superficially resemble a forest in structure and may even provide some of the same ecosystem services as native plants, some of these fast-growing exotic plants also bring significant environmental harm and negative externalities passed onto local people (van Wilgen and Richardson, 2014). Of particular concern is their role in disrupting local water cycles (Section 7.4.2), ironically the very aspect these forest restoration efforts aim to rehabilitate. The choice of species used for restoration should this be carefully considered to avoid unintended consequences later on.

The nutrient cycle

The nutrient cycle involves the cycling of essential nutrients such as carbon, nitrogen, sulphur, and phosphorus through the ecosystem. Like the water cycle, natural vegetation cover plays an important role in maintaining the nutrient cycle. That is because plant roots slow water runoff which, in turn, help soil to retain nutrients dissolved in water. Plants also form a major component of above-ground and below-ground biomass. When dead plant biomass is decomposed along with animal waste products, nutrients previously absorbed through plant roots are released back into the soil and water, where they can once again be absorbed by living plants and other consumers.

Unfortunately, vegetation cover, decomposition, and fire dynamics (discussed below) alone cannot ensure a healthy nutrient cycle. Much of Africa is nutrient impoverished because soil nutrients are lost quicker than they are replaced. One of the main causes is unsustainable agricultural practices (Sanchez, 2010), such as farming on sandy soils and in tropical forests. These areas are nutrient-poor, so crop yields are typically low. Because these areas are prone to leaching, a large proportion of synthetic fertilisers added to supplement impoverished soils leaches into groundwater or washes into nearby streams and lakes, threatening water supplies by causing harmful algae blooms and eutrophication (Section 7.1.1). To compensate, the failing farmers may resort to even more unsustainable land conversions (Wallenfang et al., 2015). Careful management of the nutrient cycle is thus critical for both biodiversity conservation and socio-economic well-being, particularly given its importance to food security (Drechsel et al., 2001). To achieve this, there is an urgent need to adopt more sustainable land management practices (Chapter 14).

Ecosystem processes are linked into multiple feedback loops, so changes in one factor are amplified elsewhere.

The energy cycle

Energy flow—a crucial component of ecosystem productivity (Section 4.2.2)—refers to the capture and storage of solar energy by primary producers (photosynthetic plants, algae, and some bacteria), and the distribution of that energy to consumers, detritivores, and decomposers. Although solar energy can appear as an unlimited resource in many ecosystems, the energy available to consumers (i.e. herbivores and carnivores) is limited because only about 10% of the energy obtained at one trophic level is passed on to the next (Figure 10.5). Being at the top of the food chain, apex predators are in a particularly vulnerable position because seemingly small disruptions at lower trophic levels will have a cumulative impact on the energy available to them. Such disruptions may include reduced prey populations (e.g. overharvesting of herbivores, Section 7.2) or foraging disruptions (e.g. a predator needing to walk further to find prey). Research from Southern Africa's Kalahari Desert has showed that such disruptions, which are amplified by predators' high-energy lifestyles (it takes a lot of energy to bring down a large ungulate!), may put apex predators such as cheetahs on a downward spiral of energy deficits (Scantlebury et al., 2014). While such impacts may not always lead to direct mortality, these insidious, subtle, and easily-overlooked sublethal impacts compromise individuals' ability to reproduce, with extinction being the end result. To avoid such a scenario, maintaining energy flow generally involves maintaining complex, species-rich ecosystems so that consumers have ample opportunities to fulfil their energy needs for finding prey, growth, reproduction, and other activities.

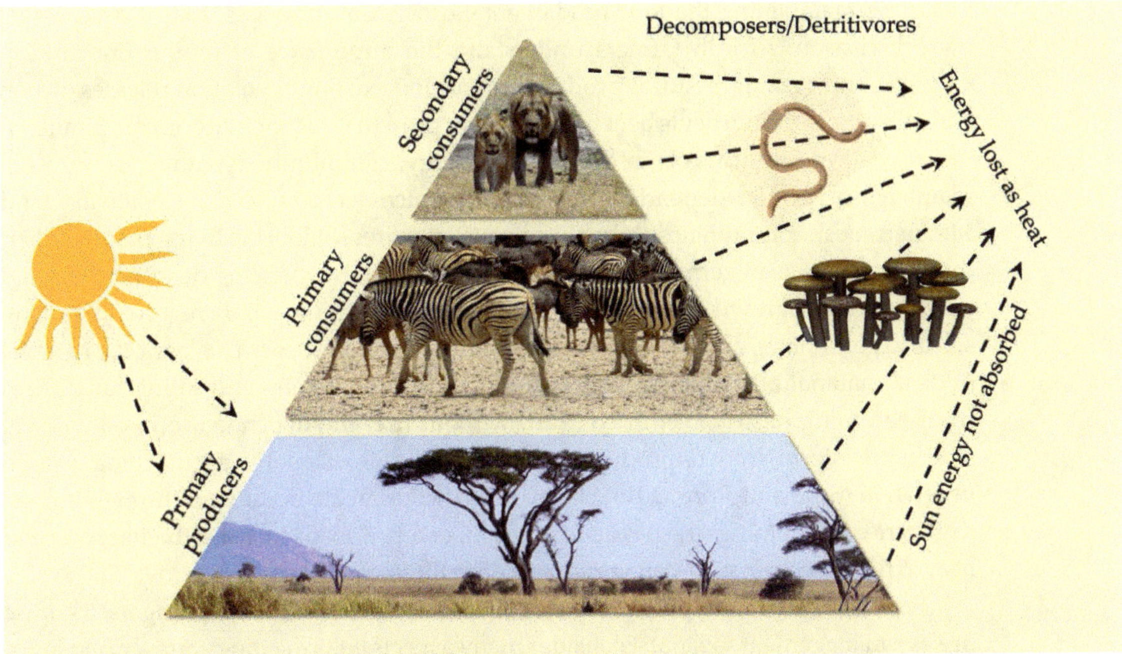

Figure 10.5 A food pyramid of a model savannah ecosystem, showing the various trophic levels and energy pathways. About 90% of energy is lost at each trophic level through respiration and animal waste excretion.

Community dynamics

In ecosystem conservation, maintaining viable populations of different interacting species is as important as maintaining important ecosystem processes, such as ecosystem productivity and ecological succession. This focus often falls on maintaining populations that form part of important mutualistic relationships such as pollination and seed dispersal (Section 4.2.5), predator-prey interactions, and even healthy levels of competitive and parasitic interactions (which allow more species to persist). Of interest is the preservation of keystone species and ecosystem engineers, which has an outsized effect on community dynamics (Section 4.2.1). As illustrated in this, and other, chapters, disrupting community dynamics through pollution, overharvesting, or any other threat facing biodiversity (Chapter 5–7), generally leads to impoverished natural communities. Impoverished communities may in turn provide opportunities for invasive species to colonise an area, further perpetuating biodiversity losses. In Chapter 11, we discuss further how populations and species can be maintained.

Fire Dynamics

Although fire is generally not considered one of the four fundamental ecosystem processes, it plays such an important role in African biodiversity management, including maintaining the four fundamental ecosystem processes, that it deserves its own discussion. African farmers understand the importance of setting fire to keep cropland and grazing pastures productive; burning existing vegetation releases carbon and other essential nutrients beneficial for plant growth into the environment. Similarly, fire also plays a critical role in the flow of energy, community dynamics, and overall maintenance of **fire-dependent ecosystems,** such as grasslands, savannahs, and Mediterranean communities. Suitably low intensity fires seldom kill living plants; rather, they encourage seed germination and seedling growth by reducing dead material that may crowd new growth, by exposing bare mineral soil (the substrate required for many seeds to germinate), and by releasing vital nutrients into the soil. This periodic removal of dead material also prevents fuel load accumulation, thereby preventing future fires from becoming destructive. In contrast, without fire, fire-dependent ecosystems will slowly transform into unproductive scrublands suffocated by encroaching woody vegetation (Smit and Prins, 2015). Then, when wildfires do occur (e.g. through human negligence or lightning) the resultant accumulated fuel loads increase the intensity and heat of fires, creating very dangerous and difficult to control scenarios.

Obviously, given the potentially destructive force of fire, land managers who use fire as a management tool must consider many aspects before setting a **prescribed burn**, also known as a controlled burn. Foremost, to prevent a fire from becoming destructive to natural communities and nearby human developments, burning must be done in a well-planned manner with careful consideration given to the area's ecology, weather forecasts, and fire-readiness of the site (Goldammer and de Ronde, 2004; Kelly and Brotons, 2017). It is also recommended that prior to burning (or any other conspicuous management operation for that matter), land managers develop a public outreach plan to explain to local people the importance of fire in ecosystems management, and the steps taken to keep them and their properties safe. To further improve community relations and education, South Africa's Working on Fire programme (Figure 10.6) provides scholarships, fire training, and employment opportunities to local youths.

Fire **management plans** that match natural fire regimes produce the best results for effective **ecosystem management**. Land managers accomplish this by ensuring that their burn plans mimic the local area's natural fire season, fire frequency, and flame intensity, while also accounting for management goals and local ecological factors such as rainfall and geology (see e.g. van Wilgen et al., 2010, 2014). The size of each burn area must also be considered. Best practices suggest not burning the entirety of a community at a time; rather, burning only portions of an area allows for more habitat heterogeneity, provides opportunities for non-burrowing animals to take refuge in unburned areas, and maximises ecosystem diversity. Bringing all of these aspects together, scientists working in Tanzania's Ngorongoro Conservation Area determined that the area would respond best if land managers burn up to 20% of their grasslands annually or biannually (Estes et al., 2006). Similarly, field **experiments** in certain South African grasslands have found that plant diversity is highest when burns occur every second year, in winter or autumn (Uys et al., 2004). Other ecosystems, such as the Cape Floristic Region's fynbos, may need to burn only once every decade (Kraaij et al.,

Figure 10.6 A fire crew from South Africa's Working on Fire programme keeps a close eye on a controlled fire set to keeps the native savannah ecosystem healthy.

2013). However, because of the high density of houses in some fynbos ecosystems, the periodic fires needed for locally-adapted vegetation to persist are often extinguished because of the threat to human settlement (van Wilgen et al., 2012).

While fire plays an important role in many African landscapes, it is important to note that overly frequent fires can be a threat even to fire-dependent communities. For example, habitat degradation resulting from too many fires in quick succession can leave a natural community vulnerable to invasions by harmful species (Masocha et al., 2011). Overly frequent fires can also prevent seedling recruitment by directly killing vulnerable young plants, and by depleting the seed bank because seedlings do not have sufficient time to mature and set seed.

Fire-sensitive ecosystems (e.g. tropical forests, high mountains, and peat bogs) must also be managed carefully to avoid fire disturbance, which can lead to habitat loss and edge effects (Chapter 5). One way to accomplish this is to educate farmers living adjacent to fire-sensitive ecosystems on how to safely manage their land with fire. Conservationists also need to be considerate when managing fire-dependent ecosystems adjacent to fire-sensitive ecosystems, as is the case with the unique patches of fire-dependent savannahs—remnants from the last Ice Age 15,000 years ago—that are surrounded by forest within Gabon's Lobé National Park (Jeffery et al., 2014). Careful fire management, led by good science, is bound to become increasingly important in the future, given that wildfires are expected to become more frequent and more intense under climate change (Pricope and Binford, 2012).

10.2.2 Minimising external threats

Human activity cannot and does not need to be eliminated from nature; in fact, the structure and diversity of many of today's natural landscapes—and to which today's wildlife are adapted to—are in part the result of past human activities (e.g. Garcin et al., 2018). Today, there are over 7 billion people on Earth, so our impacts are more pervasive than for the majority of history. There is, thus, an urgent need to utilise natural resources in such a way that future generations will also benefit from the ecosystem services that previous generations have left us. This requires a concerted effort from every sector in human society to minimise those threats we impose on the ecosystems around us. This includes preventing pollution, large-scale human disturbances, overharvesting, and habitat destruction (Chapter 5–7).

Major strides have been made in recent years towards achieving these goals. Governments are updating laws to safeguard the environment, industries are refining recycling and waste disposal methods, new techniques are being developed to remove pollutants from the environment, and individual citizens are becoming more aware of their individually small but collectively significant impacts on the environment. We should be proud of the progress being made and continue to strive for improvements. But one external threat that requires greater attention and understanding is invasive species.

Controlling invasive species

Invasive species degrade and destroy natural ecosystems by outcompeting native species, disturbing ecosystem processes, and altering the physical environment (Section 7.4). Limiting these harmful impacts can be particularly challenging since exotic species that establish themselves in a new area can build up such large numbers, become so widely dispersed, and be so thoroughly integrated into ecosystems (i.e. **naturalised**) that eradicating them entirely would be extraordinarily difficult and expensive, or as in the case of tickberry (*Lantana camara*) perhaps even impossible (Bhagwat et al., 2012). This is not only a problem facing conservation biology, but also agriculture, where invasive species often spread from one farm to another, forestry, where invasive species are spread between saw mills and along logging routes, and fisheries, where native resources are outcompeted, sometimes up-ending an entire local industry. The impact of invasive species on farming communities is particularly severe—they lose tens of billions of dollars each year while trying to combat deteriorating grazing lands, reduced crop yields, and escalating pest control expenses. One study from South Africa calculated that invasive plants result in financial losses of US $646 million each year—this figure would have been US $5 billion if invasive species control measures already implemented were absent (de Lange and van Wilgen, 2010). Consequently, a range of stakeholders have invested considerable resources in combatting invasive species.

Because invasive species are often very hard to eradicate once established (Figure 10.7), the foremost step in avoiding invasive species' harmful impacts is to avoid opportunities for new invasions (Section 7.4.1). This requires raising awareness across all levels of society about the dangers posed by invasive species, both to the natural world and to agricultural and natural resources systems. There is also a need for citizens, scientists, and industry to monitor for potential and known invasive species, and promptly implement intensive control efforts to stop establishment and spread. The Global Register of Introduced and Invasive Species (http://www.griis.org) is a free, online searchable source to facilitate these tasks, by providing information about the impact and control of invasive species. Governments can also partake in efforts to control invasive species. While most African countries screen agricultural imports for pests, countries, such as Australia and New Zealand, take this task particularly seriously, with trained officials screening each visitor (and returning residents) and package for hitchhiking species before they cross those countries' borders. Lastly, it would require increased dialogue between conservation biologists and land managers to make a careful and thorough assessment prior to the deliberate introduction of a new species, even if thought of as beneficial.

> The most important step in preventing biological invasions is to prevent the initial establishment of problem species. This requires educating people about the dangers posed by invasive species.

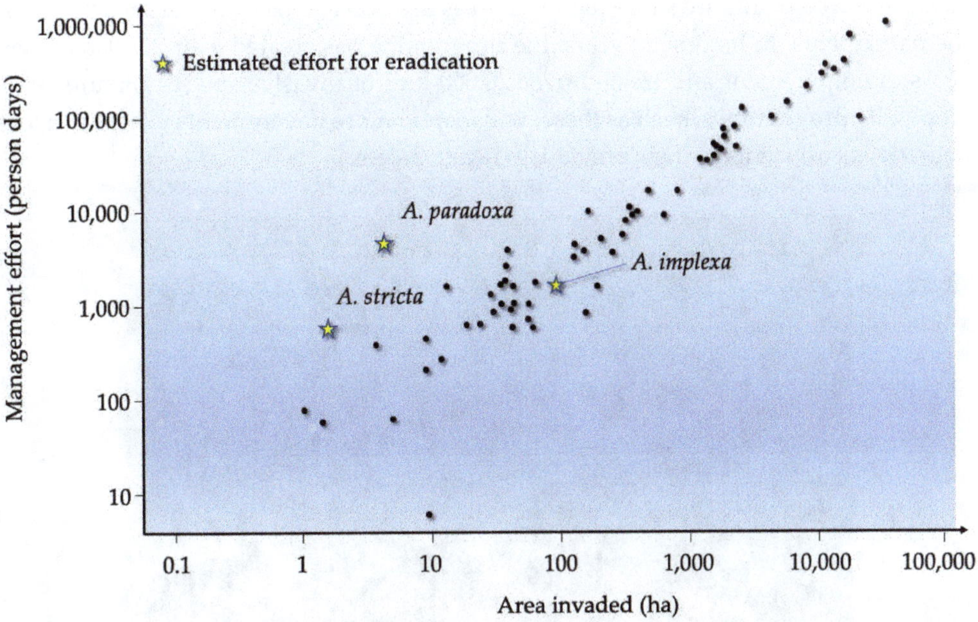

Figure 10.7 Data on the control of invasive species in South Africa have shown that the larger the infestation (a function of time passed since establishment), the more resources are required for eradication. For that reason, it is critical to avoid establishment of invasive species in the first place, and to respond promptly once new invasions have been discovered. Also shown is the effort required to eradicate three species of Australian wattle (*Acacia* spp.), based on extent of invasion.

Despite best practices, not all invasions can be prevented, and for those that do occur, an early detection and rapid response strategy offers the best chance to limit harm. This usually involves raising awareness of potential invasive species to ensure biologists and other stakeholders will recognise a new invasion, efforts to screen for such species on a regular basis, and implementing direct attack approaches, such as using herbicides, pesticides, or mechanical control once detected. While addressing a new invasion as soon as possible, it is also important to consider and contain the risks each direct attack approach carries. For example, herbicides and pesticides carry a risk of killing non-target native species via pesticide drift (Section 7.1), while mechanical control may cause disturbances such as trampling, undue soil disturbance, and even pollution.

Controlling invasive species that have become established will require substantially more resources and manpower to combat than those detected early on. Even so, it is still worth initiating control measures as early as possible since harm and resource needs will only escalate over time. To overcome these impediments to invasive species control, the South African government established an exemplary model, the Working for Water programme, in 1995. Working for Water has three goals—poverty relief, water conservation, and invasive species control—which it accomplishes by combining invasive species control with job creation and social upliftment (van Wilgen and Wannenburgh, 2016). Specifically, the programme hires and trains unemployed people to eradicate water-thirsty invasive shrubs and trees across South Africa; some of the removed plants are subsequently sold as firewood at local markets at a profit for the participants. In its first 20 years, the programme has created over 227,000 person years of employment and treated over 28,000 km^2 of invasive species (Figure 10.8). Hopefully programmes, such as these, will inspire more governments to act to restore degraded ecosystems to their previously healthy state.

Figure 10.8 Members of South Africa's Working for Water programme mechanically removing invasive Australian wattles (*Acacia* spp.). To make sure the wattles don't grow again, the stumps are also treated with a herbicide.

Another method to manage established pests is biological control, also called biocontrol. Biocontrol typically relies on one or more natural enemies from an invasive species' original range to control the pest in its introduced range (Section 4.2.7). One of the main benefits of biocontrol is that it ensures cost-effective, long-term, area-wide control of an invasive species, beyond the capabilities of chemical pesticides and mechanical control. Biocontrol also allows for opportunities to control invasive species that are hard to manage with chemical pesticides and mechanical control (at least without significant additional harm to the environment), such as submerged aquatic weeds (Coetzee et al., 2011). Third, biocontrol agents are highly host-specific, thereby eliminating the impact that chemical pesticides and mechanical control have on non-target organisms. Lastly, an effective biocontrol agent ideally eliminates the need for chemical pesticides and mechanical control, thereby reducing threats such as pesticide pollution (Section 7.1) and ecosystem degradation (Section 5.1).

Biocontrol does have some drawbacks. Primary among them is the significant upfront investment required, as candidate species first need to be found, and then extensively tested for host specificity and potential interactions with native wildlife before being released. Biocontrol also requires careful monitoring after release to determine effectiveness as well as to carefully check for impacts on non-target native species. This monitoring needs to be conducted over the long term, because biocontrol agents typically require several years before they establish self-sufficient colonies in the wild and might only then show signs of unintended impacts. Because alternative methods for controlling invasive species can also kill biocontrol agents (causing conflicting results and wasted resources), additional coordination is required before applying biocontrol and alternative pest management strategies simultaneously in the same area. Lastly, there is no guarantee that a biocontrol agent will be effective. For example, the tickberry continues to thrive despite the release of over 40 biocontrol agents (Zalucki et al., 2007). But when successful, the long-term savings from these upfront investments are generally well worth it. One study in Benin found that biocontrol of water hyacinth required a US $2 million upfront investment, but the resultant water quality improvements increased local incomes by US $84 million per year (de Groote et al., 2003). Another study from South Africa estimated a net gain of 50–3,500 times the investment, depending on the specific biocontrol agent used (de Lange and van Wilgen, 2010).

Several very successful biological control programmes have been implemented in Africa over the past century. Most famous is the rescue of the cassava crop (see Box 4.3). Another successful biocontrol programme, implemented across much of the continent, has reduced Kariba weed (*Salvinia molesta*) by over 95% within just a few years (e.g. Mbati and Neuenschwander, 2005; Diop and Hill, 2009; Martin et al, 2018). South Africa has been particularly active in the research and introduction of biocontrol agents. From 1913, when South Africa started controlling invasive cacti with hemipterans, to 2017, a total of 93 biocontrol agents have been released for the control of 59 invasive species (Zachariades et al., 2017).

While the most popular biocontrol agents generally involve insects, disease-causing pathogens can also be used for biocontrol. Feline panleukopenia virus (also known as feline distemper) was highly effective in managing a feral cat population that caused the extirpation of seabirds on Sub-Antarctic Marion Island; some birds are now even returning as breeders (Bester et al., 2002). In an effort to reduce the use of chemical pesticides on food crops, efforts are also currently underway to find fungal pathogens to control introduced pests impacting African crops, including pea leafminers (*Liriomyza huidobrensis*), originally from South America (Akutse et al., 2013), and banana weevils (*Cosmopolites sordidus*), originally from Southeast Asia (Akello et al., 2008).

Some of the most effective pest control programmes use an integrated pest management (IPM) approach that relies on using multiple pest control methods described above either simultaneously or in succession (van Wyk and van Wilgen, 2002). Strategic planning to coordinate best practices can also help offset some of the costs of invasive species control (Rahlao et al., 2010) and ensure that important pest sources are not missed (van Wilgen et al., 2007). When considering the best method to control an invasive species, it may also help to consider how our own actions inadvertently encourage invasive species. For example, an over-reliance on synthetic fertiliser has been shown to cause eutrophication (Chislock et al., 2013) and encourage growth of aquatic invasive plants (Coetzee and Hill, 2012; Bownes et al., 2012).

> The most effective pest control programmes use an integrated pest management (IPM) approach that relies on using multiple control methods either simultaneously or in succession.

Even though the impacts of invasive and other exotic species are generally considered negative, they do occasionally provide some benefits. For example, Australian pines (*Casuarina equisetifolia*) have been planted widely throughout Africa for timber, charcoal, and to stabilise eroding lands. Some people harvest invasive species to eat or to sell; examples include water hyacinth (Figure 10.9), prickly pears (*Opuntia* spp.), and Mediterranean mussels (*Mytilus galloprovincialis*). The latter has also become an important food source for the African black oystercatcher (*Haematopus moquini*, NT) (Kohler et al., 2009). Similarly, nearly 18 species of diurnal raptors, including four globally threatened species, nest and roost—sometimes in colonies numbering thousands of individuals—in stands of invasive Australian gum (*Eucalyptus* spp.) trees (Allan et al., 1997; Jenkins, 2005). Many birds also favour fruits produced by invasive plants, such as the tickberry and syringa (*Melia azedarach*); this however allows those plants to spread even further. Because they reproduce so fast, water hyacinth has been investigated as a resource for producing bioenergy (Güereña et al., 2015). A ground spider (*Prodida stella*, CR), endemic to the Seychelles and threatened by sea level rise (Gerlach, 2014), was first described from specimens collected on Australian pine, and may thus persist on trees further inland as their original range is submerged by rising sea levels. Nevertheless, assessments generally show that costs incurred from invasive species outweigh the benefits (Mwangi and Swallow, 2008). It is thus important to consider whether native species can fulfil the same functions in those cases where benefits of invasive species are touted.

Figure 10.9 Turning an undesirable weed into a cash crop: entrepreneurs from South Africa to Lake Victoria and Nigeria (pictured) have developed alternative income streams by training members of their communities in how to make handcrafts from invasive water hyacinth.

10.2.3 Adaptive management

In decades past, ecosystem management in Africa was generally conducted following *a laissez-faire* (i.e. hands-off) approach where natural processes were allowed to follow their own course, with interventions only implemented when subjectively deemed absolutely necessary. While this passive management style may have worked in an era when ecosystems were less fragmented by roads and fences, and the impact of pollution and invasive species transported along rivers and streams were limited. But maintaining healthy ecosystems (especially small ones) through limited action is becoming increasingly difficult in today's human-dominated world. Leaving concerns unattended may seem fine in the short term, but such neglect can create problems that are very difficult to contain later on. For this reason, it is increasingly necessary to actively manage ecosystems not only to achieve conservation goals, but even to just avoid degradation of current conditions.

A major challenge of active (and reactive) conservation management is that nature consists of thousands of interacting components and feedback loops. Because it is impossible to fully understand how these different components interact, management strategies are typically implemented with an incomplete understanding of how interventions may impact broader ecosystem processes.

Management actions that draw from experimentation and prior experiences often deliver the desired results. However, despite good intentions and careful consideration, some interventions may later give rise to a cascade of unintended consequences that run counter to overall conservation goals. South Africa's Kruger National Park provides a good example. Conservation managers here once thought they could better protect the local wildlife by fencing the Park and constructing artificial waterholes at regular intervals, a policy that was implemented primarily in the 1960s and 1970s (Smith et al., 2007; Venter et al., 2008; van Wilgen and Biggs, 2011). But instead of providing conservation benefits, the fences blocked dispersal routes, which caused grazing herbivores to be increasingly sedentary around waterholes, leading to overgrazing. The increased availability of surface water also allowed elephant populations to increase to a point where they became a threat to other taxa, particularly large fruit-bearing trees such as baobabs (*Adansonia digitata*). The construction of artificial waterholes in arid sections of the Park saw an expansion of plains zebra (*Equus quagga*, NT) and common wildebeest (*Connochaetes taurinus*, LC) distributions, which in turn also attracted more lions into these arid areas. This increasing grazing competition and predation pressure caused populations of four locally rare antelopes to fall by 73–88% between 1986 and 2006, prompting fears of imminent extirpations of these iconic species in one of Africa's premier protected areas.

While it is hard to escape the looming threat of unintended consequences harming biodiversity, their impacts can be mitigated. One of the first steps involves setting management goals and objectives through close working relationships with a wide variety of stakeholders, including local people (Box 10.3) and scientists who can provide additional insights into the local social-ecological context within which land managers operate. Also important is developing a monitoring protocol that enables land managers to assess whether conservation goals are being met. When monitoring shows that management actions are ineffective or detrimental, it is absolutely critical to be willing and able to integrate this improved understanding into revised management strategies. This process, whereby new knowledge gained through repeated cycles of learning is used to revise and refine conservation strategies and management goals, is known as **adaptive management** (Venter et al., 2008; van Wilgen and Biggs, 2011). Rather than punishing management errors, adaptive management embraces the idea that we live in a complex world, and that management strategies frequently need be revised to account for new knowledge, shifting priorities, and even evolving societal values. Some of the best adaptive management plans explicitly mandate regular (e.g. every 5 years) reviews, where management strategies, goals, and objectives are formally reviewed and updated.

> Despite good intentions, conservation activities may give rise to unintended consequences that run counter to overall conservation goals. Adaptive management can reduce further harm.

Box 10.3 Environmental Governance in the Serengeti Ecosystem

Alex Wilbard Kisingo

College of African Wildlife Management, Mweka, Tanzania.

✉ *akisingo@mwekawildlife.ac.tz*

The greater Serengeti ecosystem of Tanzania (Figure 10.C) represents one of the most biologically productive ecoregions in the world. In recognition of its biological importance, much of this ecosystem is safeguarded under a mosaic of government, private, and co-managed protected areas, as well as community conserved areas (Kisingo, 2013a). Among these protected areas is the world-famous Serengeti National Park, as well as the Ngorongoro Conservation Area.

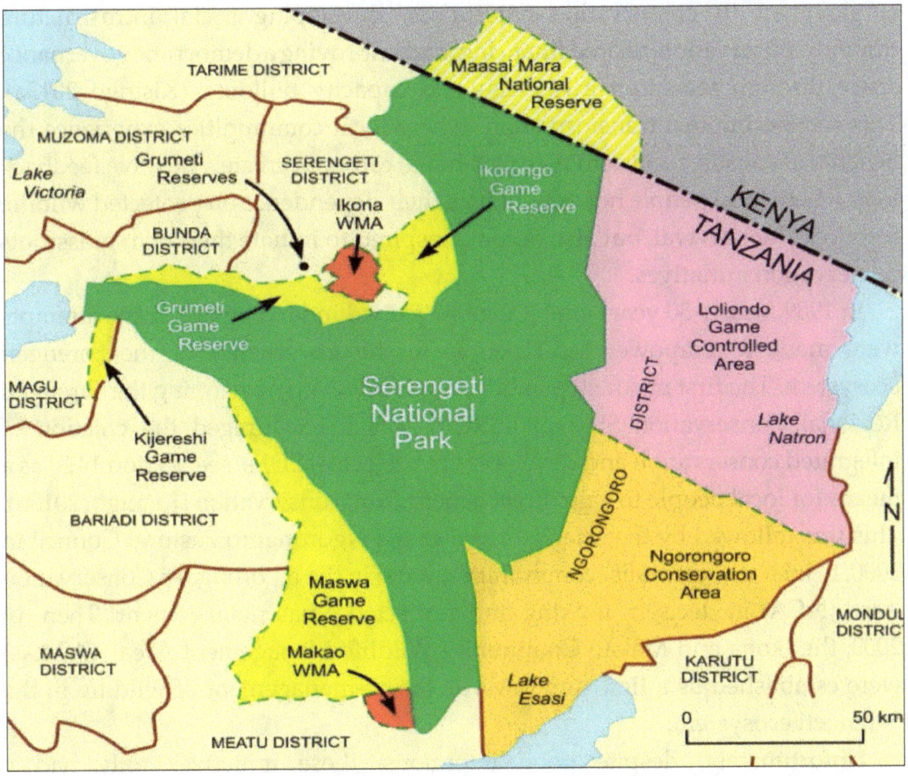

Figure 10.C A map of the greater Serengeti ecosystem, showing the location of the major protected areas in the region.

The various governance models that dictated human actions in the colonial, post-colonial, and contemporary eras have had a profound effect on the ecosystem's conservation outcomes (Polasky et al., 2008; Sinclair et al., 2008). During most of the colonial period and immediately after Tanzania gained independence in 1961, management of the ecosystem was in the hands of government, which followed a fortress conservation approach (i.e. "fences and fines"). This included evicting traditional peoples from their ancestral lands, restricting the use of wildlife and other natural resources, and imposing heavy penalties on those on the wrong side of wildlife laws. This approach severed the link between people and nature, creating an atmosphere of hostility and resistance to conservation initiatives amongst the local communities. The results have been increased subsistence and commercial poaching, human encroachment into wildlife habitats, and a general lack of community support for conservation (Kisingo 2013b). As a result, Tanzania has seen its wildlife populations reduced and migratory corridors blocked, while invasive plant species are spreading and human-conservation conflicts are intensifying.

In contrast to this counter-productive approach, involving local people in decision making and implementation can enhance attainment of conservation and social outcomes. Such an involvement can occur through training and employment in conservation enterprises, developing social infrastructure through conservation-related financing, and improving a democratic governance space through increased awareness and capacity building (Kisingo 2013a). This socio-economic transformation, where local communities experience the benefits of conservation activities first-hand, can even create a positive feedback loop where local people not only reduce their dependence on protected wildlife resources for survival, but also become inspired to initiate their own grassroots conservation initiatives.

In 1989, nearly 30 years after Tanzania gained independence, some attempts were made to empower local people in the governance of the Serengeti ecosystem. The first major step in this regard involved developing the Serengeti Regional Conservation Strategy (SRCP), which encouraged the creation of integrated conservation and development projects (ICDPs, see Section 14.3) as a means for local people to gain direct benefit from conservation (Kisingo, 2013a). This was followed by the establishment of the Ngorongoro Pastoral Council in 2000, to include pastoralist communities living in the Ngorongoro Conservation Area (NCA) in decision making and protected areas management. Then, in 2003, the Ikona and Makao Community Wildlife Management Areas (WMAs) were established as a first step towards the co-management of wildlife in the Serengeti ecosystem.

Unfortunately, despite good intentions, these initiatives only had a limited impact in empowering local communities. An important reason for this failure was a general incompatibility between local policies and national legislations, notably a legal framework that favoured a top-down approach to decision making over the wishes and values of local communities. In the NCA, communities were more involved in the provisioning of scholarships and socio-economic assistance, in effect surrendering decision making power to government authorities. Local communities thus either never had a real seat at the table during the development and implementation of management strategies, or lost what little they had over time (Kisingo, 2013a). It should thus not come as a surprise that management of the Serengeti ecosystem generally presents mixed results in terms of conservation and social outcomes. Although wildlife populations are still better off in government protected areas when compared to WMAs, neglecting these community conserved areas (which function as critical wildlife corridors) undoubtedly also negatively impacts wildlife in government protected areas.

To be more effective at meeting conservation goals, there is an urgent need to adapt and reengineer ecosystem governance structures in the greater Serengeti ecosystem. Involving more stakeholders, particularly local people, would be an important first step. This involvement should be honest and transparent. Instead of calling one or two community representatives to a workshop to secure a rubber-stamp, start by gathering input from a wide variety of stakeholders and make an effort afterwards to show how that input was considered in final plans. In this way, even those who do not get what they want will at least know that they were heard, and hopefully understand why their desires were not met. There is also an urgent need for capacity building, to develop conservation management expertise among members of local communities, rather than the current over-reliance on outside experts who do not understand local dynamics. This could start small: community members can, for example, be involved in anti-poaching efforts through the use of Village Game Scouts (VGS), a strategy that reduces operational costs in tandem with boosting local incomes. The most promising and eager scouts can then be provided with additional professional development opportunities. Empowering local communities in this way, and enabling them to benefit from conservation activities, will provide opportunities for a wider variety of people, beyond just foreign tourists, to understand how conservation actions can support and benefit livelihoods. This will result in social outcomes that are desired by local communities, and in return, conservation authorities who then gain local support for future actions.

10.2.4 Being minimally intrusive

While adaptive management often necessitates active management, it does not embrace a philosophy of intervention for its own sake. If managers try to maintain their land by intervening in every aspect in nature, conservation will become inhibitively expensive, especially as the costs of managing unintended consequences escalate. Rather, effective adaptive management plans generally embrace a philosophy of "management by exception" (Venter et al. 2008), whereby interventions are implemented only when certain pre-determined thresholds of concern are exceeded, or when monitored trends suggest that those thresholds will soon be exceeded. (For examples of such thresholds, see van Wilgen and Biggs, 2011).

Thinking back to the example from Kruger National Park, discussed above, when it became clear the four species of antelopes were on their way to extirpation, a research programme was initiated to identify the causes for these population declines. Based on this research, park managers decided that the best way forward was to close the majority of the artificial waterpoints, and move some antelopes to a predator-proof enclosure where they can safely breed (van Wilgen and Biggs, 2011). To reverse the damage caused fences, park managers also prioritised re-establishing free movement of animals by removing these fences between the park and some adjacent properties (Venter et al., 2008). While lion and zebra populations subsequently moved out of the Park's arid region as hoped, and elephant populations stabilised, numbers of the four antelope species remained stubbornly low. This prompted park managers to evaluate whether the resources invested in these locally rare but globally common ungulates could be better spent on globally rare species occurring in the park, such as black rhinoceros (*Diceros bicornis*, CR). In other words, they adapted their threshold of concern from focussing on locally rare species to prioritising globally rare species (van Wilgen and Biggs, 2011). This decision remains controversial, even among park managers concerned about the potential loss of genetic diversity within the four ungulates. But adaptive management allows for shifting priorities; park managers may very well revisit their decisions if and when the park's rhinoceros are secured, and funds are freed up for other activities.

10.3 Restoring Damaged Ecosystems

Ecosystems are regularly disturbed by natural phenomena such as floods from cyclones/hurricanes, or wildfires started by lightning. Nevertheless, natural disturbances typically lead to succession and a return to ecological conditions that can sustain high levels of biodiversity. In contrast, ecosystems that humans have damaged or destroyed through activities such as unsustainable agriculture and deforestation, overgrazing, or pollution tend to lose their ability to rebound without human intervention.

Ecological restoration is the practice of restoring damaged ecosystems to a point where their ecosystem functions and species composition resemble their original or near-original state. **Restoration ecology,** in turn, is the scientific study of restoring damaged ecosystems, communities, and populations. Ecological restoration is often the best method for providing for the long-term use of degraded sites, whether considered from the perspectives of ecology, social benefit, or even economic benefit. Consequently, and unsurprisingly, this practice and the science originally developed in response to attempts to restore economically valuable ecosystem functions: creating wetlands to prevent flooding, reclaiming mining sites to prevent pollution and soil erosion, revegetating overgrazed rangelands to increase grass production, and planting trees on cleared areas to improve agroforestry.

> Ecological restoration aims to restore damaged ecosystems to a point where their ecosystem functions and species composition resemble their original or near-original state.

Best practices in ecological restoration have undergone major advances in recent decades. In the past, restoration methods mostly aimed for quick economic benefit, which resulted in simplified ecosystems that either failed to establish or degraded after a short time. To avoid such costly mistakes, restoration plans of today increasingly aim for the permanent re-establishment of healthy ecosystems that could support sustainable industries such as ecotourism, wildlife management, carbon sequestration, and low-level grazing by livestock. Ecological restoration often also makes economic sense; a study from South Africa found that every US $1 invested in restoring ecosystem services would generate US $8.30 for the local economy (de Wit et al., 2008).

Many grassroots conservation groups are at the forefront of initiatives that use ecosystem restoration to help make the connection between healthy ecosystems and socio-economic well-being. One prime example is the Green Belt Movement, a Kenyan initiative led by rural women to combat deforestation and restore degraded forests. They do this by helping rural women work together to grow and plant trees. Since its founding in 1977, the organisation has overseen the planting of over 51 million trees, which has helped restore forests on Mount Kenya, the Aberdares, and the Mau Complex. The planted trees have prevented erosion, stored rainwater, and provided firewood, timber, and food. In addition, over 30,000 women have been trained in sustainable trades such as forestry, beekeeping, and food processing.

10.3.1 Ecological restoration approaches

There are four main approaches to ecological restoration (Figure 10.10):

- *Natural regeneration*. Degraded areas, such as abandoned fields or logged areas, are allowed to naturally reseed and return to grasslands or forests. Land managers often choose this approach when active restoration is too expensive, when earlier restoration attempts have failed, or when experience has shown that the ecosystem is resilient and can recover on its own (e.g. Crouzeilles et al., 2017).

- *Rehabilitation*. Land managers improve conditions of a degraded ecosystem by transitioning it to another, different ecosystem type. For example, land managers could rehabilitate a degraded forest by transitioning it to a tree plantation. Rehabilitation could involve replacing just a few species or many species.

- *Partial restoration*. Land managers restore some ecosystem functions and some of the species that were dominant or characteristic of the ecosystem.

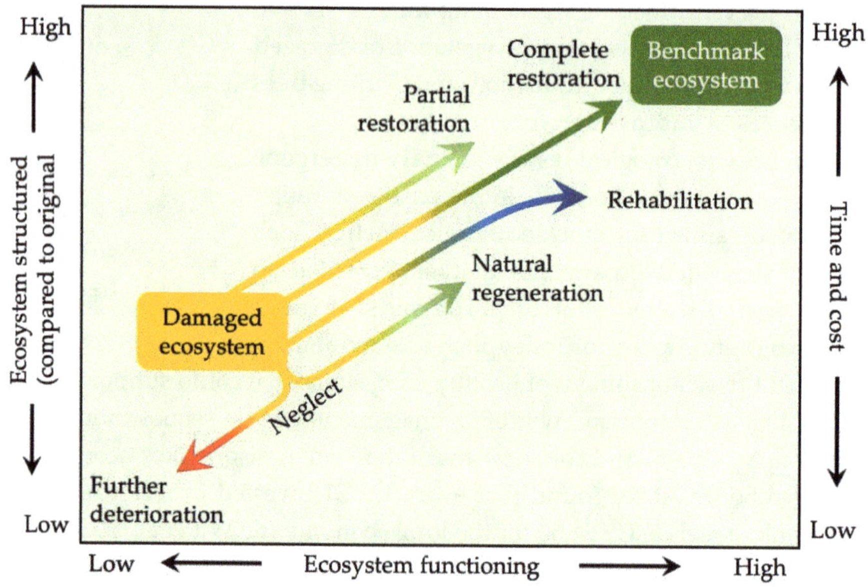

Figure 10.10 Several approaches can be followed when restoring an ecosystem, ranging from taking no action and letting the ecosystem regenerate naturally to completely restoring a degraded site. The best course of action will depend on a project's end goals and the resources available.

For example, as a part of a grassland restoration, land managers might initially replant a few key species that are hardy and contribute to ecosystem functioning; they could delay restoration of rare species until later phases.

- *Complete restoration*. Land managers restore an area to benchmark ecosystem structure, mix of species, and ecosystem functioning. Complete restoration usually requires an active programme to modify the site, reintroduce native species, and eliminate or reduce the factors that were degrading the ecosystem.

Before a restoration project is initiated, and the type of approach is decided upon, land managers must consider how quickly the ecosystem can recover, resource needs and availability, the availability of locally adapted taxa, and the work that might be required to allow the restored community to persist over the long term. Examples of specific considerations include how to prepare soils, how to handle translocated organisms, when and how much fertiliser and water to add, and how to prevent invasions by unwanted species (Galatowitsch and Richardson, 2005; Zabbey and Tanee, 2016). It is also important to remember that ecosystems generally fail to recover if the factor that caused them to become degraded in the first place is not removed or reduced. For instance, efforts to reverse desertification (Section 5.3.4) would require a reduction of grazing pressure and unsustainable agricultural practices.

To measure restoration success, biologists often aim to restore degraded areas to conditions (ecosystem functions or species composition) comparable to a chosen benchmark or **reference site**. Reference sites provide practical targets for restoration and can be used to quantitatively assess of the success of a restoration project. Comparing restoration progress against a reference site also allows land managers to intervene or adjust their methods if restoration goals are not being met. This approach, in which land managers monitor conditions and adjust their protocols as and when needed, is known as **adaptive restoration**. (For a general discussion on adaptive management, see Section 10.2.3.)

10.3.2 Major restoration targets

Many human-altered ecosystems in Africa have proven to be good candidates for ecological restoration. These include tropical rainforests, wetlands, rangelands, and coral reefs. In addition, restoration projects in urban areas (Box 10.4) have become popular in recent years in part due to the enhanced quality of life for people living in the area.

Box 10.4 Sustainable Forest Restoration Using Natural Vegetation

Samuel Kiboi

School of Biological Sciences, University of Nairobi, Nairobi, Kenya.

✉ *samuel.kiboi@uonbi.ac.ke*

Deforestation is one of the main driving forces of biodiversity loss in Africa. Many rural and urban communities rely on wood biomass for energy in the form of either charcoal or firewood. This means that they must continuously source for the firewood or charcoal by harvesting living or dead trees. In many cases, the available energy source is live trees on farmlands which are planted as border trees, or random remnants of pre-existing vegetation within the farm. In some instances, farmers who have land in less densely populated areas have portions of forested areas or woodlots which are under continuous disturbance from wood harvesting. This is more common in rangelands or areas that have lower agricultural productivity. In other areas, such as urban settlements bordering forests, such as Kibera in Nairobi Kenya, there has been extensive harvesting of firewood and sometimes selectively for medicinal purposes or wood carving (Furukawa et. al., 2011).

Given the known benefits of intact forests, including improving food security and climate change mitigation, there are currently several efforts aimed at increasing Kenya's forest cover both in protected and unprotected areas. The Kenya Forest Service has always been at the forefront of restoration in protected areas, particularly in gazetted forest areas. Despite the general enthusiasm to increase forest cover, many structural and informational challenges remain. Most reforestation programmes classify seedlings as either "exotic" or "indigenous", but do not consider which species are best suited to local conditions. In addition, despite the numerous reforestation programmes initiated by individuals, government entities, and corporations, there is generally minimal follow-up maintenance after planting, which can jeopardise an entire project. The first three years after planting are especially crucial for proper seedling establishment and require intensive management, including weeding, mulching, and protection from herbivores. Perhaps the biggest challenge to the sustainability of these reforestation initiatives is the slow growth rate of many valuable indigenous trees that does not meet short-term harvest demands while also allowing for longer-term forest regeneration.

Figure 10.D (Top) June 2016: project participants planting trees on the University of Nairobi, Chiromo campus, following the Miyawaki method; (Bottom). January 2019: less than three years later, the trees have successfully grown to provide ecosystem services to the Chiromo campus.

At the University of Nairobi, successful urban forest islands with potential natural vegetation have been established using the "Miyawaki method" (Miyawaki, 2004). This method uses native trees to restore indigenous forests at timelines shorter than if natural regeneration was allowed to take its course (Figure 10.D). To create an urban green space on the university property, we selected 16 native tree species using a vegetation science study of remnant forests around Nairobi. Within 16 months, many of the trees had established well, with the best performing species, *Ehretia cymosa*, growing to over 2 m (Kiboi et. al., 2014). This study illustrates the importance of selecting locally adapted species in forest restoration initiatives.

Sustainable restoration practices can alleviate the short-term pressure from restored ecosystems while they mature to a self-sustaining structure. Not only should locally adapted species be promoted, but also native species that can be continuously coppiced, where new shoots rapidly replace harvested branches and portions of branches. Exotic species, such as Australian gum, pine, and mesquite (*Prosopis juliflora*) often display these characteristics, but those species are often invasive with detrimental effects on native ecosystems and communities. Fortunately, many African plant species are also good candidates for sustainable restoration initiatives, including camphor bush (*Tarchonanthus camphoratus*), sickle-leaved false-thorn (*Albizia harveyi*), silver clusterleaf (*Terminalia sericea*), and weeping wattle (*Peltophorum africanum*) (Kennedy, 1998; Kaschula et al., 2005). Although coppices may have more variable increases in biomass compared to initial planted stands, it is a sustainable way of biomass management especially in areas that experience high demand for harvestable wood. In addition, planting native trees and shrubs in farmlands typically provides beneficial ecosystem services through increasing the abundance and diversity of native insectivorous birds and pollinators of crops. In these various ways, the right management practices can lead to benefits for local people, biodiversity, and sustainable conservation practices.

Tropical forests: Tropical forests cover less than 10% of Earth's land surface; yet, they contain more than half of all terrestrial species (Cortlett and Primack, 2011). When these forests are lost, we lose substantial biodiversity and ecosystem services. For this reason, tropical forest restoration initiatives in Africa and elsewhere have received much attention in recent years. Towards the end of this chapter we will discuss a major global effort focussed on restoring degraded tropical forests, known as REDD+.

> Africa has already lost over 40% of its wetlands through human activity, with current loss rates among the highest in the world.

Wetlands: Africa has already lost over 40% of its wetlands through human activity, with current loss rates among the highest in the world (Davidson, 2014).

Because of the recognised importance of wetlands in providing flood control and other ecosystem services (Section 5.5.3), damaged wetlands are frequently targeted in restoration efforts. Wetlands are defined by their hydrology; therefore, wetland restoration projects often the focus on restoring a site's original hydrology. One such example comes from South Africa, where authorities (with support from the **World Bank**) have been working on restoring Africa's largest estuarine lake at iSimangaliso Wetland Park—a multistep process that involves restoration of the estuary's hydrology, controlling invasive plants around the wetland, and improving farming practices in the surrounding area (Whitfield et al., 2013). Wetland restoration can also occur through activities like dam removals (Section 11.3.2) or replacing exotic vegetation that deplete groundwater with native vegetation to promote groundwater retention (Sirami et al., 2013). Importantly, true wetland restorations are notoriously difficult to accomplish. It can be relatively easy to replant a wetland to look as it previously looked, but to restore the foundational hydrology often requires sophisticated engineering. In many cases, partial wetland rehabilitation is the best that can be achieved.

Mangrove swamps (Figure 10.11) provide nursery grounds for many economically important fisheries, protect coastal communities against powerful storms, and prevent saltwater from intruding into freshwater systems (van Bochove et al., 2014). They are also among the world's most important carbon sinks, storing four times more carbon per hectare than other types of tropical forests (Donato et al., 2011). Yet, over 35% of the world's mangrove swamps have already been degraded by agriculture, urban expansion, pollution, and commercial shellfish farming (MEA, 2005; Giri et al., 2011). To regain these lost services, several communities are now restoring their mangroves, while also adopting more sustainable practices to reduce damage to these important habitats (Feka et al., 2009). One of Africa's most ambitious mangrove restoration projects have been initiated in Senegal, where more than 300,000 local citizens planted more than 150 million mangrove trees across 140 km^2 between 2006 and 2013 (Cormier-Salem and Panfili, 2016). Mangrove (as any other) restoration projects do need to be planned carefully to ensure success. For example, it is important to choose ecologically-appropriate species to plant, rather than the fastest growing species that promises quick (but not necessarily optimal) results. Studies from Eritrea have also shown how fertiliser runoff caused by wave action could reduce lead to project failure (Sato et al., 2005). Another concern is that mangroves are often exploited, restored, and managed as forests, while the primary determinants of their function and structure—hydrology, soils, and nutrients—are neglected (Lewis, 2005; Gopal, 2013). Recent work showed that natural regeneration of mangrove swamps may produce more diverse, resilient, and productive ecosystems compared to planting efforts (Wetlands International, 2016). These issues will need to be addressed to ensure the long-term sustainability of mangrove restoration efforts.

Seasonal drylands: Through extensive land mismanagement (primarily overgrazing and unsustainable agriculture), a large portion of Africa's seasonal drylands are undergoing desertification, the conversion of once-productive land to desolate man-made deserts—large dry unproductive dust bowls with no vegetation.

Figure 10.11 (Left) Classic air-breathing roots of a mangrove tree in Senegal. (Right) A woman collecting oysters among mangroves in Senegal's Saloum Delta.

The degradation of these lands has crippled agriculture, obliterated natural biological communities, and displaced millions of people. While many drylands seem to regenerate naturally when pressures associated with land mismanagement are removed at an early stage, extended periods of mismanagement hamper recovery by leading to a loss of natural seed banks, nutrients, and microsites that allow for seedling establishment.

Somalia is home to one of the world's most effective desertification reversal programmes. Since the early 1990s, when Somalia's national government collapsed, Somalis have been tormented by warlords and civil war. The lack of effective governance also saw the rise of an unregulated charcoal trade; groves of thorn trees hundreds of years old were set ablaze, before the so-called "black gold" was exported to Arabia. The resultant wildfires and removal of trees caused an erosion crisis, turning grazing lands that once supported a diverse pastoralist community into unproductive wastelands. The resulting famine, exacerbated by droughts, caused even more Somalis to turn to a life of crime, piracy, and terrorism in a desperate effort to support their families. To reverse this decline, the humanitarian NGO Adeso successfully persuaded a regional government to create and enforce a ban on charcoal exports. Adeso also started educating local people about the links between the environment and their own lives, and introduced sustainable alternatives to the charcoal trade, such as promoting the use of solar cookers to reduce the need for charcoal fuel. To reverse desertification and prevent further erosion, Adeso showed local communities how to construct small and simple rock dams; the dams also provide a microenvironment suitable for thorn tree seeds to germinate. Adeso has been so successful in these ventures that they subsequently expanded their work to Kenya and South Sudan.

Coral Reefs: Coral reefs are one of the world's most important marine ecosystems, both ecologically and economically. They provide food to local communities, support ecotourism industries, and protect coasts by reducing wave energy by as much as 97% (Ferrario et al., 2014). Yet, coral reefs are also one of the most threatened marine ecosystems, impacted heavily by overharvesting, pollution, sedimentation, and climate change. Nevertheless, restoring coral reefs is well worth it; a meta-analysis found that it is nearly 20 times cheaper to restore coral reefs than to construct artificial systems for coastal protection (Ferrario et al., 2014). As such, several initiatives are now in progress to restore coral reefs, ranging from transplanting corals and boosting sea urchin populations for seaweed control to creating artificial reefs that can act as substrate for coral settlements (Lindahl, 2003; Edwards and Gomez, 2007).

10.3.3 The future of ecological restoration

Research in restoration ecology has grown rapidly in recent years. Many reviews (e.g. Suding, 2011) and books (e.g. Falk et al., 2016) have recently been published on the topic. The Society for Ecological Restoration (SER) was established in 1988 to support the field, and two scientific journals (*Restoration Ecology* and *Ecological Restoration*) publish hundreds of papers each year on the topic, in addition to the papers published in other ecological and conservation journals. The growth in research provides scientists and land managers more studies and evidence to inform planning and improvement of restoration projects.

A recent development in the field involves **biodiversity offsets** (ten Kate et al., 2004; MacFarlane et al., 2016). A system generally used by developers, biodiversity offsets aim to achieve no net loss of biodiversity during economic development; some projects even aim for a net overall biodiversity gain. Developers accomplish this by compensating for the ecosystem damage (or loss of threatened species populations, Kormos et al., [2014]) that may be incurred during a development project. This compensation usually follows one or more of three main strategies: (1) reducing the extent of damage at the development site, (2) restoring or protecting natural communities at a different "receptor site" as compensation for what is being lost, and (3) enhancement of the remaining natural communities after development.

While biodiversity offsets (and other restoration initiatives in general) sound good in theory, it is important to remember that the most effective biodiversity conservation strategy remains protecting and managing intact ecosystems. Studies and practical experience have shown that ecological restoration efforts often fail to recreate key characteristics of their reference sites, including species composition or ecosystem functioning, even after years of effort and investment. It is also important to remember than some African ecosystems regenerate very slowly—tropical forests require more than

> Because restoring damaged environments takes considerable time and resources, preserving intact ecosystems should be prioritised.

100 years to develop (Bonnell et al., 2011)—so even effective restorations may take decades to provide the full range of benefits. In cases where biodiversity offsets are pursued, it is critical to ensure that these initiatives indeed offer true conservation gains by mitigating the various associated risks (Coralie et al., 2015; Gordon et al., 2015; Maron et al., 2016).

10.4 Combatting Climate Change Through Ecosystem Conservation

Complex natural ecosystems play an important role in mitigating the destructive effects of climate change. Prominently, living plants sequester greenhouse gases from the atmosphere (Zarin et al., 2015); in contrast, their loss due to habitat loss increases greenhouse gas emissions (Section 6.1). Studies have also shown how ecosystems with high complexity (Betts et al. 2018) and species diversity (Mokany et al., 2014; Isbell et al., 2015) are better buffered against climate change. Lastly, by maintaining and restoring carbon-sequestering ecosystems, we also provide opportunities for climate-sensitive to persist despite the threat of climate change pace (Section 11.4).

One of the foremost initiatives aimed at combatting climate change through ecosystem conservation and restoration is known as the **Reducing Emissions from Deforestation and Forest Degradation (REDD+,** http://www.un-redd.org) programme. Set up by the UN, REDD+ provides financial incentives to local communities and landowners that make conservation of carbon-sequestering ecosystems worth more than destroying them. Funding for REDD+ is obtained through **carbon trading** programmes, in which individuals and organisations looking to offset their emissions buy **carbon credits**. The funds obtained through REDD+ are then invested in initiatives that promote ecological restoration and reduce local dependence of intact ecosystems by creating alternative income streams such as sustainable crop, timber, honey, milk, and meat production.

The original aim of REDD+ was to safeguard primary old-growth forests, but the diversity of goals set out by REDD+ also include improving ecosystem connectivity, protecting threatened species, and preventing further loss and degradation of carbon-sequestering ecosystems other than forests. Africa has been a major beneficiary of this programme. Since its inception in 2007, REDD+ projects have been funded in 27 Sub-Saharan African countries (http://www.reddprojectsdatabase.org), affording protection for over 1.6 million ha of forest (Panfil and Harvey, 2016), and providing opportunities for thousands of Africans who would not have had access to these funds otherwise.

> REDD+ provides financial incentives to local communities and landowners by making conservation of carbon-sequestering ecosystems worth more than destroying them.

Yet the future of these opportunities is not secure. Concerns exist regarding the effectiveness of REDD+ programmes, much of which is based on problematic implementation, long-term funding security, lack of monitoring, and lack of concrete conservation goals (Phelps et al., 2011; Panfil and Harvey. 2015; Fletcher et al., 2016). For example, there are concerns that REDD+ programmes can develop into a form of perverse subsidies, such as when native vegetation is cleared to establish plantations (Figure 10.12) with trees that have a high risk of becoming invasive (Lindenmayer et al., 2012). Similarly, there are concerns about the strong emphasis on forests, possibly at the expense of other important ecosystems and ecosystem services (Bond, 2016). Conservation biologists continue to be hopeful that REDD+, as with the range of approaches described in this chapter, will provide opportunities for land managers and scientists to successfully protect and restore biodiversity now and into the future.

Figure 10.12 The Reducing Emissions from Deforestation and Forest Degradation (REDD+) programme aims to promote forest conservation by paying landowners to protect forests on their lands. However, there are concerns that some REDD+ funds have become a form of perverse subsidies, for example when native vegetation is cleared to establish plantations of invasive trees. To ensure programme sustainability, it is important to strike a balance between meeting short-term development goals and ensuring the protection of a complex and adaptable biological landscape that can provide a variety of ecosystem services over the long term.

10.5 Summary

1. Ecosystem conservation and management involves three different activities: (1) monitoring ecosystem components, (2) maintaining healthy ecosystems, and (3) restoring damaged ecosystems.
2. An ecosystem in which all the chemical, physical, and biological components and processes are functioning normally is considered healthy. Ecosystems that remain healthy through disturbance are resistant, while ecosystems that rapidly recover after disturbance are resilient.
3. Ecosystems can be monitored using direct observation, environmental or biochemical indicators, and remote sensing analysis. It is important that any monitoring method be consistent and repeatable across space and time.

4. To maintain ecosystems that can support diverse ecological communities, conservationists are guided by three complementary management principles: (1) maintain critical ecosystem processes (water cycling, nutrient cycling, energy flow, community dynamics), (2) minimise external threats, and (3) be adaptive yet minimally intrusive.
5. Ecological restoration is the practice of restoring damaged ecosystems to an agreed-upon benchmark. This can be accomplished via rehabilitation, partial restoration, complete restoration, or taking no action. The strategy followed will depend on each project's goals and resource availability.

10.6 Topics for Discussion

1. Read the articles by Bunce et al. (2008) and/or Papworth et al. (2009) about shifting baselines. Then think of a natural ecosystem in your region; it could even be an ecosystem in a protected area. How do you think that ecosystem looked 50 years ago? What about 100 years ago? And 1,000 years ago? At what time do you think the ecosystem was able to support the most diverse ecological community? What would you do to restore (or maintain) the ecosystem to this state? Would such a restoration project impact some species negatively? Is that a problem?
2. Consider all the aquatic communities in your region (ponds, marshes, streams, rivers, lakes, estuaries, coastal waters, etc.). Who is responsible for managing these ecosystems, and how do they balance the need for protecting biodiversity with the needs of society for natural resources? What additional conservation projects would you implement to help protect those ecosystems in the coming decades?
3. Imagine that the last population of a threatened bird species (which draws birdwatchers to the area) lives along a river nearby. This river also has numerous endemic species of fish, shellfish, and insects. A foreign company recently obtained permission to dam the river for hydropower generation. Beyond the impact of flooding, the dam will also cause various forms of pollution which will destroy the threatened birds' food source and nesting area. Upon writing about the challenge in the local newspaper, you receive US $1 million from an anonymous donor to save the bird. The company is willing to forego the development in exchange for the US $1 million. It will cost an additional $750,000 to implement an effective ecological restoration programme that can reverse the threatened birds' population declines. Is it better to buy out the company and not devote additional resources to ecological restoration and researching the bird? Or would you rather spend the money on finding alternative ways to protect the bird and the other endemic species? Explain your answers.

10.7 Suggested Readings

Crouzeilles, R., M.S. Ferreira, R.L. Chazdon, et al. 2017. Ecological restoration success is higher for natural regeneration than for active restoration in tropical forests. *Science Advances* 3: e1701345. https://doi.org/10.1126/sciadv.1701345 Natural regeneration is an appropriate restoration strategy under the right conditions.

Maron, M., C.D. Ives, H. Kujala, et al. 2016. Taming a wicked problem: Resolving controversies in biodiversity offsetting. *BioScience* 66: 489–98. https://doi.org/10.1093/biosci/biw038 Biodiversity offsets offer conservation opportunities as well as challenges.

Miller, B.P., E.A. Sinclair, M.H.M. Menz, et al. 2017. A framework for the practical science necessary to restore sustainable, resilient, and biodiverse ecosystems. *Restoration Ecology* 25: 605–17. https://doi.org/10.1111/rec.12475 Practical guidelines for ecological restoration success.

Panfil, S.N., and C.A. Harvey. 2015. REDD+ and biodiversity conservation: A review of the biodiversity goals, monitoring methods, and impacts of 80 REDD+ projects. *Conservation Letters* 9: 143–50. https://doi.org/10.1111/conl.12188 The UN's REDD+ programme shows promise, but several shortcomings need to be addressed.

van Wilgen, B.W., and A. Wannenburgh. 2016. Co-facilitating invasive species control, water conservation and poverty relief: Achievements and challenges in South Africa's Working for Water programme. *Current Opinion in Environmental Sustainability* 19: 7–17. https://doi.org/10.1016/j.cosust.2015.08.012 Ecosystem conservation, poverty relief, and job creation.

van Wilgen, B.W., and D.M. Richardson. 2014. Challenges and trade-offs in the management of invasive alien trees. *Biological Invasions* 16: 721–34. https://doi.org/10.1007/s10530-013-0615-8 Is the benefits gained from planting invasive species worth the costs?

Waldram, M.S., W.J. Bond, and W.D. Stock. 2008. Ecological engineering by a mega- grazer: White rhino impacts on a South African savanna. *Ecosystems* 11: 101–12. https://doi.org/10.1007/s10021-007-9109-9 Restoring ecosystem engineer populations results in a more diverse landscape.

Zachariades, C., I.D. Paterson, L.W. Strathie, et al. 2017. Assessing the status of biological control as a management tool for suppression of invasive alien plants in South Africa. *Bothalia* 47: 1–19. http://dx.doi.org/10.4102/abc.v47i2.2142 Biocontrol has many benefits

One of the following two manuscripts:

van Wilgen, B.W., and H.C. Biggs. 2011. A critical assessment of adaptive ecosystem management in a large savanna protected area in South Africa. *Biological Conservation* 144: 1179–87. https://doi.org/10.1016/j.biocon.2010.05.006 A general overview of an adaptive management programme.

van Wilgen, B.W., N. Govender, I.P.J. Smit, et al. 2014. The ongoing development of a pragmatic and adaptive fire management policy in a large African savanna protected area. *Journal of Environmental Management* 132: 358-368. http://dx.doi.org/10.1016/j.jenvman.2013.11.003 A specific overview of an adaptive management programme.

Bibliography

Acquah-Lamptey, D., R. Kyerematen, and E.O. Owusu. 2013. Using odonates as markers of the environmental health of water and its land related ecotone. *International Journal of Biodiversity and Conservation* 5: 761–69

Akello, J., T. Dubois, D. Coyne, et al. 2008. Endophytic *Beauveria bassiana* in banana (*Musa* spp.) reduces banana weevil (*Cosmopolites sordidus*) fitness and damage. *Crop Protection* 27: 1437–41. https://doi.org/10.1016/j.cropro.2008.07.003

Akutse, K.S., N.K. Maniania, K.K.M. Fiaboe, et al. 2013. Endophytic colonization of *Vicia faba* and *Phaseolus vulgaris* (Fabaceae) by fungal pathogens and their effects on the life-history parameters of *Liriomyza huidobrensis* (Diptera: Agromyzidae). *Fungal Ecology* 6: 293–301. https://doi.org/10.1016/j.funeco.2013.01.003

Allan, D.G., J.A. Harrison, R.A. Navarro, et al. 1997. The impact of commercial afforestation on bird populations in Mpumalanga Province, South Africa—Insights from bird atlas data. *Biological Conservation* 79:173–85. https://doi.org/10.1016/S0006-3207(96)00098-5

Archibald, S., R.J. Scholes, D.P. Roy, et al. 2010. Southern African fire regimes as revealed by remote sensing. *International Journal of Wildland Fire* 19: 861–78. https://doi.org/10.1071/WF10008

Bester, M.N., J.P. Bloomer, R.J. van Aarde, et al. 2002. A review of the successful eradication of feral cats from sub-Antarctic Marion Island, Southern Indian Ocean. *South African Journal of Wildlife Research* 32: 65–73. https://hdl.handle.net/10520/EJC117137

Betts, M.G., B. Phalan, S.J.K. Frey, et al. 2018. Old-growth forests buffer climate-sensitive bird populations from warming. *Diversity and Distributions* 24: 439–47. https://doi.org/10.1111/ddi.12688

Bhagwat S.A., E. Breman, T. Thekaekara, et al. 2012. A battle lost? Report on two centuries of invasion and management of *Lantana camara* L. in Australia, India and South Africa. *PLoS ONE* 7: e32407. https://doi.org/10.1371/journal.pone.0032407

Bodin, N., R. N'Gom-Kâ, S. Kâ, et al. 2013. Assessment of trace metal contamination in mangrove ecosystems from Senegal, West Africa. *Chemosphere* 90: 150–57. https://doi.org/10.1016/j.chemosphere.2012.06.019

Bond, W.J. 2016. Ancient grasslands at risk. *Science* 351: 120–22. https://doi.org/10.1126/science.aad5132

Bonnell, T.R., R. Reyna-Hurtado, and C.A. Chapman. 2011. Post-logging recovery time is longer than expected in an East African tropical forest. *Forest Ecology and Management* 261: 855–64. https://doi.org/10.1016/j.foreco.2010.12.016

Bornman, M.S., and H. Bouwman. 2012. Environmental pollutants and diseases of sexual development in humans and wildlife in South Africa: Harbingers of impact on overall health? *Reproduction in Domestic Animals* 47: 327–32. https://doi.org/10.1111/j.1439-0531.2012.02094.x

Bownes, A., M.P. Hill, and M.J. Byrne. 2013. The role of nutrients in the responses of water hyacinth, *Eichhornia crassipes* (Pontederiaceae) to herbivory by a grasshopper *Cornops aquaticum* Brüner (Orthoptera: Acrididae). *Biological Control* 67: 555–62. https://doi.org/10.1016/j.biocontrol.2013.07.022

Bradshaw, A.D. 1990. The reclamation of derelict land and the ecology of ecosystems. In: *Restoration Ecology: A Synthetic Approach to Ecological Research*, ed. by W.R. Jordan III et al. (Cambridge: Cambridge University Press).

Buckland, S.T., and A. Johnston. 2017. Monitoring the biodiversity of regions: Key principles and possible pitfalls. *Biological Conservation* 214: 23–34. https://doi.org/10.1016/j.biocon.2017.07.034

Bunce, M., L.D. Rodwell, R. Gibb, et al. 2008. Shifting baselines in fishers' perceptions of island reef fishery degradation. *Ocean and Coastal Management* 51: 285–302. https://doi.org/10.1016/j.ocecoaman.2007.09.006

Burton, M.E.H., J.R. Poulsen, M.E. Lee, et al. 2017. Reducing carbon emissions from forest conversion to oil palm agriculture in Gabon, *Conservation Letters* 10: 297–307. https://doi.org/10.1111/conl.12265

Carreiras, J.M.B, M.J. Vasconcelos, and R.M. Lucas. 2012. Understanding the relationship between aboveground biomass and ALOS PALSAR data in the forests of Guinea-Bissau (West Africa). *Remote Sensing of Environment* 121: 426–42. https://doi.org/10.1016/j.rse.2012.02.012

Chislock, M.F., E. Doster, R.A. Zitomer, et al. 2013. Eutrophication: Causes, consequences, and controls in aquatic ecosystems. *Nature Education Knowledge* 4: 10.

Coetzee, J.A., A. Bownes, and G.D. Martin. 2011. Prospects for the biological control of submerged macrophytes in South Africa. *African Entomology* 19: 469–88. https://doi.org/10.4001/003.019.0203

Coetzee, J.A., and M.P. Hill. 2012. The role of eutrophication in the biological control of water hyacinth, *Eichhornia crassipes*, in South Africa. *BioControl* 57: 247–61. https://doi.org/10.1007/s10526-011-9426-y

Coralie, C., O. Guillaume, and N. Claude. 2015 Tracking the origins and development of biodiversity offsetting in academic research and its implications for conservation: A review. *Biological Conservation* 192: 492–503. https://doi.org/10.1016/j.biocon.2015.08.036

Corlett, R., and R.B. Primack. 2011. *Tropical Rain Forests: An Ecological and Biogeographical Comparison* (Hoboken: Wiley-Blackwell). https://doi.org/10.1002/9781444392296

Cormier-Salem, M.-C., and J. Panfili. 2016. Mangrove reforestation: Greening or grabbing coastal zones and deltas? Case studies in Senegal. *African Journal of Aquatic Science* 41: 89–98. https://doi.org/10.2989/16085914.2016.1146122

Crouzeilles, R., M.S. Ferreira, R.L. Chazdon, et al. 2017. Ecological restoration success is higher for natural regeneration than for active restoration in tropical forests. *Science Advances* 3: e1701345. https://doi.org/10.1126/sciadv.1701345

Cumming, D.H.M., and G.S. Cumming. 2015. One Health: An ecological and conservation perspective. In: *One Health: The Theory and Practice of Integrated Health Approaches*, ed. by J. Zinsstag, et al. (Wallingford: CAB International).

Davidson, N.C. 2014. How much wetland has the world lost? Long-term and recent trends in global wetland area. *Marine and Freshwater Research* 65: 934–41. https://doi.org/10.1071/MF14173

Davies, A.B., C.J. Tambling, G.I.H. Kerley, et al. 2016. Effects of vegetation structure on the location of lion kill sites in African thicket. *PloS ONE* 11: e0149098. https://doi.org/10.1371/journal.pone.0149098

de Groote, H., O. Ajuonu, S. Attignon, et al. 2003. Economic impact of biological control of water hyacinth in Southern Benin. *Ecological Economics* 45: 105–17. https://doi.org/10.1016/S0921-8009(03)00006-5

de Lange, W.J., and B.W. van Wilgen. 2010. An economic assessment of the contribution of biological control to the management of invasive alien plants and to the protection of ecosystem services in South Africa. *Biological Invasions* 12: 4113–24. https://doi.org/10.1007/s10530-010-9811-y

de Wit, M., H. van Zyl, D. Crookes, et al. 2009. *Investing in natural assets: A business case for the environment in the City of Cape Town* (Cape Town: City of Cape Town).

Di Marco, M., G.M. Buchanan, Z. Szantoi, et al. 2014. Drivers of extinction risk in African mammals: The interplay of distribution state, human pressure, conservation response and species biology. *Philosophical Transactions of the Royal Society B* 369: 20130198. https://doi.org/10.1098/rstb.2013.0198

Donato, D.C., J.B. Kauffman, D. Murdiyarso, et al. 2011. Mangroves among the most carbon-rich forests in the tropics. *Nature Geoscience* 4: 293–97. https://doi.org/10.1038/ngeo1123

Drechsel, P., L. Gyiele, D. Kunze, et al. 2001. Population density, soil nutrient depletion, and economic growth in sub-Saharan Africa. *Ecological Economics* 38: 251–58. https://doi.org/10.1016/S0921-8009(01)00167-7

Dube, T., O. Mutanga, K. Seutloali, et al. 2015. Water quality monitoring in sub-Saharan African lakes: A review of remote sensing applications. *African Journal of Aquatic Science* 40: 1–7. https://doi.org/10.2989/16085914.2015.1014994

Dubovyk, O., T. Landmann, B.F.N. Erasmus, et al. 2015. Monitoring vegetation dynamics with medium resolution MODIS-EVI time series at sub-regional scale in southern Africa. *International Journal of Applied Earth Observation and Geoinformation* 38: 175–83. https://doi.org/10.1016/j.jag.2015.01.002

Edwards, A.J., and E.D. Gomez. 2007. *Reef Restoration Concepts and Guidelines: Making Sensible Management Choices in the Face of Uncertainty* (St. Lucia: Coral Reef Targeted Research and Capacity Building for Management Programme).

Estes, R.D., J.L. Atwood, and A.B. Estes. 2006. Downward trends in Ngorongoro Crater ungulate populations 1986–2005: Conservation concerns and the need for ecological research. *Biological Conservation* 131: 106–20. https://doi.org/10.1016/j.biocon.2006.02.009

Falk, D.A., M.A. Palmer, and J.B. Zedler. 2016. *Foundations of Restoration Ecology* (Washington: Island Press).

Feka, N.Z., G.B. Chuyong, and G.N. Ajonina. 2009. Sustainable utilization of mangroves using improved fish-smoking systems: A management perspective from the Douala-Edea wildlife reserve, Cameroon. *Tropical Conservation Science* 2: 450–68. https://doi.org/10.1177/194008290900200406

Ferrario, F., M.W. Beck, C.D. Storlazzi, et al. 2014. The effectiveness of coral reefs for coastal hazard risk reduction and adaptation. *Nature Communications* 5: 3794. https://doi.org/10.1038/ncomms4794

Fletcher, R., W. Dressler, B. Büscher, et al. 2016. Questioning REDD+ and the future of market-based conservation. *Conservation Biology* 30: 573–675. https://doi.org/10.1111/cobi.12680

Furukawa, T., K. Fujiwara, S. Kiboi, et al. 2011. Can stumps tell what people want: Pattern and preference of informal wood extraction in an urban forest of Nairobi, Kenya. *Biological Conservation* 144: 3047–54. https://doi.org/10.1016/j.biocon.2011.09.011

Galatowitsch, S., and D.M. Richardson. 2005. Riparian scrub recovery after clearing of invasive alien trees in headwater streams of the Western Cape, South Africa. *Biological Conservation* 122: 509–21. https://doi.org/10.1016/j.biocon.2004.09.008

Garcia-Carreras, L., and D.J. Parker. 2011. How does local tropical deforestation affect rainfall? *Geophysical Research Letters* 38: L19802. https://doi.org/10.1029/2011GL049099

Garcin, Y., P. Deschamps, G. Ménot, et al. 2018. Early anthropogenic impact on West Central African rainforests 2,600 years ago. *Proceedings of the National Academy of Sciences* 115: 3261–66. https://doi.org/10.1073/pnas.1715336115

Gerlach, J. 2014. *Prodida stella. The IUCN Red List of Threatened Species* 2014: e.T196234A2443094. http://doi.org/10.2305/IUCN.UK.2014-1.RLTS.T196234A2443094.en

Giri, C., E. Ochieng, L.L. Tieszen, et al. 2011. Status and distribution of mangrove forests of the world using Earth observation satellite data. *Global Ecology and Biogeography* 20: 154–59. https://doi.org/10.1111/j.1466-8238.2010.00584.x

Goldammer, J.G., and C. de Ronde. 2004. *Wildland Fire Management Handbook for Sub-Sahara Africa* (Freiburg: GFMC). http://gfmc.online/latestnews/GFMC-Wildland-Fire-Management-Handbook-Sub-Sahara-Africa-2004.pdf

Gopal, B. 2013. Mangroves are wetlands, not forests: Some implications for their management. In: *Mangrove Ecosystems of Asia*, ed. by I. Faridah-Hanum, et al. (New York: Springer). https://doi.org/10.1007/978-1-4614-8582-7

Gordon, A., J.W. Bull, C. Wilcox, et al. 2015. Perverse incentives risk undermining biodiversity offset policies. *Journal of Applied Ecology* 52: 532–37. https://doi.org/10.1111/1365-2664.12398

Güereña, D., H. Neufeldt, J. Berazneva, et al. 2015. Water hyacinth control in Lake Victoria: Transforming an ecological catastrophe into economic, social, and environmental benefits. *Sustainable Production and Consumption* 3: 59–69. https://doi.org/10.1016/j.spc.2015.06.003

Diop, O., and M.P. Hill, M.P. 2009. Quantitative post-release evaluation of biological control of floating fern, *Salvinia molesta* DS Mitchell (Salviniaceae), with *Cyrtobagous salviniae* Calder and Sands (Coleoptera: Curculionidae) on the Senegal River and Senegal River Delta. *African Entomology* 17: 64–70. https://doi.org/10.4001/003.017.0108

Hopcraft, J.G.C., J.M. Morales, H.L. Beyer, et al. 2014. Competition, predation, and migration: Individual choice patterns of Serengeti migrants captured by hierarchical models. *Ecological Monographs*, 84: 355–72. https://doi.org/10.1890/13-1446.1

Isbell, F., D. Craven, J. Connolly, et al. 2015. Biodiversity increases the resistance of ecosystem productivity to climate extremes. *Nature* 526: 574–77. https://doi.org/10.1038/nature15374

IUCN. 2019. *The IUCN Red List of Threatened Species.* http://www.iucnredlist.org

Jeffery, K.J., L. Korte, F. Palla, et al. 2014. Fire management in a changing landscape: A case study from Lopé National Park, Gabon. *Parks* 20: 39–52. https://doi.org/10.2305/IUCN.CH.2014.PARKS-20-1.KJJ.en

Jenkins, A.R. 2005. Lesser Kestrel *Falco naumanni*. In: *Roberts Birds of Southern Africa*, ed. by P.A.R. Hockey, et al. (Cape Town: Trustees of the John Voelcker Bird Book Fund).

Kaschula, S.A., W.E. Twine, and M.C. Scholes. 2005. Coppice harvesting of fuelwood species on a South African common: Utilizing scientific and indigenous knowledge in community based natural resource management. *Human Ecology* 33: 387–418. https://doi.org/10.1007/s10745-005-4144-7

Kelly, L.T., and L. Brotons. 2017. Using fire to promote biodiversity. *Science* 355: 1264–65. https://doi.org/10.1126/science.aam7672

Kennedy, A.D. 1998. Coppicing of *Tarconanthus camphoratus* (Compositae) as a source of sustainable fuelwood production: An example from the Laikipia Plateau, Kenya. *African Journal of Ecology* 36: 148–58. https://doi.org/10.1046/j.1365-2028.1998.00115.x

Kiboi, S., K. Fujiwara, and P. Mutiso. 2014. Sustainable management of urban green environments: Challenges and opportunities. In: *Sustainable Living with Environmental Risks*, ed. by N. Kaneko, et al. (Tokyo: Springer). https://doi.org/10.1007/978-4-431-54804-1

Kohler, S., M. Connan, J. Hill, et al. 2011. Geographic variation in the trophic ecology of an avian rocky shore predator, the African Black Oystercatcher, along the southern African coastline. *Marine Ecology Progress Series* 435: 235–49. https://doi.org/10.3354/meps09215

Kormos, R., C.F. Kormos, T. Humle, et al. 2014. Great apes and biodiversity offset projects in Africa: The case for national offset strategies. *PloS ONE* 9: e111671. https://doi.org/10.1371/journal.pone.0111671

Kraaij, T., R.M. Cowling, B.W. Wilgen, et al. 2013. Proteaceae juvenile periods and post-fire recruitment as indicators of minimum fire return interval in eastern coastal fynbos. *Applied Vegetation Science* 16: 84–94. https://doi.org/10.1111/j.1654-109X.2012.01209.x

Kyerematen, R., D. Acquah-Lamptey, E.H. Owusu, et al. 2014. Insect diversity of the Muni-Pomadze Ramsar site: An important site for biodiversity conservation in Ghana. *Journal of Insects* 2014: 985684. http://doi.org/10.1155/2014/985684

Kyerematen, R., S. Adu-Acheampong, D. Acquah-Lamptey, et al. 2018. Butterfly diversity: An indicator for environmental health within the Tarkwa Gold mine, Ghana. *Environment and Natural Resources Research* 8: 69–83. https://doi.org/10.5539/enrr.v8n3p69

Laporte, N.T., J.A. Stabach, R. Grosch, et al. 2007. Expansion of industrial logging in Central Africa. *Science* 316: 1451–1451. https://doi.org/10.1126/science.1141057

Lawrence, D., and K. Vandecar. 2015. Effects of tropical deforestation on climate and agriculture. *Nature Climate Change* 5: 27–36. https://doi.org/10.1038/nclimate2430

Lewis, R.R. 2005. Ecological engineering for successful management and restoration of mangrove forests. *Ecological Engineering* 24: 403–18. https://doi.org/10.1016/j.ecoleng.2004.10.003

Lindahl, U. 2003. Coral reef rehabilitation through transplantation of staghorn corals: Effects of artificial stabilization and mechanical damages. *Coral Reefs* 22: 217–23. https://doi.org/10.1007/s00338-003-0305-6

Lindenmayer, D.B., K.B. Hulvey, R.J. Hobbs, et al. 2012. Avoiding bio-perversity from carbon sequestration solutions. *Conservation Letters* 5: 28–36. https://doi.org/10.1111/j.1755-263X.2011.00213.x

Loarie, S.R., C.J. Tambling, and G.P. Asner. 2013. Lion hunting behaviour and vegetation structure in an African savanna. *Animal Behaviour* 85: 899–906. https://doi.org/10.1016/j.anbehav.2013.01.018

Lyons, A.J., W.C. Turner, and W.M. Getz. 2013. Home range plus: A space-time characterization of movement over real landscapes. *Movement Ecology* 1: 2. https://doi.org/10.1186/2051-3933-1-2

MacFarlane, D.M., S.D. Holness, A. von Hase, et al. 2016. *Wetland offsets: A best-practice guideline for South Africa* (Pretoria: SANBI and Department of Water and Sanitation). http://biodiversityadvisor.sanbi.org/wp-content/uploads/2014/09/Wetland-Offset-Guidelines-Version-7-For-stakeholder-comment.pdf

Maron, M., C.D. Ives, H. Kujala, et al. 2016. Taming a wicked problem: Resolving controversies in biodiversity offsetting. *BioScience* 66: 489–98. https://doi.org/10.1093/biosci/biw038

Martin, G.D., J.A. Coetzee, P.S.R. Weyl, et al. 2018. Biological control of *Salvinia molesta* in South Africa revisited. *Biological Control* 125: 7480. https://doi.org/10.1016/j.biocontrol.2018.06.011

Mashimbye, Z.E., M.A. Cho, J.P. Nel, et al. 2012. Model-based integrated methods for quantitative estimation of soil salinity from hyperspectral remote sensing data: A case study of selected South African soils. *Pedosphere* 22: 640–49. https://doi.org/10.1016/S1002-0160(12)60049-6

Masocha, M., A.K. Skidmore, X. Poshiwa, et al. 2011. Frequent burning promotes invasions of alien plants into a mesic African savanna. *Biological Invasions* 13: 1641–48. https://doi.org/10.1007/s10530-010-9921-6

Mbati, G., and P. Neuenschwander. 2005. Biological control of three floating water weeds, *Eichhornia crassipes, Pistia stratiotes,* and *Salvinia molesta* in the Republic of Congo."BioControl 50: 635–45. https://doi.org/10.1007/s10526-004-5863-1

McClanahan, T., J.M. Maina, and N.A. Muthiga. 2011. Associations between climate stress and coral reef diversity in the western Indian Ocean. *Global Change Biology* 17: 2023–2032. https://doi.org/10.1111/j.1365-2486.2011.02395.x

MEA (Millenium Ecosystem Assessment). 2005. *Ecosystems and Human Well-Being* (Covello: Island Press). https://www.millenniumassessment.org

Miyawaki, A. 2004. Restoration of the living environment based on vegetation ecology: Theory and practice. *Ecological Research* 19: 83–90. https://doi.org/10.1111/j.1440-1703.2003.00606.x

Mokany, K., S. Prasad, and D.A. Westcott. 2014. Loss of frugivore seed dispersal services under climate change. *Nature Communications* 5: 4971. https://doi.org/10.1038/ncomms4971

Mwangi, E., and B. Swallow. 2008. *Prosopis juliflora* invasion and rural livelihoods in the Lake Baringo area of Kenya. *Conservation and Society* 6: 130–40. https://doi.org/10.4103/0972-4923.49207

Naidoo, L., M.A. Cho, R. Mathieu, et al. 2012. Classification of savanna tree species, in the Greater Kruger National Park region, by integrating hyperspectral and LiDAR data in a Random Forest data mining environment. *ISPRS Journal of Photogrammetry and Remote Sensing* 69: 167–79. https://doi.org/10.1016/j.isprsjprs.2012.03.005

NASA. 2009. *ASTER Global Digital Elevation Model v. 2* (*GDEM V2*) (Pasadena: NASA JPL). https://doi.org/10.5067/ASTER/ASTGTM.002

NASA. 2013. *NASA Shuttle Radar Topography Mission Global 3 Arc Second Sub-Sampled* (*SRTM3*) (Sioux Falls: NASA LP DAAC). https://doi.org/10.5067/MEASURES/SRTM/SRTMGL3S.003

Nnoli, H., R. Kyerematen, S. Adu-Acheampong, et al. 2019. Change in aquatic insect abundance: Evidence of climate and land-use change within the Pawmpawm River in southern Ghana. *Cogent Environmental Science* 5: 1594511. https://doi.org/10.1080/23311843.2019.1594511

Panfil, S.N., and C.A. Harvey. 2015. REDD+ and biodiversity conservation: A review of the biodiversity goals, monitoring methods, and impacts of 80 REDD+ projects. *Conservation Letters* 9: 143–50. https://doi.org/10.1111/conl.12188

Papworth, S.K., J. Rist, L. Coad, et al. 2009. Evidence for shifting baseline syndrome in conservation. *Conservation Letters* 2: 93–100. https://doi.org/10.1111/j.1755-263X.2009.00049.x

Phelps, J., E.L. Webb, and L.P. Koh. 2011. Risky business: an uncertain future for biodiversity conservation finance through REDD+. *Conservation Letters* 4: 88–94. https://doi.org/10.1111/j.1755-263X.2010.00155.x

Pricope, N.G., and M.W. Binford. 2012. A spatio-temporal analysis of fire recurrence and extent for semi-arid savanna ecosystems in southern Africa using moderate-resolution satellite imagery. *Journal of Environmental Management* 100: 72–85. https://doi.org/10.1016/j.jenvman.2012.01.024

Rahlao, S.J., S.J. Milton, K.J. Esler, et al. 2010. The distribution of invasive *Pennisetum setaceum* along roadsides in western South Africa: The role of corridor interchanges. *Weed Research* 50: 537–43. https://doi.org/10.1111/j.1365-3180.2010.00801.x

Sanchez, P.A. 2010. Tripling crop yields in tropical Africa. *Nature Geoscience* 3: 299–300. https://doi.org/10.1038/ngeo853

Sato, G., A. Fisseha, S. Gebrekiros, et al. 2005. A novel approach to growing mangroves on the coastal mud flats of Eritrea with the potential for relieving regional poverty and hunger. *Wetlands* 25: 776. https://doi.org/10.1672/0277-5212(2005)025[0776:ANATGM]2.0.CO;2

Scantlebury, D.M., M.G.L. Mills, R.P. Wilson, et al. 2014. Flexible energetics of cheetah hunting strategies provide resistance against kleptoparasitism. *Science* 346: 79–81. https://doi.org/10.1126/science.1256424

Scott, J.M., B. Csuti, and F. Davis. 1991. Gap analysis: An application of Geographic Information Systems for wildlife species. In: *Challenges in the Conservation of Biological Resources: A Practitioner's Guide*, ed. by D.J. Decker, et al. (Boulder: Westview Press).

Sirami, C., S.S. Jacobs, and G.S. Cumming. 2013. Artificial wetlands and surrounding habitats provide important foraging habitat for bats in agricultural landscapes in the Western Cape, South Africa. *Biological Conservation* 164: 30–38. https://doi.org/10.1016/j.biocon.2013.04.017

Smit, I.P.J., and H.H.T. Prins. 2015. Predicting the effects of woody encroachment on mammal communities, Grazing biomass and fire frequency in African savannas. *PloS ONE* 10: e0137857. https://doi.org/10.1371/journal.pone.0137857

Smit, I.P.J., C.C. Grant, and B.J. Devereux. 2007. Do artificial waterholes influence the way herbivores use the landscape? Herbivore distribution patterns around rivers and artificial water sources in a large African savanna park. *Biological Conservation* 136: 85–99. https://doi.org/10.1016/j.biocon.2006.11.009

Suding, K.N. 2011. Toward an era of restoration in ecology: Successes, failures and opportunities ahead. *Annual Reviews in Ecology, Evolution, and Systematics* 42: 465–87. https://doi.org/10.1146/annurev-ecolsys-102710-145115

Symeonakis, E., and N. Drake. 2004. Monitoring desertification and land degradation over sub-Saharan Africa. *International Journal of Remote Sensing* 25: 573–92. https://doi.org/10.1080/0143116031000095998

ten Kate, K., J. Bishop, and R. Bayon. 2004. *Biodiversity offsets: Views, experience, and the business case* (Gland: IUCN; London: Insight Investment). https://www.iucn.org/sites/dev/files/import/downloads/bdoffsets.pdf

Torres, J., J.C. Brito, M.J. Vasconcelos, et al. 2010. Ensemble models of habitat suitability relate chimpanzee (*Pan troglodytes*) conservation to forest and landscape dynamics in Western Africa. *Biological Conservation* 143: 416–25. http://doi.org/10.1016/j.biocon.2009.11.007

Uys R.G., W.J. Bond, and T.M. Everson. 2004. The effect of different fire regimes on plant diversity in southern African grasslands. *Biological Conservation* 118: 489–99. https://doi.org/10.1016/j.biocon.2003.09.024

van Bochove, J., E. Sullivan, and T. Nakamura. 2014. *The Importance of Mangroves to People: A Call to Action* (Cambridge: UNEP). http://wedocs.unep.org/handle/20.500.11822/9300

van Wilgen, B.W., and A. Wannenburgh. 2016. Co-facilitating invasive species control, water conservation and poverty relief: Achievements and challenges in South Africa's Working for Water programme. *Current Opinion in Environmental Sustainability* 19: 7–17. http://doi.org/10.1016/j.cosust.2015.08.012

van Wilgen, B.W., and H.C. Biggs. 2011. A critical assessment of adaptive ecosystem management in a large savanna protected area in South Africa. *Biological Conservation* 144: 1179–87. https://doi.org/10.1016/j.biocon.2010.05.006

van Wilgen, B.W., and D.M. Richardson. 2014. Challenges and trade-offs in the management of invasive alien trees. *Biological Invasions* 16: 721–34. https://doi.org/10.1007/s10530-013-0615-8

van Wilgen, B.W., N. Govender, I.P.J. Smit, et al. 2014. The ongoing development of a pragmatic and adaptive fire management policy in a large African savanna protected area. *Journal of Environmental Management* 132: 358–68. http://dx.doi.org/10.1016/j.jenvman.2013.11.003

van Wilgen, B.W., G. Forsyth, and P. Prins. 2012. The management of fire-adapted ecosystems in an urban setting: The case of Table Mountain National Park, South Africa. *Ecology and Society* 17: 8. http://doi.org/10.5751/ES-04526-170108

van Wilgen, B.W., G.G. Forsyth, H. de Klerk, et al. 2010. Fire management in Mediterranean-climate shrublands: A case study from the Cape fynbos, South Africa. *Journal of Applied Ecology* 47: 631–38. https://doi.org/10.1111/j.1365-2664.2010.01800.x

van Wilgen, B.W., J.L. Nel, and M. Rouget. 2007. Invasive alien plants and South African rivers: A proposed approach to the prioritization of control operations. *Freshwater Biology* 52: 711–23. https://doi.org/10.1111/j.1365-2427.2006.01711.x

van Wyk, E., and B.W. van Wilgen. 2002. The cost of water hyacinth control in South Africa: A case study of three options. *African Journal of Aquatic Science* 27: 141–49. https://doi.org/10.2989/16085914.2002.9626585

Venter, F.J., R.J. Naiman, H.C. Biggs, et al. 2008. The evolution of conservation management philosophy: Science, environmental change and social adjustments in Kruger National Park. *Ecosystems* 11: 173–92. https://doi.org/10.1007/s10021-007-9116-x

Wallenfang, J., M. Finckh, J. Oldeland, et al, 2015. Impact of shifting cultivation on dense tropical woodlands in southeast Angola. *Tropical Conserveration Science* 8: 863–92. https://doi.org/10.1177/194008291500800402

Wegmann, M., L. Santini, B. Leutner, et al. 2014. Role of African protected areas in maintaining connectivity for large mammals. *Philosophical Transactions of the Royal Society of London B* 369: 20130193. https://doi.org/10.1098/rstb.2013.0193

Wetlands International. 2016. *Mangrove restoration: To plant or not to plant?* (Wageningen: Wetlands International). https://www.wetlands.org/publications/mangrove-restoration-to-plant-or-not-to-plant

Whitfield, A.K., G.C. Bate, T. Forbes, et al. 2013. Relinkage of the Mfolozi River to the St. Lucia estuary system—urgent imperative for the long-term management of a RAMSAR and World Heritage Site. *Aquatic Ecosystem Health and Management* 16: 104–10. https://doi.org/10.1080/14634988.2013.759081

Williams, A.E., R.E. Hecky, and H.C. Duthie. 2007. Water hyacinth decline across Lake Victoria—Was it caused by climatic perturbation or biological control? A reply. *Aquatic Botany* 87: 94–96. http://doi.org/10.1016/j.aquabot.2007.03.009

Wilson, J.R.U., P. Ivey, P. Manyama, et al. 2013. A new national unit for invasive species detection, assessment and eradication planning. *South African Journal of Science* 109: 0111. http://doi.org/10.1590/sajs.2013/20120111

Wilson, J.W., J.O. Sexton, R.R. Jobe, et al. 2013. The relative contribution of terrain, land cover, and vegetation structure indices to species distribution models. *Biological Conservation* 164: 170–76. https://doi.org/10.1016/j.biocon.2013.04.021

Zabbey, N., and F.B.G. Tanee. 2016. Assessment of asymmetric mangrove restoration trials in Ogoniland, Niger Delta, Nigeria: Lessons for future intervention. *Ecological Restoration* 34: 245–57. http://doi.org/10.3368/er.34.3.245

Zachariades, C., I.D. Paterson, L.W. Strathie, et al. 2017. Assessing the status of biological control as a management tool for suppression of invasive alien plants in South Africa. *Bothalia* 47: 1–19. http://dx.doi.org/10.4102/abc.v47i2.2142

Zalucki, M.P., M.D. Day, and J. Playford. 2007. Will biological control of *Lantana camara* ever succeed? Patterns, processes & prospects. *Biological Control* 42: 251–61. https://doi.org/10.1016/j.biocontrol.2007.06.002

Zarin, D.J., N.L. Harris, A. Baccini, et al. 2016. Can carbon emissions from tropical deforestation drop by 50% in 5 years? *Global Change Biology* 22: 1336–47. https://doi.org/10.1111/gcb.13153

11

Preventing Biodiversity Loss and Extinction

Tourists appreciating a southern right whale (*Eubalaena australis*, LC) from a whale charter boat operating from Hermanus, South Africa. Considered the "right" whale by 19th century whalers, the species was hunted to near extinction by the early 1900s, when only 300 individuals were left in the world (Reilly et al., 2013). Following the international ban on whale hunting, their populations have steadily recovered. Today it is considered safe from extinction, enabling towns such as Hermanus to base their thriving tourism industry on whale watching.

There are many examples in this textbook illustrating how species have been saved from the brink of extinction. For some, the solution was simple: halt the threats that caused their populations to decline. In other cases, more drastic steps were required, like moving the last remaining individuals into captivity until the threats have been reversed. Many species that persist with low population sizes would likely not have survived without human intervention (Figure 11.1).

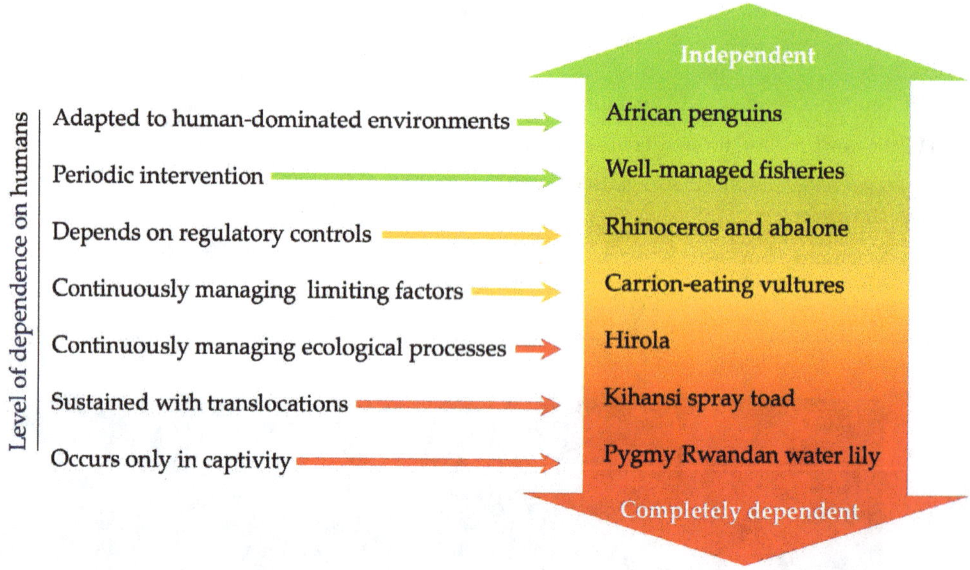

Figure 11.1 The continuum of species management approaches. Some threatened species exist under such low population sizes that they depend on active human intervention for recovery, while others can persist with minimal intervention.

In each of these success stories, the most important first steps involved determining the ecological needs of the species at risk and understanding the factors that made that species vulnerable to extinction (Section 8.5). This chapter reviews some of the most important concepts for understanding and managing those needs and risks. The concepts reviewed in this chapter include methods to study species and populations, actions that can be taken to increase population sizes, and strategies that can help maintain evolutionary processes such as genetic exchange. This chapter also considers how to manage for climate change and discuss the importance of ex situ conservation strategies.

11.1 Studying Species and Populations

To save a species from extinction, it is vital to have a firm grasp on the species' distinctive characters, in other words its **natural history**. To obtain this natural history information, 10 important factors need to be considered:

- *Population biology*: How many individuals are there in the population? How many males, females, juveniles, breeding adults, and individuals past breeding age are there? What is the species' life expectancy? How have these aspects changed over time? (see also Chapter 9)

> To save a species from extinction, it is vital to have a firm grasp on the species' distinctive characters, in other words its natural history.

- *Habitat*: In what kind of environment can the species be found? How do these ecosystems change over time and space? Does the species have a complex life history that requires multiple habitats (e.g. frogs that live on land generally need water for breeding)? What factors are important to maintain suitable habitat?
- *Distribution*: Where in the world can the species of concern be found? At what rate is its distribution increasing/decreasing? What factors drive these increases/decreases?
- *Morphology*: What are the defining traits, or range of traits, of the species' appearance? How do the species' unique morphological characteristics help it survive? Are there closely-related species that appear similar (i.e. cryptic species) and with which it can be misidentified?
- *Limiting resources*: What types of resources does the species need to survive? Are any of these resources in short supply? Does the distribution of these important resources change over time and space?
- *Physiology*: Are there any special requirements the species' physical and biochemical processes need for it to grow, survive, and reproduce? What are the conditions under which meeting these requirements is especially hard?
- *Behaviour*: How do individuals act or behave (Box 11.1)? Is the species sedentary, nomadic, or migratory? Do individuals group together, disperse at random throughout landscapes, or space themselves out at regular distances? How do these behaviours help it survive?
- *Genetics*: How much do genes vary within the species? How are the species' genetics linked to its morphology, physiology, and behaviour? Are there local genetic adaptations? Is the genetic variation in key traits sufficient to allow the species to adapt to environmental changes? Are there any deleterious genetic concerns? (Section 8.7.1)
- *Biological interactions*: In what ways do individuals of the species interact with each other and with other species? Which of these interactions are critical for survival? Are there any competitors, predators, parasites, or diseases affecting the species?
- *Interactions with humans*: How sensitive is the species to human activity? Do humans use the species in any way? Is the species sustainably harvested? Is the species associated with human-wildlife conflict (Section 14.4)?

Box 11.1 The Overlooked Role of Behavioural Ecology in the Conservation of African Mammals

Adrian M Shrader

Mammal Research Institute,
Department of Zoology and Entomology,
University of Pretoria, South Africa.
✉ *adrian.shrader@up.ac.za*

When considering the management and conservation of wild animals, topics linked to population and community ecology (e.g. carrying capacity, Hayward et al., 2007a) often come to mind. This is not surprising, as these disciplines consider broad patterns of population dynamics (e.g. birth rates and mortality rates), which are key to achieving management and conservation goals. While this information is necessary, in many instances, it fails to explain the mechanisms behind the patterns observed and answer key questions. For example, why do species prefer specific habitats? Why do some herbivores adjust their home ranges with the seasons? To answer these sorts of questions, we need to understand an animal's behavioural ecology.

Take for example the challenge of understanding the impacts that elephants cause within protected areas. A standard way to assess these impacts is to record which tree species are damaged and how many trees are affected (e.g. broken branches, bark stripping) (Boundja and Midgley, 2010). While this provides information on the trees most vulnerable to elephant damage, it does not explain why elephants are damaging the trees. Is it because the trees are a key part of the elephants' diet, or are these trees just abundant across the landscape and in the way of a moving herd? To answer these questions, we turn to behavioural ecology. By observing foraging elephants, or by walking down their feeding paths after they have left, we can determine the animals' diet, and generate an acceptability index (number eaten ÷ number available) of each tree species (Shrader et al., 2012). These data allow us to better understand the reasons behind elephant damage.

Other situations where behavioural ecology can help include reintroductions, population management, and human-animal conflict mitigation. For example, in South Africa, oribi are locally threatened by habitat loss and poaching. One conservation strategy is to relocate individuals away from known threats. Oribi are grassland specialists (Figure 11.A) that require both short and tall grasslands—therefore, release sites require a mosaic of these habitats. Moreover, within grasslands oribi perceive woodland patches to be dangerous, and tend to avoid feeding within 15 m of them (Stears and Shrader, 2015). If we do not consider how oribi utilise their environment, our estimate of available habitat at a release site may be greater than the area utilised. This mistake could reduce relocation success.

Figure 11.A The oribi is a grassland specialist that requires both short and tall grasslands and tends to forage at least 15 m from wooded patches.

With regards to population management, behavioural ecology is central to the conservation of southern white rhinoceros (*Ceratotherium simum simum*, NT) in the Hluhluwe-iMfolozi Park, South Africa. Within the park, the management policy incorporates space use and social ecology of the rhinos to facilitate population regulation (i.e. dispersal). To do this, the population can grow in the central core of the park. When rhino numbers get too high in the core, individuals naturally disperse into surrounding low-density areas, at which point they are captured by wildlife officers and transported to other areas. Thus, rhino behaviour itself is used to indicate when there are too many individuals within the fenced park (Linklater and Shrader, 2017).

Finally, behavioural ecology has helped reduce human-elephant conflict through the understanding that elephants are afraid of bees and will avoid feeding close to them. To capitalise on this fear, fences that incorporate beehives were designed and constructed around agricultural fields in northern Kenya, which helped reduce crop damage from raiding elephants. Of 32 raids recorded in the area, only one was at a farm with a beehive fence (King et al., 2011). These examples showcase how behavioural ecology can support, expand, and strengthen management and conservation of wildlife. These same principles can be applied to protect a wide range of animals across Africa, and elsewhere.

Understanding the natural history of a species directly informs conservation strategies. For example, if we know where a species occurs and what its habitat needs are, we are in a better position to prioritise which areas need to be protected or how ecosystems need to be restored. Similarly, if we know that an important food resource is missing, perhaps during a drought or due to human activities, conservationists could provide supplemental feeding until the limiting resource has recovered (Figure 11.2). Depending on the species in question, some factors play a more important role than others. For example, managing a disease outbreak may play a more important role in the conservation of a widespread migratory bird (that can spread diseases to other species), while managing for genetic diversity may play a more prominent role in the conservation of a small population of fishes restricted to only one lake. For many widespread species, different factors affect different subpopulations. In such cases each subpopulation might need to be managed as its own **evolutionary significant unit** (**ESU**; see e.g. Dubach et al., 2013) to retain unique local adaptations and genetic markers.

Figure 11.2 In some areas where diminishing food supplies threaten vulture populations, conservationists are supplementing their diets by placing carcasses at "vulture restaurants". These vulture restaurants often depend on cooperation with local farmers who donate livestock that have died.

11.1.1 Obtaining natural history data

Conservationists rely on several resources and techniques to obtain natural history information. Initial steps often involve reviewing published and unpublished literature to understand what is known (and not known) about a species. Literature reviews do have some drawbacks: they can take a long time, may uncover contradictory information, and may lack critical information relevant to a local area or specific population. For this reason, and especially when decisions need to be made under tight schedules, conservation biologists may need to speed up their initial species review by sourcing natural history information from subject matter experts who are familiar with the species or ecosystem of concern.

Conservation biologists are also increasingly recognising the importance of **traditional ecological knowledge (TEK)**—detailed insights that rural people have on the ecology, behaviour, and distribution of the species around where they live (Shackeroff and Campbell, 2007; Brook and McLachlan, 2008). For example, while termites are often considered a pest by people living in urban settings, scientists are increasingly relying on TEK to understand the important contributions of termites to food security to human health, as well as to learn about ecological sustainable methods for their control when needed (Sileshi et al., 2009).

Conservation biologists are increasingly recognising the importance of traditional ecological knowledge—detailed insights that rural people have on the species around them.

While literature reviews, expert opinions, and traditional ecological knowledge are important first steps to collect natural history information, the most reliable method remains fieldwork, where multiple individuals from the population of concern in the area of interest are observed repeatedly over time. Indeed, most of natural history information we have today was obtained during detailed notetaking by naturalists—biologists who dedicate much of their time to better understand the natural world—in the field.

Unfortunately, there are still major gaps in our understanding of the living world. Consequently, a very large number of threatened species, including better-known groups (e.g. reptiles, Tolley et al., 2016), lack the kinds of data necessary to ensure that we can give them the best chance of survival. Filling these gaps is also becoming harder since it is costly and sometimes logistically impossible (or dangerous) for naturalists to spend an extended period in the field. There is also a trade-off in the breadth and depth of data collection possible: the more area one covers, the less detailed the data; conversely, when one collects more detailed data, the scope of the study is reined in for logistical constraints. Further, there is also a limit to the number of organisms any one individual observer can study at any one time.

Recent technological advances have greatly increased our ability to overcome the logistical constraints that impede conservation fieldwork. One of the most useful developments involves the miniaturisation (and reduced costs) of animal-borne **biologging devices**, such as radio telemetry and GPS tags (Kays et al., 2015). Previously reserved for projects with large grants that focused on large animals, the big clunky devices of a few decades ago have made way for devices small enough to fit comfortably on animals as small as beetles and frogs. Some biologging devices are now also solar-powered and transmit data through Earth observation satellites in real time, allowing researchers to track the behaviours of several organisms at a time from the comfort of their offices. Even better, some tracking technologies also collect environmental data and movement data simultaneously, allowing us to better understand how wildlife responds to changing environmental conditions. These new and sophisticated datasets can then be used to better understand threats to species (e.g. Scantlebury et al., 2014; Childress et al., 2016) and inform management of protected areas (e.g. Maxwell et al., 2011).

Species distribution modelling (SDM), also known as environmental niche modelling, is becoming increasingly popular for determining a species' distribution and habitat needs. SDMs overlay species location data, obtained during field work or using biologging devices, onto a selection of relevant environmental variables (e.g. forest cover, elevation, soil type) using GIS software, after which special modelling algorithms estimate the species' ecological niche and distribution (Figure 11.3, see also Figure 10.3). This information enables conservation biologists to identify previously unknown habitat patches (which may represent undiscovered and unprotected populations) or empty habitats (which may be used in translocations, see Section 11.2). The appeal of SDMs lies in the availability of user-friendly software packages that can use very limited datasets. For example, one study from West Africa successfully combined market survey data and SDM to determine the potential for sustainable extraction of 12 medicinal plant species (van Andel et al., 2015). Another study used SDMs to develop a holistic picture of diversity and endemism patterns of nearly all 250 African bat species (Herkt et al., 2016). While distribution modelling offers very useful conservation tools, it is important to learn about the different techniques under the guidance of an expert to avoid making costly mistakes (McPherson et al., 2006; Pearson et al., 2006).

Species distribution modelling, also known as environmental niche modelling, is becoming increasingly popular for determining a species' distribution and habitat needs.

Experimentation offers powerful methods to better understand competing theories and hypotheses, and to gain insight into how specific management actions may influence population dynamics. Experimentation is often associated with controlled environments such as laboratories; however, this is often impossible and sometimes even unethical to perform laboratory experiments on threatened species. Instead, conservation researchers may opt for natural experiments, which allows for the target species or population to be studied in its natural ecosystem.

A chronosequence study is a special type of natural experiment that overcome the long-term commitment some studies require to attain meaningful results. Also called space-for-time experiments, chronosequence studies allow us to infer long-term trends over a short study period using study systems that share similar qualities but are differently aged. Chronosequence studies are particularly popular when studying ecological restoration projects (Section 10.3) since some ecological processes often require many decades to develop (Bonnell et al., 2011). In one such example, conservation biologists needed only three summers worth of vegetation surveys to

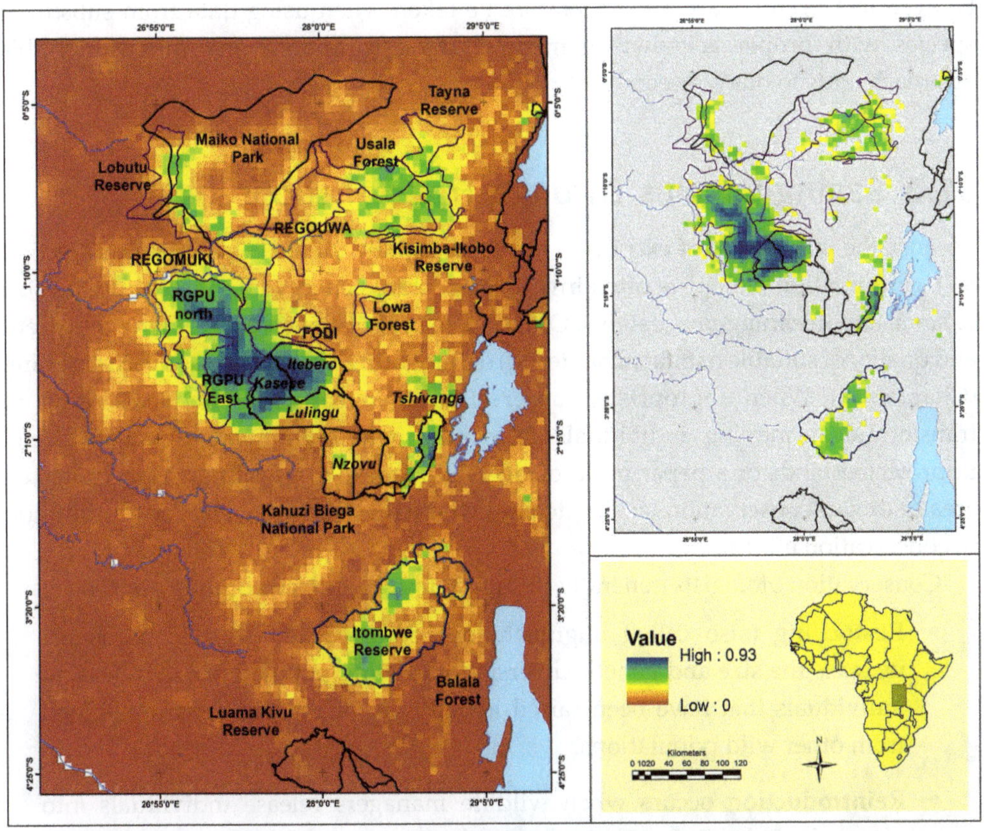

Figure 11.3 A species distribution model over the global range of the Grauer's gorilla. Purple and green areas indicate potentially suitable habitat while yellow and red areas indicate unsuitable habitat. The analysis highlighted that the gorilla is found in high-altitude forests far from deforestation activity. The map also shows which areas should be safeguarded to secure the species' survival.

show that some species recolonise coastal dune forests in the Maputaland-Podoland-Albany Biodiversity Hotspot only after 100 years since disturbance (Wassenaar et al., 2005).

Sometimes, despite their best efforts, biologists may still fail (or may not have enough time) to obtain much needed natural history information during a critical period. To overcome such a challenge, biologists have, at times, used natural history information of a **substitute species** (which is different from **surrogate species**, Section 13.3.5) to fill data gaps for a rare species (Caro et al., 2005). An example of this application comes from the USA where researchers used behavioural observations of a common butterfly to predict dispersal of another closely related butterfly that was too rare to properly study (Hudgens et al., 2012). It is important to note that using information from substitute species does have serious limits (Henry et al., 2019). For example, considering that different populations of a *single species* may have very different environmental needs and adaptations, using data from a *different species* may be even less useful. Care must therefore be taken when using data from substitute species with proper acknowledgement of the assumptions and uncertainty this approach adds to one's research.

11.2 Saving Species Through Translocations

Because the probability of extinction increases rapidly for small populations (Section 8.7), conservation biologists often invest considerable energy into increasing the size of small and declining populations. Often, these projects involve improving the extent and quality of suitable habitat (Chapter 10) or mitigating threats such as overharvesting (Chapter 12). When appropriate, conservation biologists may sometimes resort to translocations—moving individuals from sites where they are threatened (e.g. unprotected lands or a paper park) or overabundant (e.g. a well-managed protected area or ex situ conservation facility) to sites where they can offer a larger contribution to conservation efforts.

Conservation biologists generally recognise four basic translocation approaches:

- **Restocking** (also called augmentation) occurs when wildlife managers increase the size and genetic diversity of existing populations, by releasing individuals that have been raised in captivity or that have been obtained from other wild populations.
- **Reintroduction** occurs when wildlife managers release individuals into areas where they occurred in the past but not at present. The areas must be ecologically suitable and the factors that caused the extirpation must have been reduced or eliminated for a reintroduction to be successful.
- **Introduction** involves creating new populations by moving individuals to suitable areas outside that species' historical range. Introductions are usually considered when reintroductions are impossible because the species' historical range has been degraded too severely or because persistent threats will lead to reintroduction failure.
- **Assisted colonisation** (also called assisted migration) is a special class of introduction where biologists "assist" species with poor dispersal capabilities to adapt their ranges in response to environmental changes. It is anticipated that this strategy will become an important conservation tool in preventing extinctions where climate change outpaces the speed of natural migration.

Understanding a species' ecological needs is critically important for translocations, because it influences the choice of release site and type of preparations needed.

11.2.1 Important considerations for translocations

Section 11.1 broadly discussed the importance of understanding the ecological and other natural history needs when protecting threatened species. Understanding a species' ecological needs is equally, if not more, important for translocations, because it influences the choice of release site and type of preparations needed (Figure 11.4). Complementing the 10 factors mentioned in Section 11.1, the next section briefly introduces some of the most important considerations during translocations.

Figure 11.4 A team of wildlife rehabilitators release a group of Cape vultures (*Gyps coprotheres*, EN) near a vulture restaurant in South Africa. Releasing the vultures near a supplemental food source greatly enhances their chances for survival after release. The vultures have wing tags to enable monitoring of each individual after release.

Determining need and feasibility

Perhaps the most important factor to consider before starting a translocation is to determine whether it is necessary. Translocations carry risks, not only for the target population to be moved, but also the individuals left behind and for the recipient ecosystem. These risks expose translocation projects to a high risk of failure, particularly if preparations are inadequate and essential resources (e.g. funding, trained staff) are in short supply. Translocations also demand considerable resources—resources that can at times be better spent mitigating the threats the target population face. While these considerations may seem obvious, a recent review found that *most* translocations projects are initiated without proper cost-benefit analyses (Pérez et al., 2012). To improve translocation practices, conservationists seriously considering a translocation project are encouraged to review the 10 criteria outlined in Pérez et al. (2012), some of which also overlap with the considerations mentioned below.

Support from local stakeholders

It is also important to consider, at an early stage, how the public will view the translocation project. Some people may feel the resources used in a translocation are better invested elsewhere; others dislike translocations because they view it as a threat to their livelihood—this is especially true when carnivores are involved (Gusset et al., 2008a). Because of these and other potential conflicts and emotions, it is crucial that translocation projects (like any conservation activity) obtain the support from local stakeholders at an early stage. It is helpful to be transparent from the outset and to explain the project's goals, as well as the benefits the local community may gain (e.g. attract more tourists, restore a degraded ecosystem service). Good public outreach also provides opportunities to address the public's concerns and misconceptions about the project and about biodiversity conservation in general.

Identifying suitable habitat

It goes without saying that the probability for success is greatly improved when the translocated individuals are released in good quality habitat. This is particularly true for species with poor dispersal capabilities, such as plants that reproduce through vegetative propagation: the plants could die in an environment that is too sunny, shady, wet, or dry. While this point may seem obvious, many translocations fail because individuals are released in inferior habitats (Armstrong and Seddon, 2007). One of the reasons for this potential habitat mismatch is because wildlife may perceive the environment differently than humans, so a site that may look good to the human eye may lack one or more overlooked limiting resource. **Refugee species**—species forced to live in suboptimal habitat due to threats present in their preferred habitat (e.g. Ali et al., 2017)—also present a challenge to biologists who may unwittingly view inferior habitat as optimal and base conservation decisions on essentially bad information. The same challenge presents itself at **ecological traps**—unsuitable environments that an organism mistakenly perceives as optimal habitat (e.g. Sherley et al., 2017). These are some of the most important reasons why biologists need to be cautions when using species distribution models (SDM) when identifying areas suitable for translocations. To mitigate costly translocation failures, it is advisable that releases start small, and have multiple phases, to assess how released individuals respond to their new environment. Conducting experimental and adaptive releases can also reduce uncertainty by evaluating different release scenarios (Menges et al., 2016).

> Species forced to live in suboptimal habitat due to threats present in their preferred habitat may lead biologists to unwittingly view inferior habitat as optimal.

It is also important to ensure that any habitat identified as suitable is free from threats such as pollution and invasive species that may lead to declining health or even death for released individuals. A project in the Cape Floristic Region in South Africa provides a good example of how alert conservation biologists mitigated a threat that could have caused a translocation failure. The Clanwilliam sandfish (*Labeo seeberi*, EN) was once widespread in the region's Olifants-Doring River system. However, recent surveys indicated that the species had gone extinct in the Olifants River. Although biologists did find some juvenile fish in the Doring River and some of its tributaries, they also noticed that invasive fish predated on most of those juveniles before they reached adulthood (Jordaan et al., 2017). These ill-fated individuals were thus dispersing from the last remaining reproductive subpopulation persisting in the headwaters of one single Doring tributary to other parts of the river, which acted as a population sink. To prevent the species' extinction, biologists initiated a habitat restoration plan involving restoring natural stream flow regimens and eradicating predatory invasive fish in the headwaters of a second Doring tributary. They then installed barriers that prevented invasive fish from reaching the restored area before translocating 338 juvenile fish (Figure 11.5) there. With this habitat restoration plan, the biologists hope to establish a second viable population, and to improve the juveniles' chances of surviving to adulthood before they disperse back to areas where the invasive fishes occur (Jordaan et al., 2017).

Figure 11.5 (Top) Conservation biologists collecting threatened Clanwilliam sandfish for a reintroduction project in the Cape Floristic Region, South Africa.
4.0. (Bottom) A close-up view of Clanwilliam sandfish.

Considering genetics and behaviour

Translocation projects also need to consider the genetic makeup, social organisation, and behaviour of a species that is being released. It is preferable to use individuals from the same genetic stock as individuals that already occur (or have occurred) in the release area to avoid outbreeding depression and to capture local adaptations (Sections 8.7.1). Such efforts simultaneously also contribute to conservation of genetic diversity, as opposed to the pollution thereof if individuals from different genetic stock are mixed.

Group-living species, particularly those vulnerable to Allee effects (Section 8.7.2), need to be released in sufficient numbers so they can maintain their natural social organisation and behaviour. For species that need to be released in groups, it is preferable to release socially integrated animals rather than individuals unfamiliar with each other (Gusset et al., 2008b). Releasing groups of animals does have its own set of challenges. For example, social groups abruptly released from captivity may disperse explosively, possibly leading to project failure. This happened with African buffalo (*Syncerus caffer*, NT) herds translocated to South Africa's Addo Elephant National Park which fragmented into smaller groups after release, making them more vulnerable to lion (*Panthera leo*, VU) predation (Tambling et al., 2013). Fortunately, in this case, the buffaloes underwent several behavioural modifications over time, which eventually allowed their numbers to stabilise (Box 11.2). This contrasts with failed rock hyrax (*Procavia capensis*, LC) reintroductions in South Africa, where group disintegration post release exposed the animals to unsustainable predation levels (Wimberger et al., 2009).

How many individuals to release

The ultimate aim of translocation projects is to establish **ecologically relevant** populations, meaning populations that are self-sustaining, free from inbreeding, and an interactive participant of its community and ecosystem. The probability of achieving this goal increases as more individuals are being released. Because translocation projects typically do not have an unlimited supply of individuals to release, wildlife managers often rely on quantitative models (Section 9.2) to estimate the minimum number of individuals that should be released and how many times releases should occur. For example, a population viability analysis (PVA) on western lowland gorillas (*Gorilla gorilla gorilla*, CR) reintroduced to Gabon and the Republic of the Congo showed that the probability of persistence of an apparently established population could be increased significantly if more individuals were released (King et al., 2014).

> The ability to establish new populations through translocations does not reduce the need to protect threatened species still in their natural habitats.

While releasing more individuals certainly improves the likelihood of establishing a self-sustaining population, it is also important to determine how many individuals

Box 11.2 Large Predator Reintroductions: A Balancing Act

Craig J. Tambling

Department of Zoology and Entomology, University of Fort Hare, Alice, South Africa.

✉ *ctambling@ufh.ac.za*

Large predator numbers are declining, and African carnivores are no exception (Ripple et al. 2014). How to conserve African carnivores are a hotly debated topic now, with "fortress" type conservation areas considered the most viable option by many (Packer et al., 2013). In South Africa, this conservation model is the norm, and many small protected areas are now translocating large carnivores for ecotourism. However, these large carnivore translocations have repercussions for resident prey species. Understanding the ecological and biodiversity consequences of these translocations is thus important for the management of these small protected areas (Tambling et al., 2014).

In 2003, lions and spotted hyenas (*Crocuta crocuta*, LC) were reintroduced into the Addo Elephant National Park Main Camp Section after being absent from the area for over 100 years. Post-release monitoring of the six reintroduced lions indicated that at least 50% of their diet in the first two years following reintroduction was African buffalo. This was especially concerning to South African National Parks as this resident buffalo population contributes substantially to game auction sales each year, with the money raised being used to expand the national park system in South Africa (SANParks, 2009).

Following high predation rates of buffalo by lion and a 2007 buffalo census suggesting low juvenile recruitment, the coexistence of lion and buffalo in Addo was questioned. These concerns lead to a detailed assessment of buffalo behaviour and demographics between 2008 and 2011 (Tambling et al., 2012), which showed that by 2008–2009, juvenile buffalo recruitment (Figure 11.B) had rebounded to levels reminiscent of those prior to the lion reintroduction. Direct observations of the buffalo population showed drastic behavioural alteration following the high initial predation rates by lions. These behavioural changes included: (1) increased breeding herd sizes, (2) a reduction in nocturnal movement, and (3) greater use of open habitats at night and early morning when lions are hunting. These behavioural adjustments enabled the active defence of the breeding herds, reducing successful predation by lions and ensuring an increase in buffalo recruitment. Although this study suggests that prey populations are capable of behavioural adjustments to reduce predation, this is not always the case, with some species unable to respond, leading to precipitous declines in prey populations such as eland (*Tragelaphus oryx*, LC) (Leaver, 2014).

Figure 11.B After lions were reintroduced into the Addo Elephant National Park Main Camp Section, high levels of predation of buffalo (in particular, juveniles) prompted an investigation into the demographics and behaviour of the buffalo population. Results showed that buffalo were adjusting their behaviour to make greater use of open habitats, which subsequently led to improved juvenile buffalo survival.

Case studies of predator-prey interactions following large predator reintroductions highlight the management challenges faced by small reserves where ecotourism, biodiversity, and financial goals each need to be met. Due to the small size of these "fortress" reserves, a local overabundance of predators can have severe ecological effects on prey populations. However, in many reserves, the high demand for large predators for ecotourism often results in costly reactive, rather than scientifically sound proactive, management. There is, however, a growing body of research on the proactive management of large carnivores, where wildlife managers aim to replicate ecological processes (i.e. lion inter-birth intervals) to limit management interventions required to control large predator numbers (Ferreira and Hofmeyr, 2014). In small reserves, lion inter-birth intervals are shorter than in large ecosystems, and so lengthening the inter-birth intervals to that observed in large ecosystems can reduce lion population growth rate in these small reserves (Miller et al., 2015). Understanding predator-prey interactions is important regardless of the conservation model employed to protect these large charismatic species.

The ultimate aim of most translocation projects is to establish populations that are self-sustaining, free from inbreeding, and interactive participants of their communities and ecosystems.

the target community *can* sustain. In other words, the release area should contain enough suitable habitat to support the territories of *all* the released individuals. To determine how many individuals can be sustained, wildlife managers may calculate the release area's **carrying capacity**—an estimate of the maximum number of individuals an ecosystem can support. The carrying capacity concept has its roots in the livestock trade, where farmers wanted to maximise the number of animals on their land without risking overgrazing. While the concept has gained popularity in conservation biology in recent decades, calculating the carrying capacity for wildlife is very complex because of all the multi-faceted interactions that characterise healthy ecosystems. For example, the carrying capacity for a wild population can depend on factors such as food, water, shelter, soil nutrients, and sunlight availability, as well as more species-specific natural history factors such as habitat quality, home range, sex ratios (Tambling et al., 2014), and interactions with other species (Lindsey et al., 2011).

Over the past few decades, through trial and error, adaptive management (Section 10.2.3), and the collection of vast amounts of demographic data, scientists have made significant progress in calculating carrying capacity for wildlife populations. Perhaps the most progress has been made in calculating carrying capacities for large ungulates, by monitoring vegetation biomass, which in turn is affected by soil nutrients and rainfall (Fritz and Duncan, 1994). Much progress has also been made in calculating carrying capacities of predators by monitoring prey densities (Hayward et al., 2007a). For most populations, however, carrying capacity isn't explicitly calculated, but implicitly estimated based on intuition. Refining existing carrying capacity models and developing new methods for other taxa remain an active area of research that will hopefully reduce conservation biologists' over-reliance on intuition in future years. But even in the absence of carrying capacity calculations, wildlife managers can track a population's health and overall fitness. When the health of a particularly successful population or its environment starts declining, a root cause may be that too many individuals have been released, or the population is being sustained above carrying capacity.

Preparing individuals for release

Translocation projects using individuals obtained from the wild are generally much more successful than those using captive-bred individuals, given that wild individuals are already adapted to a life where they must fend for themselves. Nevertheless, some projects may have to use captive-bred individuals, particularly when the target species is extinct in the wild, or when individuals were brought to an ex situ conservation facility because it is easier to breed them under human care in controlled conditions. In such cases, a great amount of effort may be required to prepare the captive-bred individuals for releases.

> A great amount of effort may be required to prepare captive-bred individuals for translocation because they may have lost adaptations required for survival and reproduction in the wild.

A major drawback when using captive-bred individuals is that they may have lost the important adaptations required for survival and successful reproduction in the wild. Pre-release training, which varies according to the species, can sometimes overcome this drawback. For predators, it may involve providing low risk prey, such as chickens and domestic rabbits in holding facilities until their hunting skills are better developed (Houser et al., 2011). For plants propagated indoors, it may involve hardening them off by placing them outside for increasingly longer periods to gradually introduce them to sun, wind, and temperature changes during the day. To help young birds disassociate humans from food, human trainers sometimes use puppets or wear costumes (Figure 11.6) during feeding time to mimic the appearance and behaviour of wild individuals (Valutis and Marzluff, 1999). Another method, which may promote behavioural enrichment, involves **cross-fostering**, in which unrelated parents helps raise the offspring of a threatened species. In carnivore conservation, this technique has shown much promise to augment litter size and encourage gene flow using orphaned African wild dog (*Lycaon pictus*, EN) pups (McNutt et al., 2008). Interspecific cross-fostering has also been used in bird conservation, where biologists use common species to incubate eggs abandoned by threatened species (e.g. Powell and Cuthbert, 1993). However, cross-fostering using different species may lead to a new set of problems, like behavioural changes and hybridisation, if the young subsequently associate with the wrong species. A great amount of care and research are thus needed before such strategies are attempted.

Figure 11.6 Wattled cranes (*Grus carunculate*, VU) sometimes lay two eggs, but always abandon the second egg. Conservation biologists in South Africa are collecting the discarded eggs, which are then hatched in a captive breeding programme. To avoid the captive chicks associating humans with food and safety after release, handlers use special crane costumes when interacting with the birds.

Whether using captive-bred or wild individuals for translocations, individuals may have to be fed, sheltered, trained, or otherwise cared for after release to give them time to become more familiar with their new surroundings. This approach, known as **soft release**, involves keeping the released individuals in pre-release holding facilities for a period; it may also include some form of assistance after release to increase opportunities for success. Soft releases also provide an opportunity to introduce captive-bred organisms to wild individuals of the same species that can act as "instructors" for survival in the new environment, or for unfamiliar individuals to bond into cohesive units (Gusset et al., 2006).

The alternative to soft release is a **hard release**—an abrupt release of individuals from captivity without assistance such as food supplementation. While hard releases are popular (because they are relatively easy to perform), it is a risky strategy that faces a high risk to failure (Brown et al., 2007; Wimberger et al., 2009). Hard releases can however be appropriate under the right conditions (Hayward et al., 2007b). For example, hard releases are often use in **head-starting** programmes (Figure 11.7) for reptiles and amphibians (Scheele et al., 2014), where conservation biologists collect wild individuals and raise them past their most vulnerable life stages before releasing them again where they were collected.

Figure 11.7 Local children releasing leatherback sea turtles (*Dermochelys coriacea*, VU) as part of an environmental education project in Equatorial Guinea. Known as head-starting, conservationists would sometimes collect sea turtle eggs in the wild, hatched in captivity, and raise the offspring past their most vulnerable stage before releasing them back where they were found.

Post-release monitoring

A translocation project does not end after the last individual was released. Rather, ongoing monitoring should be implemented to determine whether a translocation was successful, what degree of success was achieved, whether adaptive management is needed, whether additional releases should be conducted, or whether the project should be aborted. A well-designed monitoring plan can also highlight the consequences of translocation on the broader ecosystem, such as the impact that predators introduced to a new area may have on prey populations (Box 11.2) and competing species (Groom et al., 2017). Because some responses in translocated populations can be rather subtle and take many years to show or subside, post-release monitoring should ideally be a long-term endeavour. For example, by monitoring seemingly successful elephant reintroductions across five protected areas in South Africa, researchers found that stress hormones in released animals continued to decline 24 years post release (Jachowski et al., 2013). Long-term monitoring will also help wildlife managers better understand the ultimate fate of the released individuals. Many apparently successful translocations fail because the released individuals die after several years without ever reproducing. Highlighting the importance of post-release monitoring, one study from South Africa found that 70% of captive-bred oribi (*Oribia oribi*, LC) died within two months of release, mostly due to predation (Grey-Ross et al., 2009). Another study found that reintroduced cheetahs were all killed within a year of release (Houser et al., 2011). These were expensive lessons, but post-release monitoring ensured that the reason for failures are known and can be addressed ahead of future releases.

Helping other translocation projects

Strategies used in successful translocation projects were nearly always informed by releases conducted by other wildlife managers who circulated their experiences to the wider conservation community. It is important to pay this effort forward; new translocation projects should make every effort to track and publish their results to inform others. While it is always easier to present the results of successful projects, publishing the lessons from failed projects is also important (Wimberger et al., 2010; Godefroid et al., 2011). Equally important is the publication of project costs, to enable wildlife managers to better determine under which conditions translocations represent a cost-effective conservation strategy. For example, a large African wild dog reintroduction programme in South Africa achieved their initial goal of establishing nine self-sustaining packs much more quickly than expected—five years rather than 10—yet reintroducing all these populations cost 20 times more than if the funds were used to enhance protection of existing packs within protected areas (Lindsey et al., 2005). With more information available, future conservationists would hopefully be able to have better guidelines to maximise cost-effectiveness and the likelihood of project success.

11.3 Managing and Facilitating Movement Dynamics

Some ecosystems are transient in nature—their character is temporary and will change because of disturbance and succession. Consequently, species that occupy those transient habitats are bound to be naturally extirpated at one time or another. Consider, for example, a small population of wildflowers occurring in a river's floodplain; at some stage, there is going to be a flood that will wash away those flowers. But the flooding also disperses seeds downstream, allowing for new wildflower populations to establish in suitable habitat elsewhere. These shifting populations linked by movements between them are better characterised as a **metapopulation** (a "population of populations") (Figure 11.8) consisting of several subpopulations. For some metapopulations, every subpopulation is transient: their distribution changes dramatically with each generation. Other metapopulations involve relatively permanent subpopulations with only a few individuals dispersing each generation. Some metapopulations consist of one or more **source populations** whose sizes are stable or increasing, and several **sink populations** whose sizes fluctuate depending on environmental conditions. Some sink subpopulations may undergo such dramatic fluctuations that they would be extirpated in unfavourable years were it not for **population rescue** by immigrants from source populations.

A metapopulation (a "population of populations") consists of several subpopulations linked by movements of individuals between them.

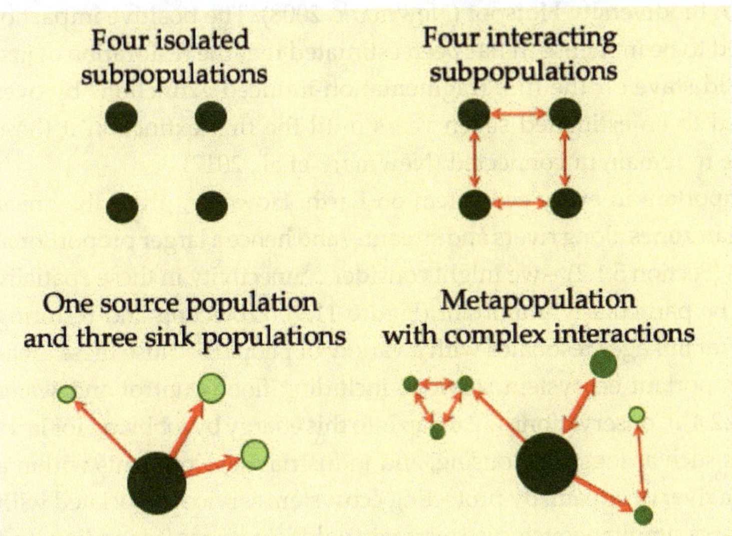

Figure 11.8 A range of metapopulation patterns is possible in nature. In this illustration, population size is represented by the size of the circle, while movement direction and intensity are indicated by the direction and thickness of the arrows.

Habitat fragmentation threatens metapopulation dynamics by reducing opportunities for dispersal across the landscape (Chapter 5). When there is too little movement of individuals between habitat fragments, the dwindling subpopulations within those fragments are at risk of extirpation or even extinction (Section 8.7). In contrast, well-connected subpopulations maintain themselves by colonising empty niches, exchanging genetic material, and adapting to changing environments. Dispersal also maintains critical ecosystem processes, such as pollination and seed dispersal (Section 4.2.5). Consequently, conservation biologists have invested significant resources in recent years to maintain and restore wildlife movements within fragmented ecosystems.

11.3.1 Connectivity in terrestrial ecosystems

Maintaining and restoring **ecosystem connectivity**—the ability of ecosystems to facilitate the dispersal of individuals between different areas—involves maintaining and restoring wildlife movements that are (at risk of being) impeded by human activities. The most popular method to maintain (or restore) connectivity in a fragmented landscape is to maintain (or restore) **habitat linkages**, also called wildlife corridors, habitat corridors, dispersal corridors, or movement corridors. All these terms refer to continuous tracts of suitable habitat with little to no dispersal barriers that connect otherwise isolated habitat patches and populations.

> Maintaining and restoring ecosystem connectivity is an important strategy for conserving wildlife whose movements are impeded by human activities.

Some of the most prominent efforts to restore habitat linkages involve habitat restoration. For example, plans are currently underway to use forest regeneration to reconnect nine forest fragments in Tanzania's East Usambara Mountain; if successful, this project would establish the largest contiguous forest block (over 3,000 km^2) in the Eastern Arc Mountain Biodiversity Hotspot (Newmark, 2008). The positive impact of this project is expected to be immense. It has been estimated that the restoration of just 80 km^2 of forest would stave off the first fragmentation-induced extinctions by over 2,000 years, compared to an estimated seven years until the first extinction if these forest fragments were to remain unconnected (Newmark et al., 2017).

Connectivity is important in every ecosystem on Earth. However, given the linear characteristic of **riparian zones** along rivers and stream—and hence a larger proportional impact of edge effects (Section 5.1.2)—we might consider connectivity in these spatially restricted systems to be particularly important (Figure 11.9). Protecting and restoring riparian zones as habitat linkages resonates with a variety of people because these areas provide a range of important ecosystem services, including flood control and water purification (Section 4.2.4). Conservationists can tap into this energy by lobbying for laws that prohibit activities such as logging, housing, and industrial developments within a certain distance from a river or stream. By protecting ecosystem services associated with riparian zones, these laws simultaneously also maintain wildlife refuges (Monadjem and Reside, 2008), source populations (Vosse et al., 2008), and habitat linkages (Bentrup et al., 2012; McLennan and Plumptre, 2012). In contrast, inadequate protection of riparian ecosystems not only compromises connectivity, but also negatively affect species not overtly dependent on these buffer areas. For example, research from Southeast Asia has shown that losing riparian ecosystems in an otherwise palm oil dominated landscape reduced stream quality, which in turn reduced local fish diversity by up to 36% (Giam et al., 2015). In contrast, protecting riparian zones were found to increase palm oil yields (Horton et al., 2018). With so many riparian areas currently being degraded and destroyed, there is an urgent need for stronger riparian protection laws (Chapter 12), and for more effective enforcement of those laws.

Figure 11.9 Protecting riparian zones such as this one along the Turkwel River in northern Kenya is an effective strategy for maintaining connectivity and securing a range of ecosystem services.

Restoring connectivity may also involve removing or otherwise mitigating human constructs that block wildlife dispersal. This is a major aim of TFCAs, which aim to restore dispersal between protected areas (Jones et al., 2012) by removing fences and other human constructs while still maintaining sustainable land tenures (Andersson et al., 2013). These efforts, accomplished through partnerships with local communities, are re-establishing historical mass migration routes, which in turn will hopefully also boost those areas' ecotourism potential (Box 11.3). Efforts to revive extinct mass migrations also seem to be paying off! For example, in Botswana, the removal of veterinary fences—meant to prevent spread of diseases from wildlife to livestock, but also cutting off the world's second largest wildebeest migration—have seen several hundred plains zebras (*Equus quagga*, NT) returning to old migration routes within four years (Bartlam-Brooks et al., 2011).

Section 5.1.1 discussed how inconsiderate fence placements threaten wildlife, while the paragraph above explained how removing fences can improve connectivity. Ironically, and illustrating the difficulties conservationists face when dealing with conflicting demands, strategically placed fences can sometimes also be used as a conservation tool. For example, researchers working on a fragmented lion population in Botswana found that the most effective way to improve this population's viability was through strategic placement of fences to direct dispersal between protected areas (Cushman et al., 2016). Strategically placed predator-proof fences may at times also be

Box 11.3 Transfrontier Conservation Areas: Managing Biodiversity Across International Boundaries

Simon M. Munthali

Kavango-Zambezi Transfrontier Conservation Area Programme, Kasane, Botswana.

TFCAs are components of a larger ecosystems that straddles the border between two or more countries, encompassing one or more protected areas as well as multiple-resource areas used by communities and private landholders. They are also managed for sustainable use of natural resources (Singh, 1998). The concept recognises that borders are political rather than ecological (Dallimer and Strange, 2015), and aims to ensure that key ecological processes continue to function where political borders have divided ecosystems, river basins, or wildlife corridors (Cumming, 1999).

TFCAs are widely being established in Africa. One of these is the 520,000 km^2 Kavango-Zambezi TFCA (KAZA)—a conservation and development initiative of Angola, Botswana, Namibia, Zambia, and Zimbabwe.

The benefits of the KAZA include:

- Re-establishment of the seasonal wildlife migration routes and connectivity among the many protected areas (national parks, community conservancies, and wildlife and forest reserves) within the region (Figure 11.C). The primary wildlife focus is the savannah elephant (*Loxodonta africana*), whose population of about 250,000 is predominantly concentrated in Chobe National Park (Botswana), Hwange National Park (Zimbabwe), and Bwabwata National Park (Namibia). Elephants need unimpeded movement to protected areas where population densities are much lower, such as Luengue-Luiana and Mavinga National Parks (Angola), and Sioma Ngwezi and Kafue National Parks (Zambia). This movement would reduce pressure on the ecosystems that are currently overpopulated and enable elephants and other species to better coexist—especially grazing herbivores that depend on the same habitats as the elephant.

- Expanding the wildlife-based economy, primarily ecotourism, into agricultural marginal areas (with predominantly Kalahari sand soils), through community-private partnerships. Through these partnerships, local communities would benefit from employment and business opportunities in ecotourism activities.

- Opportunities for local communities to participate in decision-making, and influencing policies and legislation related to natural management such as coordination of the fishing closed season between Namibia and Zambia during the fish breeding season (December–March) in the Zambezi River.

- Formation of alliances among different stakeholders (governments, private sector, NGOs, and local communities) to maximise skills and resources in promoting sustainable land use, conserving biodiversity and alleviating poverty.

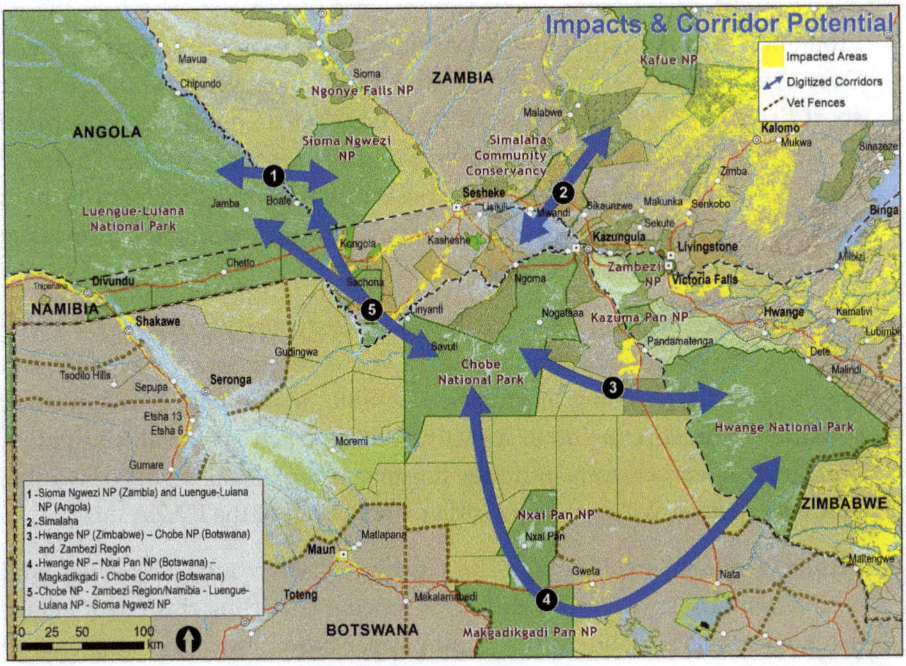

Figure 11.C Location of priority wildlife dispersal corridors between the various national parks of the KAZA TFCA.

Despite these benefits, there are obstacles to progress in attaining the benefits of the KAZA. Notable among these are social and political factors, such as increasing human population density, increasing cultivation of land, and expanding human settlements in wildlife corridors. Many of these factors trigger human-wildlife conflicts and poaching both for local consumption of bushmeat and for the illegal sale of elephant ivory. To mitigate these threats, the following strategies are being implemented:

- A Master Integrated Development Plan for the KAZA has been developed, which provides initial zoning. Its key feature is spatially allocating land into various uses (human settlement, agriculture, and protected wildlife areas, including wildlife dispersal corridors). The Master Integrated Development Plan also assists in creating awareness about the value of the wildlife corridors, which traverse communal areas.

- Promotion of conservation agriculture as a tool for improving land stewardship, intensification of agriculture, and improving crop yields per unit area of land, and therefore decreasing the likelihood of cutting down forested areas in and around wildlife corridors to plant new agricultural fields. Currently, within the KAZA, conservation agriculture is being piloted in Angola, Namibia, and Zambia. Conservation agriculture is crop production that strives to achieve acceptable profits together with high and sustained production levels while concurrently conserving the environment.
- Promotion of community-private partnerships in ecotourism development. Over the past four years, Ngoma safari lodge (Botswana), and Machenje sport fishing lodge (Zambia) have been developed specifically in support of securing wildlife corridors. They also provide incentives to the local communities for adopting wildlife conservation as a supplement to their land use practices. These lodges are in addition to the numerous existing tourist resorts in the KAZA.
- A law enforcement and anti-poaching strategy for the KAZA is being developed to coordinate transboundary law enforcement surveillance and fines to prevent poaching of protected wildlife. In addition, KAZA partner countries are integrating other security agencies, such as the military, police, immigration, and customs officials, to prevent the illegal export of wildlife products such as elephant ivory and bushmeat out of the KAZA.
- Reducing human-wildlife conflicts (Section 14.4) through improved land use planning, solar-powered electrified fencing encircling clusters of village fields and facilities and use of chilli-pepper-based olfactory repellents to deter elephants from entering crop fields.

The KAZA has made considerable progress to date in coordinating conservation efforts among the wildlife agencies and national parks across five countries in Southern Africa. The principal success has been measures to allow the continued migration of elephants along existing migration routes across international borders. The challenges ahead—from inadequate funding for wildlife patrolling and anti-poaching activities to increasing populations of rural people outside the protected areas and across migration routes—remain significant.

required to avoid human-wildlife conflict (Packer et al., 2013, but see Creel et al., 2013), and to facilitate the recovery of threatened species, as is the case for Africa's rarest antelope, the hirola (*Beatragus hunter* CR) (Ng'weno et al., 2017). The final word here is that management must remain responsive to both positive and negative impacts of tools, such as fences, rather than relegating them to bins, such as good or bad. (See also Dupuis-Desormeaux et al., [2018] for the use of fence-gaps and exclusionary fences to mitigate some negative fence impacts.)

At times, when it is impractical to establish or restore continuous habitat linkages, biologists may opt to protect and restore **stepping stone habitats** (Figure 11.10). As the name implies, stepping stone habitats are a special type of habitat linkage that facilitate dispersal along a patchwork of isolated habitat patches within a matrix of unsuitable or inhospitable habitat. Stepping stones thereby divide long dispersal events through a long stretch of inhospitable terrain up into shorter, and thus more manageable, sections. Stepping stone habitats are particularly important for migratory species that rest and refuel at stop-over sites between the end-points of their migratory route (Runge et al., 2015)—each stop-over site can be viewed as a stepping stone habitat. Prominent examples of stepping stone habitats that deserve protection include sacred forests which can act as stop-over sites for migratory forest birds; wetlands and estuaries (see Box 5.3), which can act as stop-over sites by migratory waterbirds; and small forest reserves, which can act as stepping stones between a network of other protected areas (Riggio and Caro, 2017).

> Protecting and restoring stepping stone habitats can maintain connectivity in areas where it is impractical to establish or restore continuous habitat linkages.

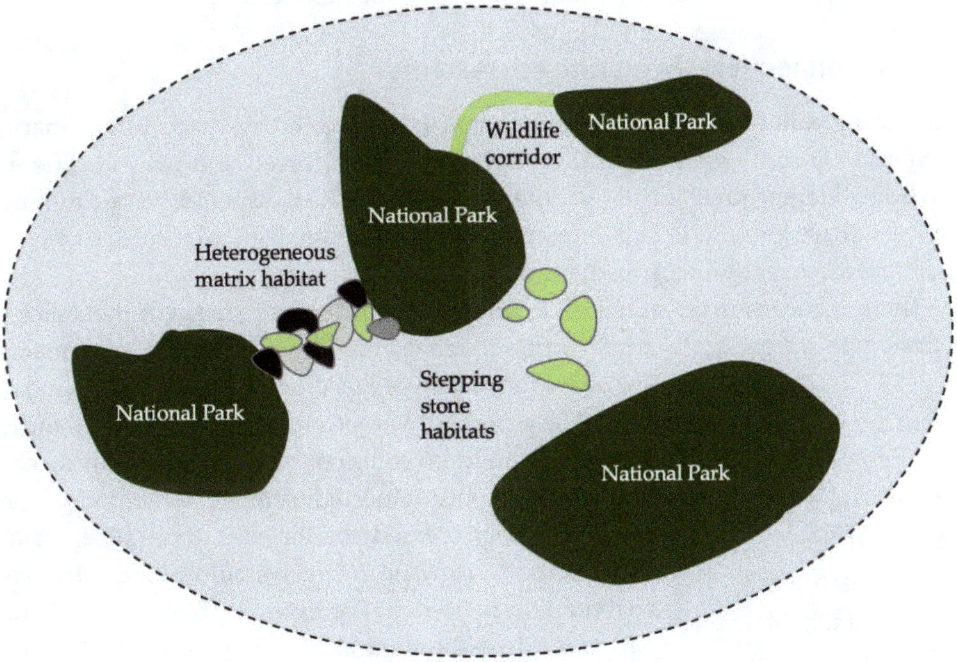

Figure 11.10 Methods to reconnect fragmented metapopulations (or maintain connectivity) can take many forms. The three main strategies are to maintain or restore wildlife corridors (e.g. to link two isolated forest patches), maintain or restore stepping stone habitats (e.g. a patchwork of wetlands or sacred forests), or facilitating movement through the matrix with sustainable land use tenures (e.g. removing fences).

11.3.2 Connectivity in freshwater ecosystems

Dams have always played an important role in hydropower generation and securing a year-round supply of water for farms, industries, and cities. Unfortunately, recent evidence suggests that reservoirs may create more problems than they solve (Section 5.3.2). Of concern is their contribution to greenhouse gases (Deemer et al., 2016), as well as their role in blocking dispersal of aquatic organisms. To counter these negative impacts, governments across the world are decommissioning and removing dams and other types of artificial water impoundments. For instance, over the past 30 years more than 1,174 dams were removed in the USA; the 72 dams removed in 2016 alone restored more than 3,000 km of streams (Thomas-Blate, 2016). Similar efforts are also underway in Europe (http://www.ecrr.org), where river restoration efforts have been initiated at over 1,100 locations across 31 countries. Unfortunately, not only are efforts to restore freshwater connectivity lagging across Africa; in many cases, even more rivers are currently being dammed (Winemiller et al., 2016).

> While dams play an important role in hydropower generation and securing a year-round supply of water, recent evidence suggests that they create many environmental problems, including blocking species dispersal.

11.3.3 Connectivity in marine ecosystems

Ecosystem connectivity is also important in marine ecosystems. Many marine organisms, including economically important species, breed and feed in different areas at different times of the year, and use established dispersal routes to move between those areas. It is thus important to protect these dispersal routes so we can maintain these marine ecosystems and ecosystem services.

There are three main strategies to maintain and restore movement dynamics of marine seascapes. First, marine corridors—zones used by whales and other marine species to move between feeding and breeding grounds—should be protected. Marine biologists in several countries successfully reduced collisions between whales and ocean-faring vessels with minor adjustments to shipping lanes that previously crossed marine corridors (Silber et al., 2012). Second, estuarine linkages should be protected, and restored where needed. For example, biologists in South Africa restored the natural flow regime of the St Lucia Estuary, Africa's largest estuarine lake, by removing dredge spoil in the estuary mouth (Nunes et al., 2018). Third, coastal habitat linkages—beaches and littoral shallows used by wildlife for dispersal, breeding, and feeding—need to be maintained. Studies from South Africa have highlighted how poor protection of connectivity pathways between coastal habitats can compromise these areas' high levels of species richness and endemism (von der Heyden, 2009; Harris et al., 2014).

> Maintaining movement dynamics in marine seascapes involves protecting and restoring marine corridors, estuarine linkages, and coastal habitat linkages.

11.3.4 Mimicking connectivity

In the absence of habitat linkages, wildlife managers may be able to mimic dispersal dynamics by sporadically translocating a few individuals between subpopulations. Managing populations in this way may be a good alternative in cases where areas earmarked for translocations are too small to sustain a single viable population. Such is the case in South Africa, where conservation biologists occasionally move threatened predators within a small and fragmented protected areas network, where none of the areas are large enough to host a viable population on their own (see Box 8.3). Managing isolated and small populations so intensively nearly always requires sound underlying principles and extensive quantitative analyses (Chapter 9) for guidance.

11.3.5 Management considerations in connectivity conservation

While intuitively appealing, there are a few potential drawbacks to connectivity that conservation planners should consider when planning to establish new habitat linkages (reviewed in Haddad et al., 2014). Prominently, connecting historically isolated populations may lead to outbreeding depression, for example when populations with different local adaptations are connected. Habitat linkages may also act as bottlenecks that expose dispersing animals to greater risks of predation and enable pests and diseases to spread easier. Care must be taken to ensure that wildlife do indeed perceive the landscape "connected"; a habitat linkage that may look good to the human eye may in fact be perceived as inhospitable habitat to wildlife (Newmark, 2008). A recent study from the Americas has shown that the habitat quality of a single stepping stone habitat can determine whether a migration is successful or not (Gómez et al., 2017).

Although the benefits for connecting landscapes for conservation generally outweigh the drawbacks (Haddad et al., 2014), it is important to carefully plan to avoid those drawbacks. Genetic studies can be useful in both determining connectivity among populations (von der Heyden, 2009; Godley et al., 2010) and help researchers detecting potential deleterious factors, such as outbreeding depression (Figure 11.11, see also Frankham et al., 2011; Ralls et al., 2018). Modelling approaches that combine a target species' movement limitations with radio tracking technologies (e.g. Godley et al., 2010) or remotely sensed environmental variables (e.g. Wegmann et al., 2014) could help to estimate whether a landscape is indeed connected. Much effort has also been invested in finding the optimal width of habitat corridors. For example, one study in lowland forests suggested that corridors that are 30–40 m wide might be adequate for migration of most species while corridors that are 200 m wide will be adequate for all species (Laurance and Laurance, 1999). This is useful guidance, but ecosystems vary, as do target species (Wilson et al., 2010; Pryke and Samways, 2012) and, thus, some corridors may need to be even wider.

> Although the benefits for reconnecting fragmented landscapes generally outweigh the drawbacks, it is important to carefully plan to avoid those drawbacks.

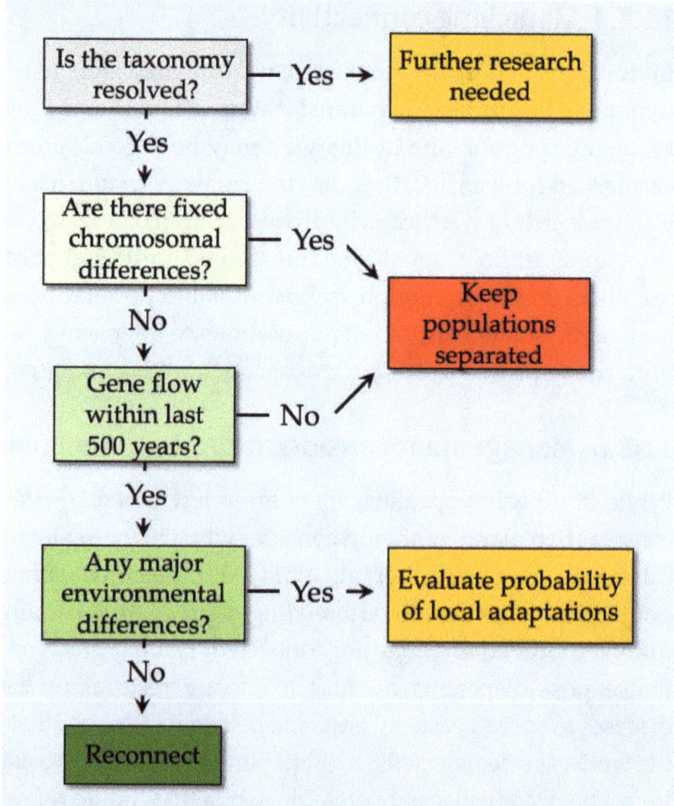

Figure 11.11 An example of a decision tree to avoid outbreeding depression, which can be used guide decisions for reconnecting fragmented landscapes.

11.4 Managing Species Sensitive to Climate Change

Earth's temperature is well on its way to exceed the 2°C increase cap set by global authorities in 2016 (***Paris Agreement***, Section 12.2.1). Many species that need to adapt to these changes are unable to do so, either because of their limited dispersal capabilities or because of human-induced habitat fragmentation (Section 6.3.5). Others that can disperse may risk decoupling of important symbiotic relationships, as the species involved may not disperse at the same speed, or the same distance (Section 6.3.2). While slowing habitat loss could slow the overall impacts of climate change (Section 10.4), preventing the extinction of many climate-sensitive species will require a range of pro-active conservation management strategies that allow species to adapt at their own pace as and when needed.

One of the most important strategies for protecting climate-sensitive species is to identify and protect their likely future habitats. This task of predicting where suitable habitats may be found in future is generally accomplished by identifying and projecting a species' climatic niche (or bioclimatic envelope) using species distribution models (SDM, Pearson and Dawson, 2003). Section 11.1.1 described how SDM use location data overlaid onto environmental variables to estimate a species' environmental niche, and how this information can then be used to predict where else a species may occur in a landscape. A similar strategy is followed when predicting a species' future climate-adapted range. Here, location data are overlaid onto present-day climate variables (e.g. average temperature and rainfall) to define the species' climatic niche; these niche limits are then projected onto the landscape of interest using future climate scenarios (Section 6.2). Much effort has also been made in recent years to incorporate aspects, such as physiology (Kearney and Porter, 2009) and biological interactions (e.g. Araújo and Luoto, 2007), in predicting future ranges.

> Preventing the extinction of climate-sensitive species will require a range of pro-active conservation strategies that allow those species to adapt at their own pace as and when needed.

Once future ranges have been identified, the next task is to recognize and protect/restore critical dispersal pathways (Section 11.3). While a general strategy of increasing ecosystem-wide connectivity will certainty also benefit climate-sensitive species, conservationists could specifically target climate adaption, by maintaining and restoring **climate corridors**—dispersal pathways between the current and future ranges (Mawdsley et al., 2009). Several efforts (e.g. Williams et al., 2005; Phillips et al., 2008; Ayebare et al., 2013) are currently underway to establish and protect species-specific and community-specific climate corridors, as predicted using advanced distribution modelling techniques. These and other studies have shown that likely climate corridors often include north–south river valleys, ridges, and coastlines to facilitate poleward distribution shifts, while habitat linkages that cross gradients of elevation, rainfall, and soil types will help climate adaptation across more complex landscapes.

Species with dispersal limitations and specialised interactions may not always benefit from increased connectivity. Instead, those species may rely on **climate refuges**—areas that are resilient to climate change and thus able to continue to support climate-sensitive communities in future. Africa offers two good examples that illustrate how climate refuges can be identified. The first study, on South African birds, identified climate refuges as areas where temperatures seldom rise above the threshold known to negatively impact a specific species' fitness (Cunningham et al., 2013). The second study, on northern Mozambique's coral reefs (McClanahan and Muthiga, 2017), identified two kinds of climate refuges: (a) areas where temperatures never reached a point where it would kill the corals, and (b) areas situated in deeper and cooler water but with the full spectrum of light, which allowed corals to thrive while avoiding heat stress. Both these studies highlight why protecting and restoring complex natural ecosystems (see also Betts et al. 2018) is so important for climate change mitigation.

> Climate-sensitive species that are dispersal-limited may not benefit from increased connectivity. Instead, they will rely on climate refuges—areas that are resilient to climate change.

Assisted colonisation is an alternative conservation strategy to save species with dispersal limitations and specialised interactions. Also called assisted migration, assisted colonisation involves the pro-active translocation of climate-sensitive species from their present ranges to their future ranges. Sometimes, even species able to self-disperse may require assisted colonisation. For example, African penguins (*Spheniscus demersus*, EN) are currently undergoing population declines because of climate change-induced shifts in fish populations on which they depend for food (Sherley et al., 2017). To re-establish this important biological interaction, conservationists are currently using assisted colonisation to establish two new penguin colonies further east from existing colonies (Birdlife South Africa, 2019), in an area where fish populations have remained healthy (Figure 11.12).

Figure 11.12 BirdLife South Africa, in partnership with CapeNature, are introducing rehabilitated African penguins to two new sites several hundred kilometres east of existing colonies. The hope is that the translocated penguins will establishing colonies that is buffered from the negative effects of climate change and fluctuating fish populations. Here members of the public are witnessing the first releases.

As with any translocation project, introducing climate-sensitive species to new areas carries significant risks, including decoupling them from critical limiting resources and symbiotic relationships. It is thus imperative to start small, by translocating only a few well-monitored individuals. If monitoring shows that the initial releases were successful, one can then plan for further releases over time. Because this strategy is still new, it is also important to disseminate your experiences to the broader conservation community, for example by presenting results at conferences or in scientific journals.

11.5 Ex Situ Conservation Strategies

The best strategy for protecting biodiversity over the long term is to protect existing wild populations in their natural ecosystems. This strategy, known as on-site, or **in situ conservation**, not only protect entire ecological communities—including thousands of species and their interactions—but also natural processes and ecosystem services. However, if the last populations of a threatened species are too small to remain viable, if they continue to decline despite conservation efforts, or if their threats do not subside, then in situ conservation may prove ineffective. In such cases, sometimes the only option left to prevent an imminent extinction is to capture those last remaining individuals and transfer them to a facility where they can be cared for under artificial, human-controlled conditions. This strategy is known as off-site, or **ex situ conservation**, and may involve individuals that were collected in the wild, orphaned, confiscated, or displaced and have nowhere else to go. Thanks to ex situ efforts, several African plants and animals that are extinct in the wild continue to survive in zoos, aquaria, and botanical gardens. Examples include four to seven species of ancient cycads (*Encephalartos* spp.) from Southern Africa, and the pygmy Rwandan water lily (*Nymphaea thermarum*, EW), which is the world's smallest water lily (IUCN, 2019).

> For species facing imminent extinction, sometimes the only option left may be to capture the remaining individuals and transfer them to captivity.

Ex situ and in situ conservation are complementary strategies (Figure 11.13; see also Conde et al., 2011). For example, many ex situ conservation programmes aim to raise enough healthy individuals to support translocation projects when appropriate habitats are available. Ex situ conservation efforts were instrumental in preventing the extinction of the live-bearing Kihansi spray toad (*Nectophrynoides asperginis*, EW). Populations of this Tanzanian endemic declined precipitously following the establishment of a hydroelectric dam, which caused the toad's waterfall spray-zone habitat to dry up. The species was subsequently declared *Extinct in the Wild* in 2009. Tanzanian conservationists, however, demonstrated good foresight by inviting zoos from the USA to collect adults for a captive breeding effort even before the dam was built. This effort is now yielding positive results: after a decade of captive breeding, the erection of an artificial sprinkler system for habitat restoration, and experimental releases (Vandvik et al., 2014), nearly 10,000 toads were released to their former range in May 2018 (Anon, 2018).

Safeguarding a well-represented sample of the world's biodiversity play only a small role in ex situ conservation efforts. Maintaining self-sustaining wildlife populations under human care not only reduce the need to collect individuals for research from the wild; it also allows researchers to study aspects such as physiology, genetics, and demographics of threatened species (Conde et al., 2019) using methods that might not be possible without animals in captivity. These studies can then provide knowledge and experience to help protect both ex situ and in situ populations. For example, the establishment of the Demographic Species Knowledge Index (Conde et al., 2019), summarise demographic data obtained from ex situ conservation facilities, play a crucial role in filling gaps in datasets for population viability analyses (Section 9.2) Ex situ facilities also play a critical role in captive breeding, head-starting, public outreach, education, and fundraising for in situ conservation. Many ex situ facilities have also become directly involved—and sometimes even taking leading roles—in

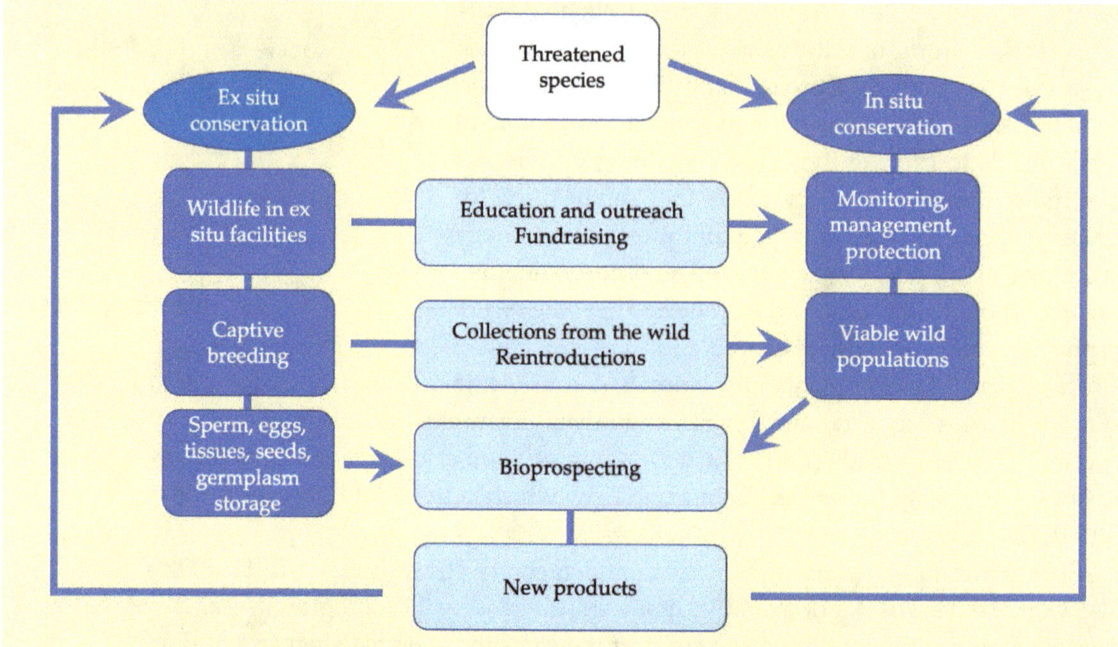

Figure 11.13 There are several ways in which in situ (on site) and ex situ (off-site) conservation can complement each other. No species conforms exactly to this idealised model, but nearly all species present some of these elements.

field conservation efforts (Wilson et al., 2019). Lastly, many ex situ facilities directly connect conservation to social and economic progress through off-site education, employment, and implementation of a range of different community development activities (Ferrie et al., 2013).

Recent efforts to increase knowledge transfer among ex situ facilities has greatly enhanced their contribution to overall conservation efforts. Facilitated by organisations such as the IUCN's Conservation Planning Specialist Group (CPSG), ex situ facilities now regularly share information on best practices for care and handling of species in human care, including aspects such as nutritional requirements, optimal housing conditions, and veterinary techniques to anaesthetize, immobilise, and reduce stress for animals when they are being moved or during medical treatments (see http://www.cpsg.org). Much of this information is stored in a central database called the Zoological Information Management System (ZIMS). Maintained by Species360, ZIMS keeps track of animal **husbandry**, medical, and breeding information on over 6.8 million animals belonging to more than 21,000 species for over 1,000 member institutions in 90 countries. Ex situ facilities that maintain these records and comply with operations standards in animal welfare, conservation, education, and research can also apply to become an accredited institution with the Pan-African Association for Zoos and Aquaria (PAAZA), or its parent organisation, the World Association of Zoos and Aquariums (WAZA). As of mid-2019, four Sub-Saharan African ex situ facilities were accredited by WAZA, and 19 by PAAZA.

11.5.1 Types of ex situ facilities

Many types of facilities help to preserve ex situ populations. Here we describe some of the most common, including zoos and aquaria for animals, and botanical gardens and seed banks for plants.

Zoos around the world currently contribute to the conservation of nearly 7,000 species of terrestrial vertebrates (mammals, birds, reptiles, and amphibians) by caring for more than 500,000 individual animals. They do not do this alone; they often work with government agencies, universities, and a variety of other organisations who use zoo animals for research, education, and other conservation activities. While zoos traditionally focussed on displaying charismatic animals that draw visitors, many zoos are now also investing in the conservation of small threatened vertebrates, as well as invertebrates, such as butterflies, beetles, dragonflies, spiders, and molluscs (many of which are also cheaper to maintain). South Africa's National Zoological Gardens, which houses more than 9,000 individual animals belonging to 705 species, is Africa's largest zoo by variety of captive species and individuals. The zoo also hosts a variety of daily school programmes meant to inspire kids to a career in conservation; these include holiday courses, a zoo club, and guided tours at night.

> Ex situ conservation facilities compliment field conservation efforts through captive breeding, public outreach, education, knowledge generation, and fundraising.

Aquaria are the aquatic version of zoos, specialised in caring, displaying, and conserving marine and freshwater biodiversity, such as fishes, corals, molluscs, and crustaceans (Figure 11.14). One such institution is South Africa's uShaka Marine World, the world's fifth largest aquarium and home to more than 390 marine species—most from the Western Indian Ocean—held in 11 million litres of seawater. Most organisms currently in aquaria have been obtained from the wild, but conservationists are constantly refining techniques to breed more species in captivity to limit wild collecting. Recent and dramatic increases in aquaculture, which currently accounts for roughly a third of fish and shellfish production globally, have made ex situ conservation of aquatic species even more important. The hope is that these ex situ populations will help maintain genetic stocks and act as insurances against disease outbreaks introduced by domestic fish, molluscs, and crustaceans.

Botanical gardens (and **arboretums,** which specialise on trees and other woody plants) are dedicated to the collection, cultivation and educational curation of living plant species. Botanical gardens across the world house more than 6 million living plants, representing over 80,000 species—approximately 25% of the world's vascular flora (Wyse Jackson, 2001). The world's oldest and largest botanical garden—the Royal Botanic Gardens in London, UK—maintains over 28,000 plant taxa, nearly 10% of plant taxa in the world. In Sub-Saharan Africa, there are at least 153 botanical gardens in 33 countries, which range from small community-organised centres to world-famous conservation hubs, such as South Africa's Kirstenbosch Botanical

Figure 11.14 (Top) Many aquaria host tours and children's programmes, some involving opportunities to touch the organisms, for additional enrichment to visitors. Photograph by Karen Schermbrucker, courtesy of Two Oceans Aquarium. (Bottom) Aquaria also provide opportunities to observe species such as this black musselcracker (*Cymatoceps nasutus*, VU) at South Africa's Two Oceans Aquarium, which many people would not have experienced otherwise.

Garden. Like zoos and aquaria, botanical gardens play a critical role in conservation efforts through public outreach and education. For example, Ghana's Aburi Botanical Garden established a model medicinal plant garden where the public can gain first-hand knowledge on how to combine conservation, cultivation, and sustainable use of medicinal plants (Gillett et al. 2002).

A few botanical gardens and research institutes have developed collections of seeds, known as **seed banks**, which take advantage of the fact that seeds of most plants can survive for long periods when stored in cold, dry conditions. The seeds deposited in seed banks may be obtained from the wild, or from cultivated specimens.

When gathering material from the wild, botanists generally target populations from across a species' geographical and habitat ranges so their collections can capture as much of each species' genetic diversity as possible. In this way, seed banks play a crucial role not only in conservation of plant species richness, but also genetic diversity. Seed banks may even be the only means some plant species are protected. Because many seeds of each species are usually collected, seed banks also provide a convenient opportunity for translocation projects. That is because safeguarded seed collections can be used to propagate not just large numbers of seedlings but, in some cases, custom-developed genetic mixtures to maximise local adaptations. The world's largest and most diverse seed bank is the Millennium Seed Bank, UK. At the end of 2018, the Millennium Seed Bank catalogued over 2.25 billion seeds from over 39,000 species; its billionth seed, from an African bamboo, was deposited in April 2007. In addition to safeguarding a portion of plant diversity, the Millennium Seed Bank has also benefitted countries, such as Botswana, Burkina Faso, and Mali through the redistribution of banked seeds to aid ecological restoration efforts.

> Seed banks contribute to conservation of genetic diversity of plants by collecting material across target species' geographical and habitat ranges.

11.5.2 Challenges facing ex situ facilities

While the contribution of ex situ conservation facilities to overall biodiversity conservation strategies is significant (Conde et al., 2011), there are some drawbacks that need to be considered. For example, due to the limited number of individuals that can be maintained under human care, especially for larger animals, there is an increased risk that captive populations may suffer from threats facing small populations, such as inbreeding depression and demographic stochasticity (Section 8.7). There is also a concern that ex situ conservation can contribute to hybridisation concerns, for example if different cryptic species are accidentally managed as a single species. To avoid these threats, many ex-situ facilities manage their captive populations jointly as a single interbreeding metapopulation. They do this through studbooks which track the origin, pedigree, and demographic history of each individual in participating facilities. By maintaining and referring to these studbooks, ex situ conservation facilities can make informed decisions regarding transfer and breeding recommendations. The establishment of a European studbook for African dwarf crocodiles (*Osteolaemus* spp.) even addressed concerns about potential hybridisation between cryptic species (Schmidt et al., 2015).

> Ex-situ facilities often manage captive populations as a single metapopulation using studbooks to track the origin and demographic history of breeding individuals.

Funding also remains an obstacle, given that ex situ facilities typically require large, long-term, funding commitments, in comparison to many in situ conservation activities. One consequence of funding limitations is that ex situ facilities mostly focus on showy or charismatic species that attract visitors, so small and less charismatic species are not always afforded equal protection (Brooks et al., 2009). Many ex situ facilities are also more inclined to house non-threatened species that are easier and less costly to care for, rather than threatened species with specialised needs (Table 11.1). For example, despite the fear of looming mass amphibian extinctions due to a disease caused by the chytrid fungus (*Batrachochytrium dendrobatidis*) (Alroy, 2015), 75% of ex situ amphibian collections consist of non-threatened species, with only 6.2% of all threatened amphibians afforded ex situ protection (Dawson et al., 2016). Neglecting threatened species in ex situ conservation efforts also creates a feedback loop, by maintaining a limited understanding on how to care for the species most in need.

Table 11.1 Number and percentages of terrestrial vertebrate species from Sub-Saharan Africa currently maintained in the world's ex situ facilities. Values in parenthesis represent percentage of all species[a], threatened species[b], and CITES-listed species[c] for each taxon class, respectively.

	Mammals	Birds	Reptiles	Amphibians	Total
Worldwide[a]	659 (55%)	1,470 (65%)	197 (27%)	44 (5%)	2,370 (47%)
Africa	110 (9%)	234 (10%)	34 (4%)	6 (1%)	384 (8%)
Asia	136 (11%)	327 (14%)	22 (3%)	2 (0%)	487 (10%)
Oceania	37 (3%)	61 (3%)	6 (1%)	1 (0%)	105 (2%)
Europe	191 (12%)	465 (20%)	73 (10%)	19 (2%)	748 (15%)
North America	145 (12%)	311 (14%)	53 (7%)	14 (2%)	523 (10%)
South America	40 (3%)	72 (3%)	197 (27%)	44 (5%)	353 (7%)
Threatened species[b]	45 (23%)	42 (20%)	22 (21%)	8 (4%)	117 (16%)
Extinct in the Wild	1 (100%)	0 (0%)	0 (0%)	1 (100%)	2 (100%)
Critically Endangered	7 (26%)	4 (19%)	5 (25%)	3 (5%)	19 (15%)
Endangered	13 (16%)	12 (15%)	2 (5%)	3 (3%)	30 (10%)
Vulnerable	24 (27%)	26 (23%)	15 (33%)	1 (2%)	66 (23%)
CITES-listed species[c]	95 (50%)	121 (62%)	45 (25%)	1 (6%)	262 (45%)
Appendix I species	30 (58%)	4 (44%)	8 (80%)	1 (6%)	43 (49%)
Appendix II species	58 (44%)	112 (62%)	37 (22%)	0 (0%)	207 (43%)
Appendix III species	7 (100%)	5 (100%)	0 (0%)	0 (0%)	12 (100%)

Source: https://zims.species360.org, current as of April-2019. Compiled by Johanna Staerk (Species360).

Fortunately, ex situ facilities have responded to these concerns by developing several innovative mechanisms that enables them to contribute more to the conservation of threatened species. For example, ex situ facilities all agree that attracting more visitors attracts more funding. To attract more visitors, zoos and aquaria are increasingly keeping animals in enclosures that are representative of their natural environments; this keeps the animals heathier and providing more opportunities to exhibit natural behaviours which, in turn, leave visitors more satisfied. Some zoos and aquaria have also established special displays where visitors can feed, touch, or otherwise interact with animals. Many ex situ facilities have also started inviting local artists to display sculptures and other artwork, which adds to the experience for visitors and attracting people that might not otherwise have visited. A rather unusual—but very successful—attempt to increase foot traffic comes from the USA, where the California Academy of Sciences hosts dance parties with laser shows, food, and drinks every Thursday night (http://www.calacademy.org/nightlife), which visitors can enjoy while visiting the Academy's aquarium and other conservation exhibits.

While the contribution of ex situ facilities to species conservation is significant, many rare species are ill-suited for ex situ efforts. Some species simply do not adapt or reproduce in captivity, while others that do relatively well in captivity experience behavioural and physiological changes or acquire diseases (Brossy et al., 1999) that prevent releases in the wild. Even so, the conservation biologists working at ex situ facilities constantly try to find ways to overcome these challenges. For example, staff at ex situ facilities sometimes use assisted reproductive techniques such as **artificial incubation** of bird and reptile eggs, or **artificial insemination** (Box 11.4) to overcome reproductive challenges (e.g. if individuals cannot mate because they are in different locations). Others use cryopreservation and **genome resource banks** for the long-term storage of embryos, eggs, sperm, or purified DNA, at least until those tissues can be used to increase a species' genetic diversity, or perhaps even to resurrect an extinct species (see de-extinction, Section 8.8). However, many ex situ conservation techniques are difficult and expensive to implement. When possible, it is almost always preferable to preserve species in situ where they can be self-sustaining, free from inbreeding, and an interactive participant of their community and ecosystem.

11.6 Thoughts on Neglected Taxa

Most of today's species-centric conservation initiatives are biased towards species that are showy, charismatic, or economically important. Consequently, conservation efforts for the vast majority of taxa are neglected, particularly in Africa where conservation funding is often more limited than elsewhere. One well-known example is known as **plant blindness**, the perception that animals take precedence above plants in conservation efforts. This isn't just a case of hurt feelings among botanists: there are likely significantly more plant than animal species that should be considered as threatened (see Table 2.1); however, thorough threat assessments are hampered because, as a group, plants receive significantly less funding compared to animals

Box 11.4 Saving the Northern White Rhinoceros with Assisted Reproduction Technologies

Morné de la Rey

Embryo Plus,
Brits, South Africa.

A few centuries ago, Earth's wildernesses enabled animals to roam and breed relatively freely. Today, sprawling cities, agriculture, and fences not only restrict animals' ability to forage, but also limit reproduction between differing gene pools. These stresses create smaller and more isolated populations which are being edged toward extinction.

There are several landscape-scale conservation initiatives to counteract these imbalances. But some species and populations are so rare that they depend on intensive management to remain viable. Assisted reproductive techniques (ART) provide promise for helping such species. Over the past 30 years, ARTs have greatly enhanced how the livestock industry preserve, improve, and proliferate genetic stock. Now, efforts are also underway to use ARTs to ensure the preservation of biodiversity.

The many types of ARTs

ARTs include a wide array of medical procedures to address infertility, and to make reproduction possible between individuals unable to do so naturally (e.g. animals in different protected areas). In this way, biologists can ensure genetic exchange while eliminating the risks inherent in translocation such as spread of diseases, adaptation to new environments, and disruption of group dynamics.

ARTs have various levels from relatively simple to very complex. The most basic technique is artificial insemination. A major advantage of this technique is that it can multiply male genetic contributions by inseminating more females than would be possible in nature. Much progress has also been made in improving viability of cryopreserved semen to overcome challenges with timing of female reproductive cycles and other logistical constraints.

As for multiplying female genetic contributions, methods involve embryo transfer and in vitro fertilisation (IVF). With multiple ovulation embryo transfer (MOET) egg fertilisation occurs naturally; with IVF, it occurs in a laboratory incubator. In both cases, an embryo is eventually transferred to a surrogate mother which will carry it until birth. Scientists are currently working on improving viability of stored germplasm, so that embryos can be cryopreserved until a suitable surrogate mother is ready.

The third technique is nuclear transfer, also known as cloning. This very delicate procedure involves replacing the haploid DNA of an unfertilised egg with diploid DNA of another; cells are then cultured, after which the embryo is transferred to a surrogate mother.

Using ARTs to save the northern white rhino

Once widespread across Central Africa, poaching has pushed the northern white rhinoceros (*Ceratotherium simum cottoni*, EW) to the brink of extinction. Today, only two females remain, both in a semi-captive setting at Ol Pejeta Conservancy, Kenya. Incapable of natural reproduction, this species is committed to extinction without drastic intervention.

A cutting-edge initiative is currently underway to use ARTs to save this iconic species. While the project's exact trajectory is still being developed, likely steps include optimising procedures for harvesting, maturing, and fertilising eggs, followed by embryo transfer into surrogate southern white rhinoceros. Some preliminary successes have also been achieved to generate stem cells from skin biopsies (Ben-Nun et al., 2011), which could be used in cloning. Genetic material (tissue samples and semen) of several northern white rhinos has been cryopreserved at various places around the world. However, there is a limited amount of sperm available (there are no males left), and so artificial insemination and IVF with northern white rhinoceros depends on embryo transfer successes. Many partners have been assembled to pool resources and ideas in support of this initiative, including Ol Pejeta Conservancy, Embryo Plus, Fauna & Flora International (FFI), Back to Africa, Dvur Karlove Zoo, Leibniz-IZW, Avantea, San Diego Zoo, and Kenya Wildlife Service.

Refining ARTs on other species

Before ARTs are implemented on the near-extinct rhinoceros, it is advisable to optimise procedures on another species. A logical choice would be the closely related southern white rhinoceros (*C. simum simum*, NT). However, the southern subspecies is also threatened, so we should look for more common mammals first.

Veterinarians at Embryo Plus routinely perform ARTs on domestic cattle, so efforts are currently focussed on building from this experience to work with wild bovines (Figure 11.D). For example, Embryo Plus recently produced the world's first African buffalo (*Syncerus caffer*, NT) through IVF; the healthy calf named Pumelelo (meaning success in isiZulu) was born in June 2016. Embryo Plus has also produced several western Zambian sables (*Hippotragus niger kirkii*) from southern sable (*H. niger niger*) surrogates using embryo transfer. Plans are also underway to investigate the viability of using eland (*Tautragus oryx*, LC) and domestic horses (*Equus ferus*) as surrogate mothers for mountain bongo (*T. eurycerus isaaci*, CR) and Grevy's zebra (*E. grevyi*, EN), respectively.

Figure 11.D (Top) The world's first African buffalo calf conceived by in vitro fertilisation. (Bottom) The world's first western Zambian sable born from a southern sable surrogate mother. Both species also breed successfully on their own, but scientists are refining their techniques on more common species before attempting them on highly threatened species.

From dream to reality

The long-term objective of the northern white rhinoceros project is to establish a viable breeding herd which can be reintroduced into secure habitats. But much work remains for this dream to become reality. While there was one successful attempt in producing a healthy bongo calf by transferring an embryo to an eland mother (Woolf, 1986), inter-species embryo transfer remains challenging. Due to a rhinoceros' size, we also need to ensure ART procedures can be performed safely without placing undue stress on the patient. Lastly, because each species' embryos have different requirements in the laboratory, extensive research is necessary before ARTs can be attempted on a new species.

Although ARTs in wildlife management is still in its infancy, we are confident that early breakthroughs hold promise for the survival of the northern white rhinoceros, as well as other threatened species that may one day benefit from these procedures.

(Negron-Ortiz, 2014). One explanation for this disparity is that plants are often seen as the backdrop of the environment rather than the critical foundation (as primary producers) of every food web on Earth. While showy plant species may indeed have highly visible roles in maintaining the environment and regional economies, neglected species may play an equally—sometimes even more—important role in maintaining ecosystems and ecosystem services (Schleuning et al., 2016).

Fortunately, the number of professional and amateur societies interested in protecting neglected taxa, such as reptiles, amphibians, invertebrates, fungi, and plants are rising. Some groups of experts are also organised into Specialist Groups (https://www.iucn.org/ssc-groups) by the IUCN. These societies and expert groups highlight the plight of neglected taxa and are willing to provide in-house expertise on best practices for protecting those species.

11.7 Summary

1. A species may be threatened by a combination of many factors, all of which must be addressed in a comprehensive conservation plan that considers its natural history.
2. New populations of threatened species can be established in the wild using either captive-raised or wild-caught individuals. Animals used in translocation projects sometimes require special care and behavioural training before release as well as care and monitoring after release.
3. Maintaining and facilitating movement dynamics is very important for protecting wildlife in their natural ecosystems. To do this, connectivity must be preserved by ensuring that habitat linkages such as wildlife corridors and stepping stone habitats that are intact, functional, and free from human-made obstacles.
4. Preventing biodiversity losses under climate change requires ecosystem preservation, maintaining and restoring climate corridors and refugia, and assisted colonisation for species unable to adapt their ranges quick enough.
5. Some species that are in danger of going extinct in the wild can be maintained in zoos, aquaria, botanical gardens, and seed banks; this strategy is known as ex situ conservation. Ex situ conservation contributes to field conservation through research, skills development, public outreach, conservation education, fundraising, captive breeding, and head-starting.

11.8 Topics for Discussion

1. How do you judge whether a reintroduction project is successful? Develop simple and then increasingly detailed criteria to evaluate a project's success.
2. Tying concepts from different chapters together, what are the biggest challenges standing in the way of conserving Africa's migratory birds?
3. Use the advanced search functions on the IUCN Red List website (https://www.iucnredlist.org) to pick one species occurring in your country that is threatened by climate change. Referring to Chapter 6, how does climate change threaten this species? What strategies can be used to prevent this species' extinction?
4. What roles do ex situ facilities play in the conservation of threatened species in Africa? Discuss two or three different roles. Do you think there are certain aspects in conservation that they can make a larger contribution to than is currently the case?
5. Find two or three examples of wild or semi-wild populations of African species maintained on other continents? Are those species threatened in their natural distribution ranges? Does maintaining populations of African species on other continents represent a successful conservation strategy? Explain your answer.

11.9 Suggested Readings

Hoffmann, M., J.W. Duckworth, K. Holmes, et al. 2015. The difference conservation makes to extinction risk of the world's ungulates. *Conservation Biology* 29: 1303–13. https://doi.org/10.1111/cobi.12519 Conservation action does make a difference, as illustrated by ungulate conservation.

IUCN/SSC. 2013. *Guidelines for Reintroductions and Other Conservation Translocations* (Gland: IUCN/SSC). https://portals.iucn.org/library/efiles/documents/2013-009.pdf Guidelines for species reintroductions and translocations.

Mawdsley, J.R., R. O'Malley, and D.S. Ojima. 2009. A review of climate-change adaptation strategies for wildlife management and biodiversity conservation. *Conservation Biology* 23: 1080–89. https://doi.org/10.1111/j.1523-1739.2009.01264.x A review of methods to combat climate change.

Menges, E.S., S.A. Smith, and C.W. Weekley. 2016. Adaptive introductions: How multiple experiments and comparisons to wild populations provide insights into requirements for long-term introduction success of an endangered shrub. *Plant Diversity* 38: 238–46. https://doi.org/10.1016/j.pld.2016.09.004 Experimentation can reduce uncertainty in population translocation.

Miller, B., W. Conway, R.P. Reading, et al. 2004. Evaluating the conservation mission of zoos, aquariums, botanical gardens, and natural history museums. *Conservation Biology* 18: 86–93. https://doi.org/10.1111/j.1523-1739.2004.00181.x Eight tough questions directed at ex situ facilities.

Nogués-Bravo, D., D. Simberloff, C. Rahbek, et al. 2016. Rewilding is the new Pandora's box in conservation. *Current Biology* 26: R87–R91. https://doi.org/10.1016/j.cub.2015.12.044 Are there limits to wildlife translocation dreams?

Pérez, I., J.D. Anadón, M. Díaz, et al. 2012. What is wrong with current translocations? A review and a decision-making proposal. *Frontiers in Ecology and the Environment* 10: 494–501. https://doi.org/10.1890/110175 Important considerations for translocations.

Sherley, R.B., K. Ludynia, B.M. Dyer, et al. 2017. Metapopulation tracking juvenile penguins reveals an ecosystem-wide ecological trap. *Current Biology* 27: 563–68. https://doi.org/10.1016/j.cub.2016.12.054 Detecting and dealing with ecological traps requires holistic thinking.

Bibliography

Ali, A.H., A.T. Ford, J.S. Evans, et al. 2017. Resource selection and landscape change reveal mechanisms suppressing population recovery for the world's most endangered antelope. *Journal of Applied Ecology* 54: 1720–29. https://doi.org/10.1111/1365-2664.12856

Alroy, J. 2015. Current extinction rates of reptiles and amphibians. *Proceedings of the National Academy of Sciences* 112: 13003–08. https://doi.org/10.1073/pnas.1508681112

Andersson, J., M. de Garine-Wichatitsky, D. Cumming, et al. 2013. *Transfrontier Conservation Areas: People Living on the Edge* (New York: Routledge).

Anon. 2018. 9,873 Kihansi spray toads return to their environment. *IPP Media*. https://go.shr.lc/2B6N7wB

Araújo, M.B., and M. Luoto. 2007. The importance of biotic interactions for modelling species distributions under climate change. *Global Ecology and Biogeography* 16: 743–53. https://doi.org/10.1111/j.1466-8238.2007.00359.x

Armstrong, D.P., and P.J. Seddon. 2007. Directions in reintroduction biology. *Trends in Ecology and Evolution* 23: 20–25. https://doi.org/10.1016/j.tree.2007.10.003

Ayebare, S., R. Ponce-Reyes, S.B. Segan, et al. 2013. *Identifying climate resilient corridors for conservation in the Albertine Rift* (Chicago: MacArthur Foundation).

Bartlam-Brooks, H.L.A., M.C. Bonyongo, and S. Harris. 2011. Will reconnecting ecosystems allow long-distance mammal migrations to resume? A case study of a zebra *Equus burchelli* migration in Botswana. *Oryx* 45: 210–16. https://doi.org/10.1017/S0030605310000414

Ben-Nun, I.F., S.C. Montague, M.L. Houck, et al. 2011. Induced pluripotent stem cells from highly endangered species. *Nature Methods* 8: 829–31. https://doi.org/10.1038/nmeth.1706.

Bennett, G. 2004. *Linkages in practice: A review of their conservation value* (Gland: IUCN). https://portals.iucn.org/library/node/8412

Bentrup, G., M. Dosskey, G. Wells, et al. 2012. Connecting landscape fragments through riparian zones. In: *Forest Landscape Restoration*, ed. by J. Stanturf, et al. (Dortrecht: Springer). https://doi.org/10.1007/978-94-007-5326-6

Betts, M.G., B. Phalan, S.J.K. Frey, et al. 2018. Old-growth forests buffer climate-sensitive bird populations from warming. *Diversity and Distributions* 24: 439–47. https://doi.org/10.1111/ddi.12688

BirdLife South Africa. 2019. *Creating new penguin colonies*. https://www.birdlife.org.za/what-we-do/seabird-conservation/what-we-do/coastal-seabird-conservation/creating-penguin-colonies/

Bonnell, T.R., R. Reyna-Hurtado, and C.A. Chapman. 2011. Post-logging recovery time is longer than expected in an East African tropical forest. *Forest Ecology and Management* 261: 855–64. https://doi.org/10.1016/j.foreco.2010.12.016

Boundja, R.P., and J.J. Midgley. 2010. Patterns of elephant impact on woody plants in the Hluhluwe-iMfolozi Park, Kwazulu-Natal, South Africa. *African Journal of Ecology* 48: 206–14. https://doi.org/10.1111/j.1365-2028.2009.01104.x

Brook, R.K., and S.M. McLachlan. 2008. Trends and prospects for local knowledge in ecological and conservation research and monitoring. *Biodiversity and Conservation* 17: 3501–12. https://doi.org/10.1007/s10531-008-9445-x

Brooks, T.M., S.J. Wright, and D. Sheil. 2009. Evaluating the success of conservation actions in safeguarding tropical forest biodiversity. *Conservation Biology* 23: 1448–57. https://doi.org/10.1111/j.1523-1739.2009.01334.x

Brossy, J.J., A.L. Plös, J.M. Blackbeard, et al. 1999. Diseases acquired by captive penguins: What happens when they are released into the wild? *Marine Ornithology* 27: 185–86

Brown, M., M. Perrin, and B. Hoffman. 2007. Reintroduction of captive-bred African Grass-Owls *Tyto capensis* into natural habitat. *Ostrich* 78: 75–79. https://doi.org/10.2989/OSTRICH.2007.78.1.11.55

Caro, T.J. Eadie, and A. Sih. 2005. Use of substitute species in conservation biology. *Conservation Biology* 19: 1821–26. https://doi.org/10.1111/j.1523-1739.2005.00251.x

Childress, B., D. Harper, B. Hughes, et al. 2004. Satellite tracking lesser flamingo movements in the Rift Valley, East Africa: Pilot study report. *Ostrich* 75: 57–65. https://doi.org/10.2989/00306520409485413

Conde, D.A., J. Staerk, F. Colchero, et al. 2019. Data gaps and opportunities for comparative and conservation biology. *Proceedings of the National Academy of Sciences* 116: 9658–64. https://doi.org/10.1073/pnas.1816367116

Conde, D.A., N. Flesness, F. Colchero, et al. 2011. An emerging role of zoos to conserve biodiversity. *Science* 331: 1390–91. https://doi.org/10.1126/science.1200674

Creel, S., M.S. Becker, S.M. Durant, et al. 2013. Conserving large populations of lions–the argument for fences has holes. *Ecology Letters* 16: 1413. https://doi.org/10.1111/ele.12145

Cumming, D.H.M. 1999. *Study on development of transboundary natural resources management areas in Southern Africa — environmental context: Natural resources, land use and conservation* (Washington: Biodiversity Support Programme).

Cunningham, S.J., A.C. Kruger, M.P. Nxumalo, et al. 2013. Identifying biologically meaningful hot-weather events using threshold temperatures that affect life-history. *PLoS ONE* 8: e82492. https://doi.org/10.1371/journal.pone.0082492

Cushman, S.A., N.B. Elliot, D.W. Macdonald, et al. 2016. A multi-scale assessment of population connectivity in African lions (*Panthera leo*). *Landscape Ecology* 31: 1337–53. https://doi.org/10.1007/s10980-015-0292-3

Dallimer, M., and N. Strange. 2015. Why socio-political borders and boundaries matter in conservation. *Trends in Ecology and Evolution* 30: 132–39. https://doi.org/10.1016/j.tree.2014.12.004

Dawson, J., F. Patel, R.A. Griffiths, et al. 2016. Assessing the global zoo response to the amphibian crisis through 20-year trends in captive collections. *Conservation Biology* 30: 82–91. https://doi.org/10.1111/cobi.12563

Deemer, B.R., J.A. Harrison, S. Li, et al. 2016. Greenhouse gas emissions from reservoir water surfaces: A new global synthesis. *BioScience* 66: 949–64. https://doi.org/10.1093/biosci/biw117

Dubach, J.M., M.B. Briggs, P.A. White, et al., 2013. Genetic perspectives on "Lion Conservation Units" in Eastern and Southern Africa. *Conservation Genetics* 14: 741–55. https://doi.org/10.1007/s10592-013-0453-3

Dupuis-Desormeaux, M., T.N. Kaaria, M. Mwololo, et al. 2018. A ghost fence-gap: Surprising wildlife usage of an obsolete fence crossing. *PeerJ* 6: e5950. https://dx.doi.org/10.7717%2Fpeerj.5950

Ferreira, S.M., and M. Hofmeyr. 2014. Managing charismatic carnivores in small areas: Large felids in South Africa. South African *Journal of Wildlife Research* 44: 32–42. https://doi.org/10.3957/056.044.0102

Ferrie, G.M., K.H. Farmer, C.W. Kuhar, et al. 2014. The social, economic, and environmental contributions of Pan African Sanctuary Alliance primate sanctuaries in Africa. *Biodiversity and Conservation* 23: 187–201. http://doi.org/10.1007/s10531-013-0592-3

Frankham, R., J.D. Ballou, M.D.B. Eldridge, et al. 2011. Predicting the probability of outbreeding depression. *Conservation Biology* 25: 465–75. https://doi.org/10.1111/j.1523-1739.2011.01662.x

Fritz, H., and P. Duncan. 1994. On the carrying capacity for large ungulates of African savanna ecosystems. *Proceedings of the Royal Society B* 256: 77–82. https://doi.org/10.1098/rspb.1994.0052

Giam, X., R.K. Hadiaty, H.H. Tan, et al. 2015. Mitigating the impact of oil-palm monoculture on freshwater fishes in Southeast Asia. *Conservation Biology* 29: 1357–67. https://doi.org/10.1111/cobi.12483

Gillett, H. 2002. *Conservation and sustainable use of medicinal plants in Ghana* (Cambridge: UNEP-WCMC). https://wedocs.unep.org/bitstream/handle/20.500.11822/7487/Conservation_sustainable_use_medicinal_plants_Ghana.pdf

Godefroid, S., C. Piazza, G. Rossi, et al. 2011. How successful are plant species reintroductions? *Biological Conservation* 144: 672–82. https://doi.org/10.1016/j.biocon.2010.10.003

Godley, B.J., C. Barbosa, M. Bruford, et al. 2010. Unravelling migratory connectivity in marine turtles using multiple methods. *Journal of Applied Ecology* 47: 769–78. https://doi.org/10.1111/j.1365-2664.2010.01817.x

Gómez, C., N.J. Bayly, D.R. Norris, et al. 2017. Fuel loads acquired at a stopover site influence the pace of intercontinental migration in a boreal songbird. *Scientific Reports* 7: 3405. https://doi.org/10.1038/s41598-017-03503-4

Grey-Ross, R., C.T. Downs, and K. Kirkman. 2009. Reintroduction failure of captive-bred oribi (*Ourebia ourebi*). *South African Journal of Wildlife Research* 39: 34–38. https://doi.org/10.3957/056.039.0104

Groom, R.J., K. Lannas, and C.R. Jackson. 2017. The impact of lions on the demography and ecology of endangered African wild dogs. *Animal Conservation* 20: 382–90. https://doi.org/10.1111/acv.12328

Gusset, M., A.H. Maddock, G.J. Gunther, et al. 2008a. Conflicting human interests over the re-introduction of endangered wild dogs in South Africa. *Biodiversity and Conservation* 17: 83–101. http://doi.org/10.1007/s10531-007-9232-0

Gusset, M., R. Slotow, and M.J. Somers. 2006. Divided we fail: The importance of social integration for the re-introduction of endangered African wild dogs (*Lycaon pictus*). *Journal of Zoology* 270: 502–11. https://doi.org/10.1111/j.1469-7998.2006.00168.x

Gusset, M., S.J. Ryan, M. Hofmeyr, et al. 2008b. Efforts going to the dogs? Evaluating attempts to re-introduce endangered wild dogs in South Africa. *Journal of Applied Ecology* 45: 100–08. https://doi.org/10.1111/j.1365-2664.2007.01357.x

Haddad, N.M., L.A. Brudwig, A.I. Damschen, et al. 2014. Potential negative ecological effects of corridors. *Conservation Biology* 28: 1178–87. https://doi.org/10.1111/cobi.12323

Harris, L., E.E. Campbell, R. Nel, et al. 2014. Rich diversity, strong endemism, but poor protection: Addressing the neglect of sandy beach ecosystems in coastal conservation planning. *Diversity and Distributions* 20: 1120–35. https://doi.org/10.1111/ddi.12226

Hayward, M.W., J. Adendorff, L. Moolman, et al. 2007b. The successful reintroduction of leopard *Panthera pardus* to the Addo Elephant National Park. *African Journal of Ecology* 45: 103–04. https://doi.org/10.1111/j.1365-2028.2006.00673.x

Hayward, M.W., J. O'Brien, and G.I.H. Kerley. 2007a. Carrying capacity of large African predators: Predictions and tests. *Biological Conservation* 139: 219–29. https://doi.org/10.1016/j.biocon.2007.06.018

Henry, E., E. Brammer-Robbins, E. Aschenough, et al. 2019. Do substitute species help or hinder endangered species management? *Biological Conservation* 232: 127–30. https://doi.org/10.1016/j.biocon.2019.01.031

Herkt, K.M.B., G. Barnikel, A.K. Skidmore, et al. 2016. A high-resolution model of bat diversity and endemism for continental Africa. *Ecological Modelling* 320: 9–28. http://doi.org/10.1016/j.ecolmodel.2015.09.009

Horton, A.J., E.D. Lazarus, T.C. Hales, et al. 2018. Can riparian forest buffers increase yields from palm oil plantations? *Earth's Future* 6: 1082–96. https://doi.org/10.1029/2018EF000874

Houser, A., M. Gusset, C.J. Gragg, et al. 2011. Pre-release hunting training and post-release monitoring are key components in the rehabilitation of orphaned large felids. *South African Journal of Wildlife Research* 41: 11–20. https://doi.org/10.3957/056.041.0111

Hudgens, B.R., W.F. Morris, N.M. Haddad, et al. 2012. How complex do models need to be to predict dispersal of threatened species through matrix habitats? *Ecological Applications* 22: 1701–10. https://doi.org/10.1890/11-1048.1

IUCN. 2019. *The IUCN Red List of Threatened Species.* http://www.iucnredlist.org

Jachowski, D.S., R. Slotow, and J.J. Millspaugh. 2013. Delayed physiological acclimatization by African elephants following reintroduction. *Animal Conservation* 16: 575–83. http://doi.org/10.1111/acv.12031

Jones, T., A.J. Bamford, D. Ferrol-Schulte, et al. 2012. Vanishing wildlife corridors and options for restoration: A case study from Tanzania. *Tropical Conservation Science* 5: 463–74. https://doi.org/10.1177/194008291200500405

Jordaan, M., A. Lubbe, C. Bragg, et al. 2017. *Labeo seeberi. The IUCN Red List of Threatened Species* 2017: e.T11071A100162293. http://doi.org/10.2305/IUCN.UK.2017-3.RLTS.T11071A100162293.en

Kays, R., M.C. Crofoot, W. Jetz, et al. 2015. Terrestrial animal tracking as an eye on life and planet. *Science* 348: aaa2478. http://doi.org/10.1126/science.aaa2478

Kearney, M., and W. Porter. 2009. Mechanistic niche modelling: Combining physiological and spatial data to predict species' ranges. *Ecology Letters* 12: 334–50. https://doi.org/10.1111/j.1461-0248.2008.01277.x

King, L.E., I. Douglas-Hamilton, and F. Vollrath. 2011. Beehive fences as effective deterrents for crop-raiding elephants: Field trials in northern Kenya. *African Journal of Ecology* 49: 431–39. https://doi.org/10.1111/j.1365-2028.2011.01275.x

King, T., C. Chamberlan, and A. Courage. 2014. Assessing reintroduction success in long-lived primates through population viability analysis: Western lowland gorillas *Gorilla gorilla gorilla* in Central Africa. *Oryx* 48: 294–303. https://doi.org/10.1017/S0030605312001391

Laurance, S.G., and W.F. Laurance. 1999. Tropical wildlife corridors: Use of linear rainforest remnants by arboreal mammals. *Biological Conservation* 91: 231–39. https://doi.org/10.1016/S0006-3207(99)00077-4

Leaver, J. 2014. *Options for eland: A multi-scale assessment of antipredatory responses of a vulnerable prey species to their major predator in the Eastern Cape, South Africa.* MSc thesis (Port Elizabeth: NMMU). http://hdl.handle.net/10948/6570

Lindsey, P., C.J. Tambling, R. Brummer, et al. 2011. Minimum prey and area requirements of the Vulnerable cheetah *Acinonyx jubatus*: implications for reintroduction and management of the species in South Africa. *Oryx* 45: 587–99. https://doi.org/10.1017/S003060531000150X

Lindsey, P.A., R. Alexander, J.T. du Toit, et al. 2005. The cost efficiency of wild dog conservation in South Africa. *Conservation Biology* 19: 1205–14. https://doi.org/10.1111/j.1523-1739.2005.00088.x

Linklater, W., and A.M. Shrader. 2017. Rhino challenges: Spatial and social ecology for habitat and population management. In: *Conserving Africa's Mega-diversity in the Anthropocene: The Hluhluwe-iMfolozi Park Story*, ed. by J.P.G.M. Cromsigt, et al. (Cambridge: Cambridge University Press). https://doi.org/10.1017/9781139382793

Mawdsley, J.R., R. O'Malley, and D.S. Ojima. 2009. A review of climate-change adaptation strategies for wildlife management and biodiversity conservation. *Conservation Biology* 23: 1080–89. https://doi.org/10.1111/j.1523-1739.2009.01264.x

Maxted, N. 2001. Ex situ, in situ conservation. In: *Encyclopedia of Biodiversity*, ed. by S.A. Levin (San Diego: Academic Press).

Maxwell, S.M., G.A. Breed, B.A. Nickel, et al. 2011. Using Satellite tracking to optimize protection of long-lived marine species: Olive ridley sea turtle conservation in Central Africa. *PLoS ONE* 6: e19905. https://doi.org/10.1371/journal.pone.0019905

McClanahan, T.R., and N.A. Muthiga. 2017. Environmental variability indicates a climate-adaptive center under threat in northern Mozambique coral reefs. *Ecosphere* 8: e01812. https://doi.org/10.1002/ecs2.1812

McLennan, M.R., and A.J. Plumptre. 2012. Protected apes, unprotected forest: Composition, structure and diversity of riverine forest fragments and their conservation value in Uganda. *Tropical Conservation Science* 5: 79–103. https://doi.org/10.1177/194008291200500108

McNutt, J.W, M.N. Parker, M.J. Swarner, et al. 2008. Adoption as a conservation tool for endangered African wild dogs (*Lycaon pictus*). *African Journal of Wildlife Research* 38: 109–13. https://doi.org/10.3957/0379-4369-38.2.109

McPherson, J.M., W. Jetz, and D.J. Rogers. 2006. Using coarse-grained occurrence data to predict species distributions at finer spatial resolutions—possibilities and limitations. *Ecological Modelling* 192: 499–522. http://doi.org/10.1016/j.ecolmodel.2005.08.007

Menges, E.S., S.A. Smith, and C.W. Weekley. 2016. Adaptive introductions: How multiple experiments and comparisons to wild populations provide insights into requirements for long-term introduction success of an endangered shrub. *Plant Diversity* 38: 238–46. https://doi.org/10.1016/j.pld.2016.09.004

Miller, S.M., C.J. Tambling, and P.J. Funston. 2015. GrowLS: Lion (*Panthera leo*) population growth simulation for small reserve management planning. *African Journal of Wildlife Research* 45: 169–77. https://doi.org/10.3957/056.045.0169

Monadjem, A., and A. Reside. The influence of riparian vegetation on the distribution and abundance of bats in an African savanna. *Acta Chiropterologica* 10: 339–48. http://doi.org/10.3161/150811008X414917

Negrón-Ortiz, V. 2014. Pattern of expenditures for plant conservation under the Endangered Species Act. *Biological Conservation* 171: 36–43. https://doi.org/10.1016/j.biocon.2014.01.018

Newmark, W.D. 2008. Isolation of African protected areas. *Frontiers in Ecology and the Environment* 6: 321–28. https://doi.org/10.1890/070003

Newmark, W.D., C.N. Jenkins, S.L. Pimm, et al. 2017. Targeted habitat restoration can reduce extinction rates in fragmented forests. *Proceedings of the National Academy of Sciences* 114: 9635–40. https://doi.org/10.1073/pnas.1705834114

Ng'weno, C.C., N.J. Maiyo, A.H. Ali, et al. 2017. Lions influence the decline and habitat shift of hartebeest in a semiarid savanna. *Journal of Mammalogy* 98: 1078–87. https://doi.org/10.1093/jmammal/gyx040

Nunes, M., J.B. Adams, and G.M. Rishworth. 2018. Shifts in phytoplankton community structure in response to hydrological changes in the shallow St Lucia Estuary. *Marine Pollution Bulletin* 128: 275–86. https://doi.org/10.1016/j.marpolbul.2018.01.035

Packer, C., A. Loveridge, S. Canney, et al. 2013. Conserving large carnivores: Dollars and fence. *Ecology Letters* 16: 635–41. https://doi.org/10.1111/ele.12091

Pearson, R.G., and T.P. Dawson. 2003. Predicting the impacts of climate change on the distribution of species: Are bioclimate envelope models useful? *Global Ecology and Biogeography* 12: 361–71. https://doi.org/10.1046/j.1466-822X.2003.00042.x

Pearson, R.G., W. Thuiller, M.B. Araújo, et al. 2006. Model-based uncertainty in species range prediction. *Journal of Biogeography* 33: 1704–11. https://doi.org/10.1111/j.1365-2699.2006.01460.x

Pérez, I., J.D. Anadón, M. Díaz, et al. 2012. What is wrong with current translocations? A review and a decision-making proposal. *Frontiers in Ecology and the Environment* 10: 494–501. https://doi.org/10.1890/110175

Phillips, S.J., P. Williams, G. Midgley, et al. 2008. Optimizing dispersal corridors for the Cape Proteaceae using network flow. *Ecological Applications* 18: 1200–11. https://doi.org/10.1890/07-0507.1

Plumptre, A.J., S. Nixon, D.K. Kujirakwinja, et al. 2016. Catastrophic decline of world's largest primate: 80% loss of Grauer's gorilla (*Gorilla beringei graueri*) population justifies Critically Endangered status. *PloS ONE* 11: e0162697. https://doi.org/10.1371/journal.pone.0162697

Powell, A.N., and F.J. Cuthbert. 1993. Augmenting small populations of plovers: An assessment of cross-fostering and captive-rearing. *Conservation Biology* 7: 160–68. https://doi.org/10.1046/j.1523-1739.1993.07010160.x

Pryke, J.S., and M.J. Samways. 2012. Conservation management of complex natural forest and plantation edge effects. *Landscape Ecology* 27: 73–85. https://doi.org/10.1007/s10980-011-9668-1

Ralls, K., J.D. Ballou, M.R. Dudash, et al. 2018. Call for a paradigm shift in the genetic management of fragmented populations. *Conservation Letters* 11: 1–6. https://doi.org/10.1111/conl.12412

Reilly, S.B., J.L. Bannister, P.B. Best, et al. 2013. *Eubalaena australis. The IUCN Red List of Threatened Species* 2013: e.T8153A44230386. http://doi.org/10.2305/IUCN.UK.2018-1.RLTS.T8153A50354147.en

Riggio, J., and T. Caro. 2017. Structural connectivity at a national scale: Wildlife corridors in Tanzania. *PLoS ONE* 12: e0187407. https://doi.org/10.1371/journal.pone.0187407

Ripple, W.J., J.A. Estes, R.L. Beschta, et al. 2014. Status and ecological effects of the world's largest carnivores. *Science* 343: 12341484. https://doi.org/10.1126/science.1241484

Runge, C.A., J.E.M. Watson, S.H.M. Butchart, et al. 2015. Protected areas and global conservation of migratory birds. *Science* 350: 1255–58. http://doi.org/10.1126/science.aac9180

SANParks. 2009. Sought-after disease-free Addo buffalo to go on auction. *SANParks News*. https://www.sanparks.org/about/news/?id=1246

Scheele, B.C., D.A. Hunter, L.F. Grogan, et al. 2014. Interventions for reducing extinction risk in Chytridiomycosis-threatened amphibians. *Conservation Biology* 28: 1195–205. https://doi.org/10.1111/cobi.12322

Schleuning, M., J. Fründ, O. Schweiger, et al. 2016. Ecological networks are more sensitive to plant than to animal extinction under climate change. *Nature Communications* 7: 13965. https://doi.org/10.1038/ncomms13965

Schmidt, F., F.A. Franke, M.H. Shirley, et al. 2015. The importance of genetic research in zoo breeding programmes for threatened species: The African dwarf crocodiles (genus *Osteolaemus*) as a case study. *International Zoo Yearbook* 49: 125–36. https://doi.org/10.1111/izy.12082

Scott, J.M., D.D. Goble, J.A. Wiens, et al. 2005. Recovery of imperilled species under the Endangered Species Act: The need for a new approach. *Frontiers in Ecology and the Environment* 3: 383–89. https://doi.org/10.1890/1540-9295(2005)003[0383:ROISUT]2.0.CO;2

Shackeroff, J.M., and L.M. Campbell. 2007. Traditional ecological knowledge in conservation research: Problems and prospects for their constructive engagement. *Conservation and Society* 5: 343

Sherley, R.B., K. Ludynia, B.M. Dyer, et al. 2017. Metapopulation tracking juvenile penguins reveals an ecosystem-wide ecological trap. *Current Biology* 27: 563–68. https://doi.org/10.1016/j.cub.2016.12.054

Shrader, A.M., C. Bell, L. Bertolli, et al. 2012. Forest or the trees: At what scale do elephants make foraging decisions? *Acta Oecologica* 42: 3–10. http://doi.org/10.1016/j.actao.2011.09.009

Silber, G.K., A.S.M. Vanderlaan, A.T. Arceredillo, et al. 2012. The role of the International Maritime Organization in reducing vessel threat to whales: Process, options, action and effectiveness. *Marine Policy* 36: 1221–33. http://doi.org/10.1016/j.marpol.2012.03.008

Sileshi, G.W., P. Nyeko, P.O.Y. Nkunika, et al. 2009. Integrating ethno-ecological and scientific knowledge of termites for sustainable termite management and human welfare in Africa. *Ecology and Society* 14: 48. http://www.ecologyandsociety.org/vol14/iss1/art48

Singh, J. 1998. The lessons learnt: The development and management of transboundary parks world-wide. In: *Study on the Development and Management of Trans-boundary Conservation Areas in Southern Africa* (Gabarone: RCSA).

Stears, K., and A.M. Shrader. 2015. Increases in food availability can tempt oribi antelope into taking greater risks at both large and small spatial scales. *Animal Behaviour* 108: 155–64. http://doi.org/10.1016/j.anbehav.2015.07.012

Tambling, C.J., D.J. Druce, M.W. Hayward, et al. 2012. Spatial and temporal changes in group dynamics and range use enable anti-predator responses in African buffalo. *Ecology* 93: 1297–304. https://doi.org/10.1890/11-1770.1

Tambling, C.J., J.W. Wilson, P. Bradford, et al. 2014. Fine-scale differences in predicted and observed cheetah diet: Does sexual dimorphism matter? *South African Journal of Wildlife Research* 44: 90–94. https://doi.org/10.3957/056.044.0109

Tambling, C.J., S.M. Ferreira, J. Adendorff, et al. 2013. Lessons from management interventions: Consequences for lion-buffalo interactions. *South African Journal of Wildlife Research* 43: 1–11. https://doi.org/10.3957/056.043.0116

Thomas-Blate, J. 2017. Celebrating a great year for dam removals in 2016. *American Rivers*. https://www.americanrivers.org/2017/02/celebrating-great-year-dam-removal-2016

Tolley, K.A., G.J. Alexander, W.R. Branch, et al. 2016. Conservation status and threats for African reptiles. *Biological Conservation* 204: 63–71. http://doi.org/10.1016/j.biocon.2016.04.006

Valutis, L.L., and J.M. Marzluff. 1999. The appropriateness of puppet-rearing birds for reintroduction. *Conservation Biology* 13: 584–91. https://doi.org/10.1046/j.1523-1739.1999.97443.x

van Andel, T.R., S. Croft, E.E. van Loon, et al. 2015. Prioritizing West African medicinal plants for conservation and sustainable extraction studies based on market surveys and species distribution models. *Biological Conservation* 181: 173–81. https://doi.org/10.1016/j.biocon.2014.11.015

Vandvik, V., I.E. Måren, H.J. Ndangalasi, et al. 2014. Back to Africa: Monitoring post-hydropower restoration to facilitate reintroduction of an extinct-in-the-wild amphibian. *Ecosphere* 5: 1–16. https://doi.org/10.1890/ES14-00093.1

von der Heyden, S. 2009. Why do we need to integrate population genetics into South African marine protected areas planning? *African Journal of Marine Science* 31: 263–69. https://doi.org/10.2989/AJMS.2009.31.2.14.886

Vosse, S., K.J. Esler, D.M. Richardson, et al. 2008. Can riparian seed banks initiate restoration after alien plant invasion? Evidence from the Western Cape, South Africa. *South African Journal of Botany* 74: 432–44. https://doi.org/10.1016/j.sajb.2008.01.170

Wassenaar, T.D., R.J. van Aarde, S.L. Pimm, et al. 2005. Community convergence in disturbed subtropical dune forests. *Ecology* 86: 655–66. https://doi.org/10.1890/03-0836

Wegmann M, L. Santini, B. Leutner, et al. 2014. Role of African protected areas in maintaining connectivity for large mammals. *Philosophical Transactions of the Royal Society B* 369: 20130193. https://doi.org/10.1098/rstb.2013.0193

White, P.S. 1996. Spatial and biological scales in reintroduction. In: *Restoring Diversity: Strategies for Reintroduction of Endangered Plants*, ed. by D.A. Falk, et al. (Washington: Island Press).

Williams, P., L. Hannah, S. Andelman, et al. 2005. Planning for climate change: Identifying minimum-dispersal corridors for the Cape proteaceae. *Conservation Biology* 19: 1063–74. https://doi.org/10.1111/j.1523-1739.2005.00080.x

Wilson, J.W., R. Bergl, L.J. Minter, et al. 2019. The African elephant *Loxodonta* spp. conservation programmes of North Carolina Zoo: Two decades of using emerging technologies to advance in situ conservation efforts. *International Zoo Yearbook* 53: *in press*. https://doi.org/10.1111/izy.12216

Wilson, J.W., R.L. Stirnemann, Z.S. Schaikh, et al. 2010. The response of small mammals to natural and human-altered edges associated with Afromontane forests of South Africa. *Forest Ecology and Management* 259: 926–31. http://doi.org/10.1016/j.foreco.2009.11.032

Wimberger, K., C.T. Downs, and M.R. Perrin. 2009. Two unsuccessful reintroduction attempts of rock hyraxes (*Procavia capensis*) into a reserve in the KwaZulu-Natal Province, South Africa. *South African Journal of Wildlife Research* 39: 192–201. https://doi.org/10.3957/056.039.0213

Wimberger, K., C.T. Downs, and R.S. Boyes. 2010. A survey of wildlife rehabilitation in South Africa: Is there a need for improved management? *Animal Welfare* 19: 481–99.

Winemiller, K.O., P.B. McIntyre, L. Castello, et al. 2016. Balancing hydropower and biodiversity in the Amazon, Congo, and Mekong. *Science* 351: 128–29. http://doi.org/10.1126/science.aac7082

Woolf, N.B. 1986. New hope for exotic species. *BioScience* 36: 594–97. https://doi.org/10.2307/1310192.

Wyse Jackson, P.S. 2001. International review of the ex situ plant collections of the botanic gardens of the world. *Botanic Gardens Conservation News* 3: 22–33.

Permissions

All chapters in this book were first published by Open Book Publishers; hereby published with permission under the Creative Commons Attribution License or equivalent. Every chapter published in this book has been scrutinized by our experts. Their significance has been extensively debated. The topics covered herein carry significant information for a comprehensive understanding. They may even be implemented as practical applications or may be referred to as a beginning point for further studies.

The contributors of this book come from diverse backgrounds, making this book a truly international effort. We would like to thank all the contributing authors for lending their expertise to make the book truly unique. They have played a crucial role in the development of this book. Without their invaluable contributions this book wouldn't have been possible. They have made vital efforts to compile up to date information on the varied aspects of this subject to make this book a valuable addition to the collection of many professionals and students.

This book was conceptualized with the vision of imparting up-to-date and integrated information in this field. To ensure the same, a matchless editorial board was set up. Every individual on the board went through rigorous rounds of assessment to prove their worth. After which they invested a large part of their time researching and compiling the most relevant data for our readers.

The editorial board has been involved in producing this book since its inception. They have spent rigorous hours researching and exploring the diverse topics which have resulted in the successful publishing of this book. They have passed on their knowledge of decades through this book. To expedite this challenging task, the publisher supported the team at every step. A small team of assistant editors was also appointed to further simplify the editing procedure and attain best results for the readers.

Apart from the editorial board, the designing team has also invested a significant amount of their time in understanding the subject and creating the most relevant covers. They scrutinized every image to scout for the most suitable representation of the subject and create an appropriate cover for the book.

The publishing team has been an ardent support to the editorial, designing and production team. Their endless efforts to recruit the best for this project, has resulted in the accomplishment of this book. They are a veteran in the field of academics and their pool of knowledge is as vast as their experience in printing. Their expertise and guidance has proved useful at every step. Their uncompromising quality standards have made this book an exceptional effort. Their encouragement from time to time has been an inspiration for everyone.

The publisher and the editorial board hope that this book will prove to be a valuable piece of knowledge for students, practitioners and scholars across the globe.

Index

Printed in the USA
CPSIA information can be obtained
at www.ICGtesting.com
LVHW082209201023
761596LV00009B/1638

9 781641 167888